The Fortunes of Francis Barber

[signature]

Well,

14th October 2015

ꙅꟽꙅ

The Fortunes of Francis Barber

The True Story of the
Jamaican Slave Who Became
Samuel Johnson's Heir

Michael Bundock

Yale
UNIVERSITY PRESS

NEW HAVEN AND LONDON

1 2 0594809 3

Published with assistance from the Annie Burr Lewis Fund.

Published with assistance from the foundation established in memory
of Philip Hamilton McMillan of the Class of 1894, Yale College.

Yale University Press books may be purchased in quantity for educational, business, or promotional use.
For information, please e-mail sales.press@yale.edu (U.S. office) or sales@yaleup.co.uk (U.K. office).

Set in Fournier MT type by IDS Infotech, Ltd.

Printed in the United States of America.

978-0-300-20710-1
Catalogue records for this book are available from the Library of Congress and the British Library.

This paper meets the requirements of ANSI/NISO Z39.48–1992 (Permanence of Paper).

10 9 8 7 6 5 4 3 2 1

For Kate

Contents

1. The House in Gough Square

On a summer's day in 1752, two conspicuously odd figures are making their way through the hubbub and grime of London's Fleet Street. The street is mobbed with people of all kinds—merchants off to do business, beggars after a penny for gin, travellers hurrying to catch the stagecoach, and pedlars trying to sell their wares—but these two stand out. Each on his own would attract attention, but there seems to be something particularly comical about the sight of the two of them together; some street children catch sight of them, mutter comments, and grin at each other as the pair pass by.

Walking westwards from the stinking Fleet Ditch, the couple turn a corner by an inn, and disappear into a dark alley. They pause while one of them presses a coin into the hands of a sleeping figure curled up in a doorway, then pass on and emerge into a large courtyard. This is their destination: a rather imposing house in the corner of the square is their home.

A little while later, both are to be found in the garret at the top of the house. They are on their own, with nobody to remark on their oddity or to comment on the scruffy appearance of their surroundings. The room is spacious, some twenty-five feet long, and with windows on three sides, so that daylight streams in and catches the dust which hangs everywhere in the air. It is untidy, and cheaply furnished: a couple of very battered chairs, and several desks showing marks of frequent use. There are books, some of them valuable folios, on bookcases, on the desks, and on the floor, and papers piled up in heaps. This is clearly a place of work, perhaps of a literary or scholarly kind, but it is not easy to guess what the nature of that work is.

Standing at a desk at one end of the garret, the older of the two dominates the room. He is a heavily built man, forty-two years old and very tall by the standards of the day—he stands almost six feet in height. But although he is powerfully built, his appearance is disconcerting. His clothes are shabby and stained, and the wig which perches on his head is tattered, and even burnt in places, as if its wearer had once leaned too close to a candle—as indeed he had. Worse, his face is disfigured, with a long scar down one side of his neck, and one sightless eye partially closed.

The man is reading a book—in fact, it would be more accurate to say he is devouring it. He handles it roughly, bending back the cover in a way which will do the expensive binding no good at all. It is obvious that he is not reading for pleasure. He scans the pages very fast, holding the book close to his one good eye and occasionally pausing to underline a passage in the text or to jot a note in the margin. As he works, he mutters and grunts to himself, occasionally emitting a strange whistling sound, "Tooo, tooo." From time to time, his face is convulsed by some kind of nervous twitch. It would be easy to take him for some kind of madman.

Anyone who made such an assumption would be astonished to discover the truth about this man. He is Samuel Johnson, and the work he is engaged in—compiling a dictionary of the English language—will, in a few years' time, make him one of the most famous figures in the land. He will become so emblematic of his time that it will often be referred to later as the "Age of Johnson."

Further down the room another figure sits at one of the rough desks: a boy, about ten years old, Johnson's Fleet Street companion. While Johnson reads, the boy entertains himself, scribbling on one of the many scraps of paper left lying around. Sometimes he draws pictures. Like many other children of his age he practises writing his name over and over: "Francis Barber, Francis Barber." He also writes out repeatedly another word which any child might write in this time and place, "England, England," and one which is more surprising, "antique/an."

Like Johnson, Francis Barber stands out in the London crowd, though not for his size or his mannerisms, but for another reason: he is black. While black faces are not unknown in London, they are unusual; indeed, a black servant is regarded as a fashionable novelty. But there is something else which is different about Barber, something which sets him apart from Samuel Johnson and indeed from almost all other Londoners. Francis Barber was born a slave. He lived on a Jamaican sugar plantation until he was brought to England by his owner, and has only recently joined Johnson's household in Gough Square; for him it means entering a whole new world.

More than 250 years later, on a damp autumn night, I find myself walking down Fleet Street, heading for Gough Square. The name of the street carries a weight of historical baggage, but there is little sense of the past in the present buildings; many of the shops could be found on any suburban high street. But to turn off Fleet Street into the alleys which run north and south is to step back in time. Johnson, that great Londoner, once declared (according to his biographer, James Boswell) that "if you wish to have a just notion of the magnitude of this city, you must not be satisfied with seeing its great streets and squares, but must survey the innumerable little lanes and courts." This is the area he had in mind when he said those words, as he lived for over thirty years in a succession of houses in the courts around Fleet Street.

I turn into Wine Office Court, a small covered alley whose name hints at the time, three hundred years ago, when it was home to the licensing office. On the corner is a pub, Ye Olde Cheshire Cheese. The name is a cliché but for once it seems almost justified: the claim on the sign outside—"Restored 1667"—is true. On the wall a list of famous visitors includes, inevitably, Samuel Johnson. Well, perhaps: he certainly liked a tavern, and his home is not far away.

Walking a few paces farther on I pass some substantial Georgian houses, one of which was home in the 1760s to Johnson's friend, the Irish author Oliver Goldsmith. The alley is no longer covered over, but there are tall buildings to the right and left, and not much sunlight can get down here; the paving stones are slippery, and tinged with green. The alley broadens out and divides into two. Taking the left fork, I walk the twenty yards into Gough Square.

The square itself is attractive and retains some of its eighteenth-century atmosphere, but most of the surrounding buildings are modern and nondescript; during the Second World War the area was bombed so flat you could see all the way to St. Paul's Cathedral. Many of the offices seem to be occupied by barristers, and in a curious echo of Johnson's day a yellowing wig can be glimpsed hanging on a peg in one such office, a reminder that we are close to the heart of legal London. The light from the windows ensures that even at seven o'clock in October the square is well lit. Only at the weekend, when the area is deserted, is there a sense of how it might have looked when Johnson and Barber lived here: dark and rather threatening.

In the northwest corner of the square, number seventeen stands out from the other buildings. It is a solid four-storey house, built in the early eighteenth century. A plaque announces that "Dr. Samuel Johnson" once lived here. Visitors usually enter by a modern doorway at the side of the house, but tonight the front door is open. The door, which is up a few steps, is stout, and a massive chain can be pulled across, for added security. There is a bar across the fanlight. In the mid eighteenth century, with no streetlights,

Samuel Johnson's House in Gough Square (1881), by John Crowther. (City of London, London Metropolitan Archives, Chadwyck-Healey Collection, SC/GL/CHA/007/C1/13)

and with only a rudimentary police force, the house must have presented a tempting target to burglars. It would have given the impression of being occupied by a man of means (although to any burglar the contents of the house would have come as a severe disappointment).

I have come to attend a lecture, which is to take place in the famous garret where Johnson compiled his dictionary. The subject is celebrity in the eighteenth century, but what we hear is not an account of the great names of the period—Johnson, David Garrick, Henry Fielding, and the rest. Rather, we are reminded that there are different stories to be told of Georgian London, of other people who achieved their fifteen minutes of fame and then slipped from sight: the boxer George Taylor, the gentleman highwayman James MacLaine, and Hannah Snell, who, disguised as a man, served as a soldier.[1]

After the lecture, I wander around the house and look at the portraits of Johnson's friends and contemporaries which cover the walls. To examine these pictures is to return from the forgotten figures of the eighteenth century I have been hearing about to the well-known characters, so familiar from Boswell's *Life of Johnson*. It is a sort of eighteenth-century *Who's Who*: Boswell himself, the statesman Edmund Burke, the novelist and diarist Frances Burney, Oliver Goldsmith, and the painter Joshua Reynolds.

Among the famous names, however, one portrait stands out from all the others. The subject is a black man, quite young—perhaps in his twenties or thirties. He is good-looking, with high cheekbones and clear skin. He appears to be quite slight, although the voluminous coat he is wearing makes it hard to be sure of this: it falls in deep folds across his chest. Around his neck he wears a white stock, which comes high up his throat. The artist has set him, slightly incongruously, in the open air, against a backdrop of white clouds and blue sky. The expression on his face is solemn, if not melancholy, and he stares into the distance to his right-hand side. The overall impression is one of nobility, and yet the inscription beneath the painting states that this is Francis Barber, "Dr. Johnson's servant." How did this young man come to take his place among some of the most famous figures of his time?

This book sets out to tell two stories. The first is that of the remarkable journey of Francis Barber, from a sugar plantation to the heart of literary London. Born the property of a slave-owner, Barber had no prospect of any kind of independent existence, yet he made a life of his own in eighteenth-century England and ended up as the heir of one of the most celebrated men of the day, and one of the most famous of all time.

The other story is intertwined with the first: it is an account of an unlikely friendship, that between Francis Barber and Samuel Johnson. The former Jamaican slave and the man of letters had at first little or nothing in common, yet their relationship lasted for thirty-two years, changing and developing over time. During much of that period the two lived in the same household in a state of increasing interdependence.

There are numerous biographies of Johnson, and each of them mentions Francis Barber, but inevitably their primary concern is with the great writer. Barber often appears as little more than the passive beneficiary of Johnson's charity, someone whose sole function is to show Johnson in a good light. But in truth there was much more to their relationship—and far more to Francis Barber.

The story of Barber's life also has a wider significance: it opens up a window to an unfamiliar world. The history books record that there were thousands of black Britons in the eighteenth century, but the lives of individuals within that community have been little explored, in most cases because the records simply do not exist. The vast majority are completely forgotten; we know little about them apart from their names, and often not even that. Francis Barber, however, occupies a unique position. Because of his close connection with Samuel Johnson, Barber appears, at least passingly, in many accounts of the period. In biographies of Johnson like those by James Boswell and by Johnson's executor, John Hawkins, Barber has a walk-on part and he also makes occasional appearances in the letters and diaries of other contemporaries, such as Hester Thrale and Frances Burney. His story allows us an unusual glimpse into the black community of eighteenth-century Britain, and a reminder of a time when there were slaves on the streets of London.

Tracking the clues about Barber's life is not always easy, and some surprising claims have been made about him. Barber never published a word, but he appears in Robert Winder's history of immigration, *Bloody Foreigners*, as "a poet and protégé of Johnson."[2] In a poll which appeared in the London *Evening Standard* ranking great black Britons, Barber is listed as a "writer." (He was placed thirty-first, well below Olaudah Equiano, but above Ignatius Sancho.)[3] In *Bury the Chains*, Adam Hochschild's fine account of the struggle to abolish slavery, Barber is described as Johnson's "valet-butler-secretary," making him sound like a character from the pen of P. G. Wodehouse.[4]

Such descriptions of Barber may be inaccurate, but their existence testifies to a continuing interest in his life. That interest is also vividly demonstrated by Barber's frequent appearances in works of fiction: a select list would include John Wain's radio play *Frank*, Maureen Lawrence's prize-winning stage play *Resurrection*, S. I. Martin's *Incomparable World*, and most recently Caryl Phillips's novel *Foreigners*.[5]

But what is the true story of Francis Barber, and of his relationship with Samuel Johnson? To answer this question we must enter a world very different from Johnson's London, but one that is intimately linked to it. The place to begin the search is an environment as vicious as the house in Gough Square is civilized.

2. "The Dunghill of the Universe"

How should our search for Francis Barber begin? Perhaps we should follow the example of the opening pages of the most celebrated biography ever written, James Boswell's *Life of Samuel Johnson*:

> Samuel Johnson was born at Lichfield, in Staffordshire, on the 18th of September, N. S. 1709 . . . his baptism is recorded, in the register of St. Mary's parish in that city, to have been performed on the day of his birth.[1]

Names, places, dates: hard facts, reminding us that Boswell was first and foremost a lawyer. He is careful to identify his sources, too, pointing to the parish register as if to say, "You don't have to take my word for it—here is the evidence." And if we take up the challenge, we can still read the entry for Johnson's baptism in the parish register of St. Mary's, Lichfield, for 1709, "Sept. 7. bapt. Sam. son of Mich. Johnson gent."[2] The difference in the dates may cause a modern reader to pause, but Boswell is there before us, keen to avoid uncertainty or ambiguity: the change to the Gregorian calendar had occurred in 1752, and Boswell is careful to note that the date he gives is according to the "N. S." (new style) calendar.

Boswell goes on to tell us the name and occupation of Johnson's father, his mother's name and family origins, and his brother's name (Nathaniel). We discover that Michael Johnson was "of obscure extraction," but his wife, Sarah (Ford) Johnson, was of an "ancient race of substantial yeomanry."

Samuel Johnson is firmly rooted in a place, a time, and a family; the record of his early life is one of solidity and certainty. For Francis Barber, none of this is true. To begin with, by what name should we call him? During his lifetime, he was referred to variously as Quashey, Francis, Frank, the Blackamoor, poor Blacky, the Ethiopian, and sometimes, in the newspapers of the time, by no name at all—"the Doctor's negro servant." Francis Barber may be the best we can do, but even this is misleading. The name has a very English quality about it, especially in the form in which Johnson used it, "Frank Barber." The effect is even greater when their names are linked, as they often are—Sam Johnson and Frank Barber. They have a certain ring to them: respectability, moderation, ordinariness. *Johnson and Barber* could be a long-established firm of lawyers. There is no hint of the unfamiliar or the unsettling. No one would have been surprised to hear such a name in eighteenth-century London. Imagine if, instead, his name had been Quobna Ottobah Cugoano or Ukawsaw Gronniosaw (two other black Britons of the time).

When and where was he born, and who were his parents? Barber left no autobiography of any kind, but on two occasions he talked about his early years to another person who wrote down Barber's recollections. The first record of such a conversation is a very unusual document. On 15 July 1786 James Boswell, who was then at work on his *Life of Johnson,* wrote a letter to Barber, requesting that he would "oblige me with Answers to the following Questions for the Life of your late excellent Master." Boswell went on to set out a series of questions in eight numbered paragraphs, leaving spaces for Barber to fill in the answers—it was perhaps the first time a written questionnaire had been used in the research for a biography. The original letter survives in Boswell's private papers, and the answers to the questions have been written on it, but they are in Boswell's handwriting. What seems to have happened is that Barber brought the letter back to Boswell, who went through the queries one by one, writing on the letter Barber's responses.[3] Boswell's first questions and Barber's answers were as follows:

> 1. Where was you born? When did you come to England? . . . Born in Jamaica. Came to England with Colonel Bathurst father of Dr. Bathurst in 1750. Was seven or eight years old.[4]

Here, in just twenty-one words, we have the fullest known account of the first seven or eight years of Barber's life. In other answers to the questionnaire (to which we will return later) he spoke about his later life.

The second document to record Barber's origins was created thirteen years after Boswell's questionnaire. On 4 October 1799 Barber had to

complete a Poor Law examination, an enquiry taken on oath before a Justice
of the Peace to see whether he was entitled to financial support from the
parish. It is a standard form in which the examiner has filled in the gaps. It
declares:

> Examination of [Francis Barber . . .] Who said that he is about the
> age of [Fifty-two] Years, and that he was born, as he has been
> informed and verily believes in the: [Island of Jamaica in the West
> Indies of which Island his parents were Natives.][5]

In both accounts Barber says that he was born in Jamaica, but when did
this take place? In the answers to Boswell's questionnaire Barber said that he
came to England in 1750, when he was seven or eight years old. If this was
correct, then Barber must have been born in 1742 or 1743. But in the 1799
Poor Law examination he declared that he was "about 52 years old," which
would mean he was born around 1747. Which date, if either, is correct?
A man's age is an important part of his identity: when we read about his life,
we want to know how old he was when he married, when he died, and at
other key events. Boswell understood this; not only does he start his *Life of
Johnson* by telling his readers the date of Johnson's birth, he also records
Johnson's age at the top of each page of the book, so that with a glance we
can locate any event in its place in Johnson's life.

Of one date we can be reasonably certain: Francis Barber's arrival in
England. Barber recollected that it was 1750 when he was brought from
Jamaica by his owner, Colonel Richard Bathurst, and, as we shall see, this is
consistent with the dates of other events in the lives of both Barber and
Colonel Bathurst.[6] If Barber was born in 1742 or 1743, then he would have
been seven or eight years old when Bathurst brought him to England, but
if he was born in 1747, he would have been only three years old when he
accompanied Bathurst on the voyage. Like much about Barber's early years,
the date of his birth remains uncertain, but the earlier date seems more
probable.

So far as his parents were concerned, Barber recorded in the Poor
Law examination only that they were natives of Jamaica. He may have
known little or nothing about them, as one of the consequences of the slave
system in Jamaica was that anything approximating conventional family
life (as that was judged by European standards) was very difficult, if not
impossible, to maintain. A couple might have different owners, with all the

practical problems that entailed. If they were owned by the same master their relationship could easily be broken up by their owner's decision to sell, or by his death or bankruptcy. Partners could be separated, and a parent divided from a child.[7]

Barber came to be the property of Colonel Bathurst in one of two ways: either Bathurst purchased him, or the young boy was the child of a woman slave whom Bathurst owned. There is a possible early glimpse of Barber in some Jamaican deeds of sale dated August and September 1749. A few months before Colonel Bathurst took Barber to England, he sold the sugar plantation where he had lived for almost twenty years—2,600 acres of land, together with all the buildings, livestock, sugar, rum, and 143 slaves. However, the sale excluded "one mulatto child of Colias a negroe man named Shadrach and negroe boy named Quashey and a negroe woman named Nancy." In another copy of the deed, the names appear as Coolas, Shadrac, Quashey, and Nanny, and it is recorded that the "said Nanny is since manumitted and made free by Richard Bathurst."[8] So Bathurst kept four slaves back from the sale and gave one—the woman Nancy, or Nanny— her freedom.

Of the two child slaves Bathurst still owned after the 1749 sale, it is most probable that the "negroe boy named Quashey" was the slave he brought to England the following year. The distinction between a "negroe boy" and a "mulatto child" (whose appearance indicated that he or she was of mixed race) was a significant matter in the colonial West Indies, and Colonel Bathurst referred to Francis Barber in 1756 as "a negroe whom I brought from Jamaica."[9]

The name "Quashey" may tell us something about Barber's origins. Many Jamaican slaves were Coromantines, the English term loosely used to refer to Akan speakers brought from the African Gold Coast (present-day Ghana). They seem to have made a particular effort to retain what they could of their own culture, often giving their children Akan day-names, indicating on which day of the week they had been born. The Akan day-name for a boy born on a Sunday was "Quashey."[10] Had Barber's forbears been brought from the Gold Coast?

In any society the naming of a child is an important event, but its significance is by no means universal. When Michael and Sarah Johnson named their sons Samuel and Nathaniel the choice of biblical names said something about their religious beliefs, and perhaps also about their hopes for their children. In Jamaica, a slave's name was chosen not by the parents, but by the slave-owner. As a result, it carried completely different overtones: naming a slave was a statement of ownership and control and an exercise of power. Both the names chosen and their form emphasised the distinction between the black slave and the white free—and by implication the inferior status of the former. White people invariably had at least two names, including a family surname, but slaves had a single name such as Quamino or Caesar, or a name which indicated their age or origins—Old Coobah or Creole Jack. Some slave names had a more explicitly demeaning effect, and it was not uncommon for slaves to carry the same names as livestock, such as Prince, Pompey, Jumper. In some cases, the intent to demean was apparent— Monkey, Villain, Strumpet.[11] It seems that Barber was at first called "Quashey"; he might as well have been called "slave." In these pages I usually refer to him as Quashey up to the point when he became Francis Barber. It serves as a reminder that he did not begin life as Francis Barber, and that his origins were in slavery.

Naming could also give rise to a sense of continuity—or a lack of it. Both Samuel Johnson's name and the baptismal record, "son of Michael Johnson," preserved his history as part of the Johnson family. In Jamaica, in contrast, the naming of slaves ignored their parentage and showed complete disregard for family relationships. The effect was to create a fracture in the historical record. In his book *Searching for the Invisible Man*, Michael Craton set out to record the oral histories of numerous Jamaicans, in order to learn more about slavery and plantation life.[12] What he discovered instead was a startling but eloquent absence. Little knowledge of the past had been preserved, and what had been passed down was only from recent history. Anyone who wants to know more of the family into which Samuel Johnson was born can look in the 283 pages and twenty-nine pedigrees of Aleyn Lyell Reade's massive volume, *The Reades of Blackwood Hill and Dr. Johnson's Ancestry*.[13] Anyone who wants to know about Francis Barber's family is left scrabbling for clues. We know that Bathurst kept Quashey when he sold the rest of his slaves in 1749, and it is very likely that this was the young Francis Barber. But can we trace his story any further back, and find out how Bathurst obtained the young slave?

There is just one possible reference to Quashey's mother. Two years before Colonel Bathurst sold his estate, he purchased three slaves. The deed of sale, dated 23 September 1747, records the purchase by Bathurst of "a negro woman slave named Grace and her two children Luckey and Quashy. Consideration 5£ currency."[14] Could this be the "Quashey" whom Bathurst kept back when he sold his estate in 1749, and was Grace his mother? If so, it tells us that at a very young age Barber was separated from his mother and brother—Grace and Luckey were not among the slaves whom Bathurst retained. But once again the record slips from our grasp. We cannot be sure that this was the same boy, as the name appears again and again in Jamaican slave records. Quashey, or Quashy, was one of the most common names for a male slave, so much so that it came to be almost a generic term for a male slave. It was synonymous with an attitude of subservience and passive acceptance.[15]

One central fact, though, is certain: as the child of a woman slave, Quashey was born a slave. For the first seven or eight years of his life, he lived in a slave society. If we know little of Quashey's parents, we know rather more about the environment in which he spent those early years, and about another important figure in his life, his owner, Colonel Richard Bathurst. When Quashey was born the Bathurst family had been plantation owners in Jamaica for over sixty-five years. The Bathursts had been beneficiaries of the policy of Charles II towards his unruly colony.

The history of Jamaica as a British possession was undistinguished. In 1655, Oliver Cromwell sent a substantial expedition—over 8,000 men—against the Spanish West Indies. They launched a poorly planned assault on Hispaniola, the island which is now divided between Haiti and the Dominican Republic. This failed miserably, and 1,000 British men were lost in the attack. Abandoning this attempt, they turned their attention to the nearby island of Jamaica, which was virtually undefended. They managed to seize the island, although it still took another five years to achieve a final victory over the Spanish troops. The island was fertile, but the settlers were unable to take advantage of this fact. Illness and agricultural incompetence decimated the occupying forces as well as later arrivals, and large numbers of them died. Within five years, the number of the occupying troops had fallen to 2,200.[16]

Many of the soldiers, along with other settlers, joined forces with the buccaneers who came to Jamaica in large numbers from elsewhere in the Caribbean. Under the leadership of the notorious Henry Morgan they made the island the base for attacks on ships, or raids on the coastal settlements of Cuba, Hispaniola, and Central America. For a while, in the late 1650s and early 1660s, this activity was not only tolerated but actively encouraged by the British governor of Jamaica, Edward D'Oyley, as the buccaneers' actions were directed mainly against the Spanish. But when the Spanish had been finally driven out, the buccaneers remained—there were estimated to be as many as 1,500 of them in 1670.[17] The island became difficult to govern, and Port Royal, the capital, became notorious for the riotous behaviour of its population of prostitutes, convicts, and drunks.

The occupation of Jamaica was beginning to look like a disastrous venture. But on his restoration to the throne, Charles II decided to take steps to establish the colony on a firm basis. The buccaneers, who lived in the north of the island, stood in the way of that development. So a new policy was adopted: immigrants from England were to be persuaded to settle in the undeveloped areas in the north, in an attempt to squeeze out the buccaneers. In 1661 a royal proclamation was issued:

> For the encouragement of our subjects, as well such as are bred upon the said island, as all others that shall transport themselves thither to reside and plant there, we have thought proper to declare and publish that thirty acres of improveable lands shall be granted and allotted to every such person, male or female . . . to them and their heirs for ever.[18]

After an initial period of failure, the settlers began to establish themselves, to develop plantations and to produce a variety of cash crops—cotton, cocoa, and, above all, sugar.

The model for the production of sugar had been developed in Barbados in the mid seventeenth century. Until then it had been in short supply in Britain and remained a luxury product which only the wealthy could afford. But two developments changed all that in a short space of time, turning it into an item of mass consumption. First, the demand for the sweetener increased dramatically among the general public as the taste for coffee, and later tea, grew, and both became available to all social classes: in the period from 1650 to 1800 the consumption of sugar in Britain increased by 2,500 percent.[19] Second, between 1640 and 1660 the Barbados planters switched from tobacco and cotton—with which they had not had much success—to sugar. They learnt new production techniques from sugar plantations in Brazil which were controlled by the Dutch from 1630 to 1645, and adapted them to great effect. Another lesson they learnt from the Dutch was the use of slaves in sugar production.

The first British planters had relied for labour upon poor, white inden-tured servants, but these did not provide a very reliable workforce, and in any event not many of them stayed on when their indentures expired. A further problem was that there were simply not enough of them to do the labour-intensive work, especially as the planters began to see the benefits of increased production. The solution was the import of slaves from Africa in increasing numbers, providing a cheap and reliable source of labour.

Jamaica was much larger than Barbados, and its fertile soil offered great prospects to sugar planters. In 1664 Sir Thomas Modyford, who had been a successful sugar plantation owner for twenty years in Barbados, was appointed governor of Jamaica, a post he held until 1671. He encouraged many of his fellow Barbados planters to move to Jamaica. Sugar was soon established as the surest way to wealth, commanding high prices and paying low English import duties. The planters responded by expanding their plan-tations and increasing production. It marked the creation of a plantation society: for 150 years, the production of sugar was to be at the heart of Jamaican life and the basis of hundreds of fortunes.

The number of plantations soared. In 1671 there were 146 plantations, of which 57 were growing sugar, but within thirteen years this number had grown to 690 plantations, 246 of them for sugar. One of these was owned by an incomer from England, John Bathurst, who in 1674 had been granted by Charles II an area of land in the parish of St. Mary, bounded to the east by the Orange River and to the south by the Stoney River. It was a very substan-tial amount of land. In 1670 a survey showed that forty-four planters held 1,000 acres or more, and sixteen held 2,000 acres or more. The Orange River estate was 4,000 acres, to which a further 2,200 acres in other parishes were later added.[20] Bathurst became a figure of some consequence on the island, and was on several occasions elected a member of the Assembly of Jamaica, representing St. Mary's parish.[21] In 1685, when the cartographer Philip Lea drew up a map of Jamaica showing all the principal plantations, the Orange River estate appeared, marked with the name "Bathurst."

Bathurst's estate, Francis Barber's first known home, was a sugar plan-tation. Every aspect of life on the estate revolved around the production of sugar, and every grain was precious. A law of 1711 made it an offence to sell or give away sugar or sugarcane without a ticket (evidence of the plantation owner's permission). The penalty was "whipping, not exceeding thirty-one lashes."[22] Producing sugar involved intensive, backbreaking manual labour, both in the fields, digging, hoeing, planting, and reaping, and in the factories, distilling and boiling. Each part of the process was dependent on slave labour.

The large plantations required great numbers of workers—the rule of thumb was one slave per acre of land growing sugarcane. The birthrate amongst slaves was low (and the infant mortality rate high), largely due to a combination of disease, malnourishment, and overwork. So what became known as the slave-trading triangle developed. Slaves were bought in Africa, in modern-day Liberia, Ghana, or Nigeria, and crammed into slave ships for the Middle Passage, the two-month journey across the Atlantic to the Caribbean or to the American colonies. In the 250-year period between 1607 and 1857 some 1,020,000 slaves were sent on the route from Africa to Jamaica.

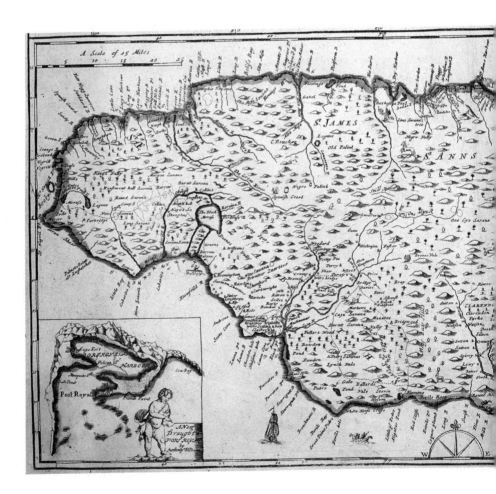

A new Mapp of the Island of Jamaica (1685), by Philip Lea. The map shows the names of the plantation owners. In the detail two properties are marked "Bathurst." The Orange River plantation, Francis Barber's first known home, is the one shown at the bottom, to the north of the Orange River. (British Library, maps 80710(5) © British Library Board)

Those who survived the crossing—on average 15.1 percent of the slaves died on the voyage—were inspected by the plantation owners, and the fittest and strongest were bought to be used for the production of sugar and the other cargoes which the slave ships carried back to Britain.[23]

Slaves were imported into Jamaica on a massive scale. In 1662, when the first Jamaican census was taken, the population of the island was 4,207, of whom 554 (just 13.2 percent) were black. By the time of the 1730 census the population had grown to 83,765, of whom 75,535 (84.7 percent) were black. These included a small number of freed blacks, but the vast majority were slaves. By 1740 the Orange River estate was one of nineteen sugar plantations in St. Mary's parish, owning 4,484 slaves between them. In 1752 (about ten years after Barber's birth) there were some 110,000 slaves in Jamaica.[24] Some of them, like Barber, had been born there, second- or third-generation slaves, but most were the victims of the slave trade.

The system of chattel slavery was formalised and enshrined in a series of Acts of the Jamaican Assembly.[25] The first Jamaican legislation dealing with slavery was passed in 1661, and the first complete slave code in 1696. Section 4 of the Act of Jamaica of 1674 spelt out the legal status of slaves with absolute clarity: "All negroes lawfully bought as bondslaves shall here continue to be so and further be held and judged and taken to be goods and chattels." In addition, there were aspects of Jamaican slavery which were universally recognised, although never formally laid down. There appears never to have been any express legal provision in Jamaica providing that the child of a slave inherited slave status from the mother. Nevertheless, this was the unquestioned practice.

Slaves were chattels, not in a metaphorical but in a literal sense. They were items of property, and could be bought, sold, lent, or given away in the same way as any other goods. Quashey was the property of Richard Bathurst, who had inherited the Orange River plantation from his father, John, in about 1730. Bathurst was colonel of the North Side Regiment of the militia, a sort of part-time police force which dealt with troublesome whites, rebellious slaves, and runaways. Every free white male had to belong to the militia regiment for his parish, his rank reflecting his standing as a landowner; Bathurst's colonelcy was an indication of his status, as was his election to the Jamaican Legislative Assembly in 1722.

Bathurst's money and position made him part of the plantocracy, the wealthiest plantation owners, who saw themselves as the social superiors of other whites—the tradesmen, employed overseers, clerks, and smallholders. In their own eyes, they were an élite group whose position demanded respect. They could certainly afford all the trappings to support this self-image, including the great houses where they could display their books and paintings and indulge their substantial appetites for food, drink, and slave women. But the reality was that many had failed at previous occupations in Britain, and some had been forced to flee the country. The social pretensions and high militia ranks of such men were the subject of mockery in Britain. In 1698 the satirist Ned Ward wrote a hugely popular travel account, *A Trip to Jamaica: With a True Character of the People and Island.* The portrait it painted was unlikely to leave a reader in any doubt as to Ward's opinion of the island and its people:

> The Dunghill of the Universe, the Refuse of the whole creation . . . the Receptacle of Vagabonds, the Sanctuary of Bankrupts, and a Close-stool for the Purges of our Prisons. The generality of the men look as if they had just nock'd off their fetters . . . They are all *Colonels, Majors, Captains, Lieutenants,* and *Ensigns* . . . A Broken *Apothecary* will make there a topping *Physician;* a *Barbers Prentice,* a good *Surgeon;* a *Bailiffs Follower,* a passable *Lawyer,* and an *English Knave,* a very *Honest Fellow.*[26]

It is a portrait which needs to be borne in mind in relation to Bathurst. He was often referred to as Colonel Bathurst, and in tracing Francis Barber's story it is convenient to use Bathurst's militia rank in order to distinguish him from his son (also called Richard), who played an important role in Barber's life. But he should be thought of more as the leader of a neighbour-hood watch or community police force than as a commissioned colonel in the regular army.

Bathurst's plantation was large, but its situation was unfavourable. Although the island as a whole was very fertile, the parish of St. Mary was poor for planters and slaves alike. It was one of the last parts of Jamaica to be settled, mainly because much of the area was hilly or mountainous and, according to the account published by Edward Long in 1774 in his *History of Jamaica,* extremely wet for most of the year, and cold. These conditions often proved fatal to those slaves who were sent there immediately on their arrival in Jamaica or transferred there from the parishes in the south of the island, where it was warmer and dryer. Sugarcane grown in the area was of poor quality.[27] It was also a dangerous area for slave-owners such as Bathurst. Long noted that it had been "frequently disturbed with insurrections of negro slaves, so it has 4 barracks, at 2 of which there is usually a small cantonment of soldiers." All these circumstances made it a difficult plantation for Bathurst to work profitably.

How did the Orange River estate look through the eyes of the young Quashey? For a start, it was a black world: everywhere he looked, in the thatched huts where the slaves lived, in the little plots nearby where they tried to grow food, and in the fields where they worked, he saw black men, women, and children. There were at least 148 slaves living on the estate. Even some of the authority figures were black—the women who looked after slave children such as Quashey, and the head drivers, slaves appointed to direct the work of their fellow slaves working in the field gangs. We know of no white person on the plantation other than Bathurst (his wife, Catharine, having died in 1726), but there were probably a handful of others: it was usual to have a white overseer, and a few other whites in positions where slaves were not trusted, such as managers of the mill or the boiling house. At some level, even a child such as Barber must have registered the fact that it was the few whites who exercised power: they were the ones who gave orders and dealt out punishments or rewards. The large majority, the slaves, obeyed or suffered.

On a substantial plantation such as the Orange River estate, it made sense for the slaves to live near their place of work, and at some distance from the great house—planters did not want their slaves close by, where they might trouble them with their noise and smell.[28] (One Jamaican smallholder lived some 130 yards from his slaves, but he somewhat improbably noted in his diary in 1781 that "Pompey frequently lets such loud farts that we hear him plain & loud to my house.")[29] The slaves lived in small family groups in huts close to the fields. Here they cooked, ate, slept, and sometimes made music at night (much to the annoyance of the whites). When Bathurst sold the estate in 1749 it included fifty slave huts, which suggests that about three people occupied each hut.[30]

From the sounding of the conch shell at four a.m., the waking moments of the field slaves were dominated by work. For six days a week they would work twelve-hour days, from dawn until dusk—the seventh day was for work on the slaves' own plots. Our picture of Jamaican slavery is usually of adults at work in the plantations, but in fact child slaves such as Quashey were as much part of the sugar-production process as adults. One planter of a later period, Thomas Roughley, published in 1823 a guide to the efficient running of a plantation, *The Jamaica Planter's Guide*, based on his twenty years' experience. In addition to describing the work of the adult field slaves, he laid down a pattern for the use of children. Such a slave should be taken from the mother at the age of one (to enable her to work) and given to a "well-disposed matron." At the age of three, he or she would be put in "a little playful gang," where each child would have "a little basket, and be made somewhat useful by gathering up fallen trash and leaves, and pulling up weeds."[31]

At the age of five or six, children would join the "Third Gang," sometimes called the "weeding" gang: "the supple hand of the negro child is best calculated to extract weeds and grass." In planting time, each child would carry a small basket of dung, and would walk in front of the mature slaves, throwing dung in the cane holes. An experienced woman slave superintended the Third Gang, armed with a pliant, serviceable twig, "more to create dread, than inflict chastisement."

Cutting the sugar cane (1823), by William Clark. A rare depiction (foreground) of a child slave in the West Indies. The painting is from the same year as Thomas Roughley's *Jamaica Planter's Guide,* well after Barber's time. (Plate IV from *Ten Views in the Island of Antigua,* by William Clark [London: Thomas Clay, 1823], British Library, 1786.c.9, c13321–20 © British Library Board)

At twelve years old, the children would join the "Second Gang," along with the elderly and the weak, doing fieldwork of a relatively undemanding kind—heaping manure, planting corn, cleaning and banking young canes. "How pleasing," wrote Roughley, "how gratifying, how replete with humanity it is to see a swarm of healthy, active, cheerful, pliant, straight, handsome creole negro boys and girls going to, and returning from the puerile field work allotted to them, clean and free from any disease or blemish."[32]

At eighteen the children would graduate to the "First Gang," the mature slaves who did the heavy work of planting and harvesting—intense, physical labour of the hardest kind, often carried out in brutal heat. Jamaican weather records for 1764 show that in the hottest months the mean daily temperature was about 80°F, and in January (the coolest point of the year) it was about 75°F.[33] The peak temperatures were, of course, much higher. The slaves would continue to labour throughout their lives until they died or became unable to work anymore.

Fortunately for Quashey it seems that he escaped the fate of the child field slaves. Some distance from the slave huts stood Bathurst's home, the great house where he was able to live in considerable style. It was common for planters to have numerous domestic slaves to cook, clean, wait at table, and generally attend to their owners' every wish. The life of these house slaves was in many ways better than that of field slaves: the work was lighter, they were more likely to obtain favours, and they were better fed and clothed. Quashey must have had some such household role, as Bathurst was to take him along when he returned to England: the services of a young field slave would have been of no value to Colonel Bathurst, but a young houseboy could be very useful.

Quashey left no account of his impressions of his first home. The records of slavery which have survived are the records of the slave-owners: how can we capture the experience of the slaves and, in particular, a child slave? For some sense of this, we could look at the accounts written by former slaves, such as Olaudah Equiano or Ukawsaw Gronniosaw, or turn to the campaigning publications of well-informed abolitionists like James Ramsay. We could examine the official reports which were eventually published as the campaign against slavery intensified. All of these would be helpful in building up a picture of slave life in Jamaica.

But there is one remarkable source which takes us into the very heart of Quashey's world. One of the most extraordinary surviving records of life in

Jamaica is the diary of Thomas Thistlewood, over 10,000 manuscript pages which provide a detailed account of daily life on a sugar plantation.[34] Thistlewood sailed to Jamaica from England in 1750 (the year when Bathurst took Quashey to England), and lived there until his death in 1786. He was at first the overseer of a large sugar estate, much like the Orange River plantation, and then became the owner of a smallholding. Living in the same setting as Quashey, at almost exactly the same time, he left a record which is invaluable for understanding Quashey's experience.

Of course, Thistlewood's account is written from the perspective of a white slave-owner, but it is still very revealing. What makes the diary so valuable is that it was not written for anyone else to read. Thistlewood was not trying to defend his way of life, nor that of planters in general. (It would never have occurred to him that it might need defending.) His account is telling, precisely because it is intended only to record. It is the matter-of-fact tone which makes it both chilling and compelling.

As the owner of a smallholding, Thistlewood was not a member of the plantocracy, as Bathurst was. Nevertheless, he was able to live in a grand style which he could not have hoped to achieve in England, and which would have astonished many a wealthy man in the mother country. He records a meal with three friends, not an unusual event:

> Had mutton broth, roast mutton and broccoli, carrots and asparagus, stewed mudfish, roast goose and paw paw, apple sauce, stewed giblets, some fine lettuce, crabs, cheese, mush melo, etc. Punch, porter, ale, cider, Madeira wine and brandy, etc.[35]

The following day he noted, "Very unwell." One fact that Thistlewood does not note is that the food was prepared and served by slaves, who would often go hungry.

Thistlewood was intelligent and well-read. When he arrived in Jamaica, he brought with him 75 books. While he was there he had many more sent over from England, and he borrowed and lent books. Unlikely as it seems, Jamaica was (as Thistlewood's biographer, Trevor Burnard, points out) a small corner of the enlightenment. Thistlewood read Chaucer, Montesquieu, Voltaire, Montaigne, Bolingbroke, Gibbon's *Decline and Fall of the Roman Empire*, Milton's *Paradise Lost*, Pope's *An Essay on Man* and *The Tatler* essays, as well as books on history, geography, and medicine.[36] He read

Samuel Johnson's *Adventurer* essays, and on one occasion recorded an account of Johnson, given by a friend who claimed to know very well "the author of the noted dictionary . . . a tall stout man, and a great sloven . . . his beard would frequently be 1/2 or 3/4 of an inch long, and did not put on a clean shirt perhaps above once in 2 or 3 weeks, in which condition he would frequently go and dine with noblemen at their houses."[37]

Such literary interests did not make life better for Thistlewood's slaves. As greed and hunger could live side by side on the plantations, so literature and culture coexisted with brutal violence:

> Friday, 2nd May, 1777: In the evening flogged Lincoln, for disobedience in not fishing for me as I ordered him . . . Put him in the bilboes [iron fetters], and then flogged Dick for not bringing him to me . . . Also flogged Strap for going with grass to the Bay to sell without coming for a ticket . . . and other impudent tricks.

> Monday, 12th May 1777: Dr King lent me An *Inquiry into the Nature & Causes of the Wealth of Nations*, by Adam Smith.[38]

These records of floggings are not at all unusual: the pages of Thistlewood's diary are full of casual records of extreme violence. At one time or another, he whipped all of his slaves, often for the most trivial of reasons. Violence was an everyday event: it was part of the atmosphere. Slave-owners lived in fear of what the slaves might do if not kept at all times in a state of subjugation, and they were intent on maintaining control. They did so partly by giving rewards (food or time off work) but, much more important, by the ever-present threat of punishment. The usual methods were flogging or chaining, but on occasion other ways were used, not just to inflict extreme pain, but to humiliate and to degrade. On 30 July 1756, Thistlewood recorded in his diary that he caught two runaways:

> Punch catched at Salt River and brought home. Flogged him and Quacoo well, and then washed and rubbed in salt pickle, lime juice & bird pepper; also whipped Hector for losing his hoe, made New Negro Joe piss in his eyes & mouth etc.[39]

On 1 August, another runaway, Hazat, was captured: "Put him in the bilboes both feet; gagged him; locked his hands together; rubbed him with molasses & exposed him naked to the flies all day, and to the mosquitoes all night." One slave, Derby, was driven by hunger to eat sugar canes: "Derby . . . catched by Port Royal eating canes. Had him well flogged and pickled, then made Hector shit in his mouth."[40]

Women slaves were just as likely to be flogged as the men, but they had much more to fear from Thistlewood, as his diary entries reveal:

Friday, 1st July 1757: About 7p.m. *cum* Phoebe, the cook, *Sup. Lect* [with Phoebe, the cook, on the bed] in North Room.

Saturday, 2nd July . . . At night *cum* Illa, B*is.* [with Illa, twice]

Sunday, 3rd July: . . . At night *cum* Phib.[41]

Such sexual abuse of slaves was commonplace among white Jamaicans. Thistlewood also offered his slaves to visitors: "Saturday, 19th May 1759: At night Mr Cope came. Slept here, had Little Mimber; but suspect he has the clap." On this occasion Thistlewood did not allow his (well-founded) concerns about venereal disease to limit his predatory activities. Five days later he recorded: "In the evening, *Cum* Little Mimber, a Creole, *Sup Lect. in meo domo* [on the bed in my home] parlour."[42]

Thistlewood's diary reveals that in his 37 years in Jamaica, he had sex 3,852 times, with 138 women.[43] On just over half of those occasions, his partner was Phibbah, a slave who was his long-term mistress. On most of the other occasions he would give the woman money. The issue of consent did not arise. There was simply no question of resistance, as the women knew the consequences only too well: "Egypt Susannah and Mazerine whipped for refusal."[44]

Of course, Thistlewood was not Bathurst, and it is possible that Quashey was much more fortunate than Thistlewood's slaves. But brutal punishments were a feature of plantation society: even a pro-slavery propagandist such as Edward Long could deplore some legal penalties as "highly tyrannical and cruel."[45] Thistlewood's diary tells us a great deal about the environment in which Quashey was born and brought up. The values and attitudes which were accepted by all whites in Jamaica permitted Thistlewood to see himself as a respectable member of society—and to be perceived as such by whites who knew him. Jamaican slave society provided an agreeable home for such a man, a world in which white men were free to act precisely as they pleased towards their slaves. Thistlewood's biographer points out that during all his years of residence he records only one occasion when a white was punished for ill treatment of slaves—John Wright murdered four of his partners, but escaped penalty until he killed a mistress who was mulatto. Even then he was permitted to escape jail by leaving the country.[46]

It was this world of Jamaican slavery in which Quashey spent his first seven or eight years. He saw the same sights, and breathed the same atmosphere of fear and brutality, and they remained with him. In 1756 Samuel Johnson wrote that Jamaica was "a place of great wealth and dreadful wickedness, a den of tyrants and a dungeon of slaves."[47] We do not have to look far to find the source of his information: living in his household at that time was an eyewitness, Francis Barber, the former slave Quashey.

Some members of the plantocracy were themselves repelled by their experience of Jamaica. One such was Colonel Bathurst's son, Dr. Richard Bathurst. He was born in Jamaica in 1722, but left the island in 1738 and never lived there again, though he occasionally visited. On one such visit some years later, he described Jamaica, in a letter to his friend Samuel Johnson, as "this execrable region," and added, "Nothing I think but absolute want can force me to continue where I am."[48]

When Colonel Bathurst inherited the plantation sometime in the 1730s, it was a substantial business. But it proved a difficult estate to run, and by the late 1740s it was on the verge of financial collapse. In August 1749, with his affairs in chaos, the Colonel was forced to sell his land, which had by then been reduced from its original 4,000 acres to 2,600 acres. For him it was a disaster, but for his son Richard it was a source of relief and delight: "My dear friend Dr. Bathurst," said Johnson, "declared he was glad that his father, who was a West-Indian planter, had left his affairs in total ruin, because having no estate, he was not under the temptation of keeping slaves."[49]

Following the collapse of his business, Colonel Bathurst decided to leave Jamaica for good and make his home in England. It was a crucial moment in the life of the young Quashey. Bathurst could easily have sold him, leaving him to spend the rest of his days in Jamaican slavery, but something made him decide not to do so. When he sailed for England in 1750, he did not travel alone: accompanying him on the three-month voyage was his child slave. Bathurst's decision to take Quashey with him was a life-changing one, and it raises an important question. Why would a former plantation owner, sailing to England to spend his last days there, take with him a seven-year-old slave?

In fact what Bathurst did was not unusual: there were many instances of planters or others bringing a slave with them when they went to Britain from the colonies. When Benjamin Franklin, one of the future founding fathers of the United States, travelled to London from Pennsylvania in 1757 with his son William, they brought with them their slaves Peter and King. In 1768 a Scots plantation owner, John Wedderburn, took his slave Joseph Knight back to Scotland from Jamaica, and the following year another Scots merchant called Charles Steuart brought his slave James Somerset from Virginia to England. (As we shall see, Knight and Somerset were to play crucial roles in the ending of slavery in Scotland and England, respectively.)[50]

There were a number of reasons for bringing slaves back to England. Partly it was just a matter of personal convenience: any white person who had lived in the colonies was accustomed to being served by slaves, and would not wish to travel without such service on the lengthy voyage or once they arrived. The alternative was a servant, but it might be difficult to find one who was able and willing to go to England. There was also the financial aspect—a servant would require wages, but a slave did not have to be paid. Added to this was the risk that a servant might be taken all the way to England only to leave his or her master for some other post. Slaves, on the other hand, had no such option and could never leave (though they could be discarded or sold in England if they were no longer required).

Another motive for taking a young slave to England was display. There was nothing remarkable or prestigious in possessing a servant in London at this time: there were many thousands of them, working in all kinds of households. A young black boy or girl, however, was an exotic novelty, a status symbol much more likely to attract attention, especially when dressed up in a smart livery. A visitor to England in 1735 recorded, "Passing out at the *Spring-Garden* Passage a Hackney Coach with a little *Blackmoor Boy* was waiting on two *fine Ladies*."[51] For these fine ladies and others like them, a black child was the latest fashion accessory.

There was another reason, however, why some black children were brought from the colonies to England. Sexual relations between master and slave were commonplace in Jamaica, and not just amongst the Thomas Thistlewoods of the plantations. Some planters formed long-term relationships with slave women, but there were also countless other encounters. There were very few single white women in Jamaica who might have made suitable wives or sexual partners for the planters, but there were thousands of readily available slave women, who were not in a position to object.[52] (In any event the availability of white women does not seem to have made much difference: even planters who were married and whose wives and children were living with them often openly conducted sexual relationships with slaves.)[53] Most domestic slaves were women, and they were particularly vulnerable. All this was an open secret: in 1784 one writer recorded that plantations were being run by either "a dissipated, careless, unfeeling young man, or a grovelling lascivious, old bachelor (each with his half score of black or mulatto pilfering harlots)."[54]

Not surprisingly, many planter–slave sexual encounters resulted in children. Such children would still be slaves (as they would inherit slave status from the mother), but their owners might accept a degree of special responsibility for them: they were often given favoured positions, perhaps being used as house slaves or as skilled workers, rather than having to labour in the fields. Richard S. Dunn, the historian of the Jamaican planters, writes of these children that "the planter sometimes baptized them into the Church of England, released them from slavery, articled them as apprentices, or set them up as small farmers and craftsmen." Financial provision was often made for them in wills or deeds.[55]

This was the world which Colonel Bathurst had inhabited for his entire life, and for much of that time he was a single man. In 1721 he married Catharine Phillips at St. Andrew's, Jamaica, but she died just five years later, and by the time he left Jamaica in 1750 Bathurst had been a widower for twenty-four years.[56]

This context, both of life in Jamaica and of the circumstances of Colonel Bathurst, may shed some light on a number of facts about Quashey. As we have seen, one of the two possible routes by which he became Bathurst's slave was by his birth to one of Bathurst's women slaves (the other being by purchase). The fact that he accompanied Bathurst to England indicates that he was not a field slave but a house slave—in other words, that he had been placed in a particularly desirable post. To this knowledge about Barber can be added the details of two later events. The first is that on arrival in England the young boy was baptised, and the second is that when Colonel Bathurst made his will in 1754 he left to the boy who had by then become Francis Barber "his freedom and twelve pounds in money."[57] These matters give rise to an unanswerable question: was Quashey simply a favoured slave—or was he Colonel Bathurst's son?[58]

Bathurst's only known reference to Francis Barber is in his will, where, as we have seen, he stated that he had brought the young boy from Jamaica. He said nothing about Barber's parentage. The only occasion on which Barber is known to have referred to his parents was in his Poor Law examination of 1799, when he stated on oath that he had been "informed and verily believes" (the standard language of the examination) that his parents were natives of Jamaica. Colonel Bathurst had been born there, but it is very unlikely that Barber would have referred to him alongside his mother as a native of Jamaica, so it seems that Barber did not believe that Bathurst was his father. Or perhaps he believed that he was, but was unwilling to acknowledge the fact in a public declaration. Such uncertainty is one outcome of his having been being born in a slave-owning society. That stage of Quashey's life, however, was now at an end as he set sail with Colonel Bathurst, bound for England.

3. A New Name

When Colonel Bathurst and Quashey arrived in England in 1750 they lived at first in London, staying with the Colonel's son, Dr. Richard Bathurst. We do not know where his home was, but it may have been in Fenchurch Buildings, off Fenchurch Street. Dr. Bathurst was certainly living there in September 1754, when he took up a post at the Middlesex infirmary.[1]

One can only guess at the shock which Quashey experienced when he arrived in the capital city. London, to anyone arriving for the first time, was an overwhelming assault on the senses. Travellers often commented on the stench: the city had open sewers, and horse manure, human urine, rotting food, dead animals, and rubbish of all kinds accumulated in the streets. In a parliamentary debate in 1738 on a plan to pave the streets of London, Lord Tyrconnel had described the capital as "a city famous for wealth, and commerce, and plenty, and for every other kind of civility and politeness, but which abounds with such heaps of filth, as a savage would look on with amazement." (The sentiments may have been Lord Tyrconnel's, but the wording was that of the reporter of the debate, Samuel Johnson.) Adding to this stink was the coal smoke which poured from houses and workshops, creating a near-permanent fog—a visitor to the city could smell it from several miles away. Then there was the noise: horses' hooves, the iron wheels of wagons and coaches on cobblestones, and the cries of hawkers, beggars, and the watermen on the Thames.[2]

Above all, there were the people, great numbers of them in the streets and the courtyards. In Jamaica in 1752 there were some 120,000 people on an island of 4,200 square miles: in London in 1750 there were 675,000 in a city of about 15 square miles.[3] And it was in the population that the contrast with Jamaica was at its most obvious—Quashey was now a black person in a white society.

Quashey's presence was not, however, a complete novelty: there was nothing new about blacks forming part of the population. As far back as 1596 Queen Elizabeth had proclaimed:

> Her Majestie understanding that there are of late divers black-moores brought into this realme, of which kinde of people there are allready here to manie . . . Her Majesty's pleasure therefore ys that those kinde of people should be sent forth of the lande.[4]

Clearly there was a black community in the late sixteenth century which was sufficiently sizeable and conspicuous to trouble the queen (although the threatened expulsion never took place). African slaves had been brought to England from the 1570s onward, but the numbers became much more significant in the latter part of the seventeenth century and throughout the eighteenth, with the development of the colonies and the growth of the slave trade. In 1723 the *Daily Journal* reported, " 'Tis said there is a great Number of Blacks come daily into this City, so that 'tis thought in a short Time, if they be not suppress'd, the City will swarm with them."[5] When Quashey arrived in England the sight of a young black boy in London would not have been unknown, but it would have been less common outside the capital. In 1761 the slave Olaudah Equiano visited the Isle of Wight and recorded that "a black boy about my own size . . . having observed me from his master's house, was transported at the sight of one of his own countrymen, and ran to meet me with the utmost haste . . . he soon came close to me, and caught hold of me in his arms as if I had been his brother."[6]

For some white Londoners the increasing size of the black community was an unwelcome development, which threatened both the purity of the race and the jobs and well-being of the "native population." In 1765 "F. Freeman" wrote to the *London Chronicle* proposing a tax on "Negroe and East-India servants, who of late years are become too abundant in this kingdom . . . The mixture of their breed with our own ought by no means to be encouraged . . . In their employments they . . . stand in the way of our own people, and by so much of the means of subsistence as they obtain, they lessen the degree of our native population. . . . I have heard their numbers of both sexes estimated at the lowest to be thirty thousand in the whole kingdom."[7] (It is likely that this correspondent had West Indian interests: the vast majority of such warnings about the threat to the "breed" and the taking of jobs from "our own people" came not from the population at large, but from the very active and vocal West Indian propagandists.)[8]

The figure of 30,000 for the size of the black population was pure guesswork, as were all the different figures cited in the mid eighteenth century—1,400, 14,000, 15,000, 20,000. There were simply no reliable statistics as to the number of black Britons, and the size of any estimate could be affected by the perspective of the person providing it. A clear example of this is provided by comments made on the size of the black population during the *Somerset* case of 1772, when the legality of slavery was challenged. Edward Long, a virulent opponent of sexual relationships between blacks and whites who had every reason to exaggerate the size of the black population, wrote a booklet on the judgment in which he at first estimated the black population of Britain to be 3,000. But he then discovered that other figures had been cited. During the trial of the case John Dunning (counsel for the slave-owner) claimed that there were 14,000 slaves in Britain "from the most exact intelligence I am able to procure at present." In replying his opponent, Serjeant Davy, stated the number as "14,000 or 15,000." The figures of "14,000 or 15,000" were then repeated by the judge, Lord Mansfield. Samuel Estwick, a pro-slavery propagandist, used this reference in a pamphlet on the case, but he gave only the higher figure of 15,000. When Edward Long read Estwick's publication he promptly added a postscript to his own pamphlet, changing his own estimate of the figures from 3,000 to 15,000.[9] The reality was that such guesses were completely unreliable, but the higher figure better served the purposes of Long's propaganda.

The most extensive and detailed research into the issue has been conducted by Kathleen Chater, who describes in her book *Untold Histories* how she systematically trawled parish records and other sources for the period from 1660 to 1807. She found references to 550 black people in the London area over the period from 1742 to 1772, and concluded that "there were probably only a few thousand black people in London in the early 1770s."[10] In 1786 the Committee for the Relief of the Black Poor estimated that there were between 3,000 and 5,000 black people in London.[11] (Numbers had increased with the arrival of black loyalists who had fought for Britain against their former masters during the American War of

Independence.) The earliest certain figure, based on seven lists of black people in England drawn up in 1786–1787, shows an absolute minimum of 1,114.[12] To set these figures in context, the population of London is thought to have been about 675,000 in 1750, and it is estimated that it grew from around 500,000 to 958,863 between 1700 and 1801, suggesting that in the late eighteenth century fewer than 1 percent of the population of the city were black. The population of England was some 6.5 million in 1751, and 7.1 million in 1771.[13]

Shortly after the young Quashey's arrival in London, another important event occurred in his life. It was recorded by John Hawkins, a lawyer who was close to Johnson and who became his first major biographer. In his 1787 *Life of Samuel Johnson* he wrote that Colonel Bathurst "arrived in England from Jamaica, and brought with him a negro-servant, a native of that island, whom he caused to be baptized and named Francis Barber."[14] The modern reader might pass without pause over that innocuous phrase "caused to be baptized," but contemporary readers of Hawkins's book would have realised its implications. For the vast majority of English people baptism was a commonplace event; it was important, but it was a normal part of growing up in a country where the Church of England had established status. The position was very different for anyone who, like Quashey, had been born a slave. For such a person baptism carried a level of meaning which it did not have for a free man.

The effect of the baptism of a slave was the subject of a fierce debate which had been going on since the seventeenth century.[15] The underlying issue was the basis on which someone could continue to be held as a slave. A number of justifications of slavery had been suggested, but one recurring theme was that the practice was justifiable because those who were enslaved were not Christians, but heathens. One of the first English court cases to address the problem of slavery, *Butts v. Penny* in 1677, involved a situation in which the plaintiff claimed that the defendant had taken a hundred of his slaves. The plaintiff sued the defendant by way of an action for trover, a form of action used to recover property. The defendant argued—somewhat technically—that a man could not be a piece of property, and therefore an action for trover could not be brought to recover a man. But the court found that "the negroes were infidels, and the subjects of an infidel prince," and that "negroes being usually bought and sold among merchants, as merchandise, and also being infidels, there might be a property in them sufficient to maintain trover."[16]

At first sight it might seem that this justification of slavery would be welcome to slave-owners, but in fact it was problematic for them because it simultaneously provided support for the institution and undermined it. If a person could be held in slavery only because he was an infidel, it followed that a Christian could not be enslaved, and a slave who converted to Christianity must be set free. It became a widespread belief amongst slaves (and a fear amongst slave-owners) that baptism freed a slave, or prevented a person from being enslaved, and this belief took hold throughout Britain and the colonies.

The London baptismal records for the period bear witness to this. They include numerous entries which stand out because of the advanced age of the person being baptised, and also their colour or origin—"a more," "a blackmore," "a negro," "an Indian," or "a dark man." On 16 February 1743 the parish records of St. Bride's, Fleet Street, recorded the baptism of "William Eaton, an adult Negro. Aged about 17." At St. Katharine by the Tower, "Henry Phillips a Black 27 years" was baptised on 1 February 1746, and "John Mathews a mulatto 19 years" was baptised on 12 February 1748. Most of these entries are names with nothing more about the person being baptised, but occasionally there is a hint of a life story of the person being baptised, as when the register of St. Sepulchre, Holborn, records the baptism on 12 October 1749 of "Philip Bailey, a negro 31 years old born in Guinea."[17]

Some owners were prepared to go to great lengths to prevent such baptisms. In November 1760, *Lloyd's Evening Post* reported that a runaway slave had been brought to church in Westminster to be baptised. Her owner heard of the plan and intervened:

> The mistress of the girl, getting intelligence of it, while the Minister was reading the churching service, seized upon her in the face of the congregation, and violently forced her out of the Church, regardless of her cries and tears; telling the people about her that she was her slave, and would use her as she pleased.[18]

The newspaper commented, "We should be glad to be informed, first, whether it is in the power of a master or mistress of a Negro slave to prevent her being baptized after her arrival in England? Secondly, whether in this free country such a Negro still continues a slave after baptism?"

Many people were asking the same questions, but slaves and owners would have given different answers. "I have been baptized; and by the laws of the land no man has a right to sell me," declared the slave Olaudah Equiano to his owner in London in 1762.[19] His owner was not impressed: he promptly sold Equiano, who was forcibly taken to sea, and off to the West Indies.

The view of slavery as based on irreligion created conflict between slave-owners and clergymen, especially missionaries in the colonies whose actions in baptising slaves threatened to undermine property interests. Many colonial legislatures solved the problem by passing laws explicitly declaring that a slave who converted to Christianity was not thereby freed. But there was no such legal provision in Britain, so a group of West Indian merchants obtained an influential legal opinion on slavery which supported their position. The opinion was given in 1729 by two leading lawyers, the Attorney-General (Sir Philip Yorke) and Solicitor-General (Sir Charles Talbot), who stated:

> We are of opinion, that a slave coming from the West Indies to Great Britain or Ireland doth not become free and Baptism doth not bestow freedom on him, nor make any alteration to his temporal condition in these kingdoms.[20]

Pro-slavery interests made sure the opinion was widely publicised in Britain and the colonies, and it was quoted in sermons and letters, and printed in full in many newspapers. It has often been described by historians as a "judgment," but it had no such status; it was simply the professional view of two highly regarded law officers. But opinions of this kind often circulated amongst lawyers in manuscript or in printed collections, and they could carry great weight.[21] In this instance the views of the two lawyers acquired much greater authority twenty years later when they were adopted by the judge in the case of *Pearne v. Lisle*.[22] This matter was decided in 1749, just a year before the boy who was to be baptised "Francis Barber" arrived in England. Its outcome was not entirely surprising, as the judge was the former Sir Philip Yorke, now Lord Hardwicke, the Lord Chancellor. He stated:

> There was once a doubt, whether, if they [slaves] were christened, they would not become free by that act, and there were precautions taken in the Colonies to prevent their being baptized, till the opinion of Lord Talbot and myself was taken on that point. We were both of opinion, that it did not at all alter their state.

It was this religious and political controversy which formed the back-drop to Quashey's baptism. No mention of the baptism can be found in the

London parish registers; either the relevant entry has not survived or the baptism took place elsewhere. Barber himself left no record of the occasion. We know of the event only because two of Johnson's biographers refer to it. In the account given by John Hawkins it is Colonel Bathurst who arranged the baptism. However, an alternate version of events is provided by another friend and biographer of Samuel Johnson, William "Conversation" Cooke. In *The Life of Samuel Johnson, LL.D.*, published in 1785, Cooke claimed that it was Johnson, not Bathurst, who had Barber baptised:

> Francis Barber was but ten years old when he took him under his care and at a time when the Doctor was but ill qualified, in point of circumstances, to maintain him. The first thing he did was to have him made a *Christian*.[23]

As a friend of Johnson, Cooke had some qualifications to write about his life, but he is a much less reliable source than Hawkins. Cooke knew Johnson only in his last years, and even then he was not particularly close to him. His biography was rushed out, appearing only two weeks after Johnson's death in an obvious attempt to cash in on interest in Johnson, and was full of mistakes: it was the subject of a damning review in the *Gentleman's Magazine*.[24] Hawkins, in contrast, knew Johnson well, including at the time when the baptism took place; they were friends for over thirty years. It seems probable therefore that it was Colonel Bathurst who had Barber baptised. This may seem surprising, given the significance which both slaves and their owners attributed to baptism, although it becomes more comprehensible if Bathurst was in fact Barber's father.

At his baptism Quashey the Jamaican slave ceased to exist, and became instead "Francis Barber." The reason for this choice of name is not known. The rites of the Church of England required that there should be at least two sponsors for the baptismal candidate, and it was common in cases of slave baptisms for the person baptised to take the surname of one of these sponsors, so it is possible that this is the source of the Barber name.[25] Another possibility is that Bathurst simply decided to adopt it as a common and easy to use surname, perhaps prompted by the fact that a family named Barber had lived near him in Jamaica.[26]

Barber did not stay for long with Colonel and Dr. Bathurst. According to the account of his early life which he gave to James Boswell, he was sent to school at Barton in Yorkshire, and stayed there for between two and three years. This raises an obvious question: why should Barber have been sent some 250 miles to go to school? It was certainly not because of the reputation of the establishment. Barton was (and is) a very small village, in what was then the North Riding of Yorkshire. It lay just off the main coaching road, about five miles from Richmond. The school was a very small one which had been established in a cottage in 1702, and was run by the Perpetual Curate, the Revd. William Jackson.[27] (Baptism would have been a prerequisite of attendance at a church school, so this confirms that Barber was baptised before he was sent to Yorkshire.)

There is some evidence that the choice was influenced by cost. Colonel Bathurst left Jamaica because of his financial difficulties, and his son Richard was finding it hard to make a living from his medical practice. Expense would have been a key factor in the choice of school. There is a hint of this in a letter from Johnson's friend Thomas Percy, Bishop of Dromore, to James Boswell. Writing in 1788, Percy recalled that Barber had been "placed by his Master at one of the cheap schools in Yorkshire."[28]

But cost alone cannot have determined the selection of the Barton school, as there must have been many cheap schools in London or nearby to which Barber could have been sent. Viewed from London, the principal feature of Barton was probably the very fact of its distance from the capital. It would have been a good place to conceal any kind of embarrassing or discreditable connection. Some schools in that part of Yorkshire were to become notorious in the nineteenth century as useful out-of-the-way places to which illegitimate or otherwise unwanted children could be sent. They became a byword for brutality and neglect when they were attacked by Charles Dickens in *Nicholas Nickleby:* the fictional Dotheboys Hall was in part based on a school in Bowes, in the North Riding, and there were a number of similar establishments in that area.[29] If Colonel Bathurst felt he had done enough for the young boy by bringing him to England and having him baptised, and now wanted him out of sight, Barton was a good choice. One thing was clear: Colonel Bathurst did not want the young Barber nearby.

We do not know how Bathurst became aware of the school's existence, but perhaps it was via Samuel Johnson (a close friend of Dr. Bathurst), who had a connection with that area. His cousin, the Revd. Cornelius Harrison, had been Perpetual Curate of Darlington, just eight miles from Barton, from 1727 until his death in 1748.

At some point in 1750 Barber made the long journey to Yorkshire. From Jamaica to London to Barton, within the space of a few months: it is not hard to imagine what a disorienting experience it must have been. In Jamaica Barber had been a slave, but there was at least some sense of community as he was a part of the black majority. In London, the black population formed a very small part of the whole, but Barber was by no means unique. In Barton, Barber's was almost certainly the only black face to be seen. There was nothing at all to the place—a church, an inn, and a few houses gathered round the village green. In such a place a black boy was a conspicuous novelty.

So far as we know, Barber never saw Colonel Bathurst again. He spent the next two years in Barton, during which he must have received at least a smattering of elementary education. Then, in 1752, Barber was brought back to London. But there is nothing to suggest that Colonel Bathurst was in any way involved in this decision: Barber recalled that when he returned to London he was then "with Dr. Bathurst a short time," but significantly he makes no mention at all of Colonel Bathurst.[30] (At some point the Colonel moved to Lincoln—he was living there in 1754 when he made his will, and he died there the following year.) It was Dr. Bathurst who became the central figure in Barber's life at this time, and who was to play a crucial role in it.

As we have seen, Dr. Richard Bathurst had been born in Jamaica in 1722.[31] His mother died when he was four years old, and his father sent him to Peterhouse, Cambridge, at the age of sixteen. Bathurst obtained a degree in medicine in 1745, but he never made much money as a physician. John Hawkins, who knew Bathurst at this time, put his failure down to lack of influence: "He possessed the qualities that were most likely to recommend him in his profession; but, wanting friends, could make no way in it." It was not for want of trying: "He studied hard, dressed well, and associated with those who were likely to bring him forward, but he failed in his endeavours." When his father and Francis Barber came to stay with him, there was little money to spare. According to Hawkins, "in the course of ten years' exercise of his faculty, [Dr. Bathurst] had never opened his hand to more than one guinea."[32] In 1754 he was appointed physician at the Middlesex infirmary, a fifteen-bed charity hospital for "the sick and lame of Soho" which had opened in 1745. The infirmary did not provide him with much income; its own finances were precarious, and many physicians stayed for only two or three years. Bathurst's employment there did not last long. Two months after his appointment he took six months' leave of absence to visit Jamaica to sort out his father's affairs. In the event it took him longer to deal with matters than he had hoped. He returned to London the following year but had to go back to Jamaica in November 1756, at which point he resigned from the hospital.[33]

Bathurst's lack of success may have been in part due to the fact that he also had literary ambitions. In the early 1740s, while he was still studying, he became acquainted with Samuel Johnson, then a struggling jobbing writer, and they formed a close friendship. Johnson promoted Bathurst's writing, sending to the publisher George Strahan a proposal for a "Geographical Dictionary" to be compiled by Bathurst, and publishing items by Bathurst in the *Literary Magazine*, of which Johnson was, for about a year, the editor. It was in the first issue of this magazine in 1756 that Johnson denounced Jamaica as a "den of tyrants, and a dungeon of slaves," and one of Bathurst's contributions appeared only a few pages later.[34]

Bathurst was particularly congenial to Johnson, with his passionate nature and his shared politics. "Bathurst was a fine fellow!" said Johnson. "He hated a fool, & he hated a rogue, & he hated a Whig—he was a very good hater!"[35] There were other attitudes they had in common, not least their vehement opposition to slavery. Then, too, Bathurst was a doctor; Johnson always admired medical men and numbered many among his closest friends. In 1748 Bathurst became a founding member of Johnson's Ivy Lane club, which met every Tuesday at the King's Head beefsteak house for dinner and conversation. Its nine members included three physicians. The friendship between the two men was amongst the most important of Johnson's life: many years after Bathurst's death (which occurred in 1762), Johnson referred to him as "My *dear dear* Bathurst, whom I loved better than ever I loved any human creature."[36]

When Barber returned to London from Yorkshire in 1752 he stayed for a little while with Dr. Bathurst. The young boy's future was in Bathurst's hands, and he soon arrived at a momentous decision: Barber should join the household of Samuel Johnson as his servant. Dr. Bathurst's role in the move is confirmed by Johnson, who wrote that Barber had been "given me by a Friend whom I much respect."[37] The first transforming journey of Barber's life had been across the Atlantic: the second was across London. In early April of 1752, Barber climbed the stone steps to the door of the house in Gough Square, to meet the intimidating figure of Samuel Johnson.

4. Johnson

There could hardly have been a greater contrast than that between the slight, young Francis Barber—then probably aged about ten—and Samuel Johnson. At this stage in his life, the forty-two-year-old writer looked like a boxer who was past his prime. Portraits of him in later life show him as rather portly, but when Barber met him he was tall and muscular though ungainly, and towered over most people. "He is upwards of six feet" wrote Boswell's friend, the Revd. William Johnson Temple, "and proportionably large and gross, big-boned, clumsy and awkward. You would rather take him for an Irish chairman, London porter, or one of Swift's Brobdingnaggians, than for a man of letters."[1]

Even a man of letters had to walk the threatening streets of London, and Johnson's uncommon size and strength had on occasion saved his purse, and possibly his life. Once, while walking in a darkened street, he was attacked by four robbers but fought them off single-handedly until the watch could be summoned. On another occasion Johnson encountered two large dogs, fighting ferociously. Boswell recounted that "as one who would separate two little boys who are foolishly hurting each other, he ran up to them, and cuffed their heads till he drove them asunder."[2]

What he possessed in the way of strength, however, he lacked in the way of control over his body. This was not just a matter of clumsiness or awkwardness, but something much more serious and perhaps neurological in origin: it has been suggested that he may have suffered from Tourette's syndrome.[3] As he made his way along the street, his lurching movements attracted attention and mockery. Laetitia-Matilda Hawkins (daughter of

Johnson's biographer, John Hawkins) recalled that "he made his way up Bolt Court in the zigzag direction of a flash of lightning; submitting his course only to the deflections imposed by the impossibility of going further to right or left."[4] He always walked with his left arm folded across his chest, and his left hand under his chin, thrusting his legs out to the side in a motion memorably captured by Boswell: "When he walked, it was like the struggling gait of one in fetters."[5]

Even when he was at ease, he was not still. "His mouth is in perpetual motion, as if he was chewing," wrote the novelist Frances Burney. "He has a strange method of frequently twirling his Fingers, & twisting his Hands;— his Body is in continual agitation, *see sawing* up & down; his Feet are never a moment quiet;—&, in short, his whole person is in perpetual motion."[6]

On more than one occasion people meeting Johnson for the first time had serious doubts about his sanity. Boswell reported that when the artist William Hogarth was visiting Samuel Richardson, he "perceived a person standing at a window in the room, shaking his head, and rolling himself about in a strange ridiculous manner. He concluded that he was an ideot, whom his relations had put under the care of Mr. Richardson, as a very good man." That person was Johnson. The painter Ozias Humphry, observing Johnson for the first time, recorded that "I could hardly help thinking him a madman for some time, as he sat waving over his breakfast like a lunatic."[7]

Nor did Johnson improve on closer inspection, as numerous accounts over the years indicated. "His appearance was very forbidding," wrote Boswell, describing him as a young man in 1734, "he was then lean and lank, so that his immense structure of bones was hideously striking to the eye, and the scars of the scrophula were deeply visible." When Boswell met Johnson for the first time in May 1763 he wrote that "Mr. Johnson is a Man of a most dreadfull appearance." Frances Burney recorded in 1778 that "this man . . . has a Face the most ugly, a Person the most awkward, & manners the most singular, that ever were, or ever can be seen." To add to the disconcerting effect of his appearance, he had, according to Joshua Reynolds's sister Frances, a "loud and imperious voice" which "had an intimidating influence on those who were not much acquainted with him."[8] This was the startling figure Francis Barber first encountered at 17 Gough Square. It was not a meeting calculated to set a ten-year-old at ease.

If the person Barber met was alarming, the atmosphere of his home in Gough Square was one of deep gloom. Only a few years earlier, when

Samuel Johnson (c. 1769–70), by Joshua Reynolds. Frances Reynolds noted, "As for his gestures with his hands . . . sometimes he would hold them up with some of his fingers bent, as if he had been seized with the cramp." (MS Eng 1411, reproduced courtesy Hyde Collection, Houghton Library, Harvard University)

Johnson had taken possession of the house, it had seemed to mark a great upturn in his fortunes, a leap forward after many years of struggle, but now his affairs, both professional and personal, were at a very low ebb.

The path to Gough Square had been a long one, and mostly uphill. Samuel Johnson was born in 1709 in Lichfield, Staffordshire, the eldest son of a bookseller and his wife, who had married late in life. From very early on, and in spite of his disabilities, he was recognised as a prodigy who in some way would make his mark in the world. He was gifted with a remarkable memory, devouring the many books which formed his father's stock. When he entered Pembroke College in October 1728, an Oxford degree was within his grasp as the first step on his road to distinction.

It was many years before he took the second step. The chance he had been given was snatched away from him when he was forced to leave Oxford without a degree after thirteen months, as his father could no longer afford to pay the fees. He had no choice but to return to Lichfield, the local boy who had not made good. There, at the age of about twenty, he suffered a serious nervous collapse, the first of a number of such episodes which occurred throughout his life. For a time he worked, with a conspicuous lack of enthusiasm, in his father's bookshop, but he then determined on becoming a schoolmaster. It was an ambition which he pursued tenaciously; though his regard for some of his own teachers had been low, education was something which he valued very highly (a fact which was to stand Barber in good stead). Over the next seven years he applied for six posts: two applications resulted in work which lasted only a few months, and the others were met with rejections. His lack of a degree was a significant obstacle, but so was his appearance. One application was turned down because he was "a very haughty, ill natured Gent" and had a way of "distorting his Face."[9] His failure was compounded with loss when, a year after he left Oxford, his father died.

His recovery came from an unexpected direction. In 1735 he married Elizabeth Porter, the widow of a mercer in Birmingham; she was twenty years Johnson's senior, and the mother of three children. The match provided Johnson with vital emotional support, but it was bitterly opposed by her family. Johnson was several notches down the social scale and was impecunious, with no obvious way of supporting a wife. Elizabeth Porter did have money, however, and Johnson used it to set up a school near Lichfield. Like all his previous ventures into education it failed, and he determined instead to make his living as a writer.

In 1737 he travelled to London with a half-finished play, *Irene,* in his pocket. From then until 1762 (when he received a royal pension) he lived precariously by his pen in any way that he could. The work poured out: essays, reviews, biographies, translations, political tracts, sermons, poems, and accounts of the proceedings in Parliament—anything which might make money. Johnson was, however, no mere Grub Street hack. His poems *London* (1738) and *The Vanity of Human Wishes* (1749) attracted notice (not least, from Alexander Pope), and *An Account of the Life of Mr Richard Savage* (1744) created a new kind of biography, telling the story of his friend, the poet, wastrel, and killer Richard Savage in a way that was both deeply sympathetic and unillusioned.

Gradually Johnson acquired a reputation, at least in the small world of London editors, booksellers, and publishers. Beyond that circle, however, he had made little impact. In 1746 his old Lichfield mentor Gilbert Walmesley described him as "a great genius—quite lost both to himself and the world."[10] Nor did increasing professional recognition bring with it much in the way of tangible benefits: Johnson remained poor.

Then on 18 June 1746, everything changed for Johnson. On that date he met over breakfast with a consortium of booksellers and signed a contract to write a dictionary of the English language. It was a massive undertaking for one man, and the fact that the booksellers were willing to entrust it to Johnson is an indication of the regard they had for his abilities. The payment agreed was £1,575, payable in instalments as the work progressed. For the first time in his life Johnson had a guaranteed income. He was confident that it would take him three years to write the book, at which rate he would earn, on average, £10 per week. Admittedly, he would have to pay all his expenses from this income, including his clerks (whose wages cost him 23s per week), but this would still have left him a handsome sum.

Since his arrival in London, Johnson had moved from one set of lodgings to another in the courts and alleys around the Strand and Fleet Street— anywhere that was cheap. He now took a lease on the house in Gough Square, paying rent of about £26 a year. It was a place of work for him and his assistants, and a home for Johnson and his wife Elizabeth (whom he usually called "Tetty"). Johnson's relationship with Tetty had not always been an easy one, and they had spent some time apart, but the dictionary contract promised a new start, with financial stability and a comfortable home. They moved into the house and set up the garret as Johnson's place of work.

In spite of Johnson's newfound security, however, the work did not proceed well. It took much longer than he had estimated, and early in 1750 he realised with horror that he had made a false start, and that his methodology would need to be fundamentally revised.[11] The discovery was devastating, coming as it did over three years into the work. Publication would be further delayed, and the booksellers started to make anxious enquiries about their investment. Johnson responded angrily to their request for a meeting: "I shall *not* see the Gentlemen Partners till the first volume is in the press."[12] On several occasions he had to borrow money to pay debts as they fell due.

Then, on 17 March 1752, came the heaviest blow of all: Tetty died. Her death, the end of their sixteen-year marriage, plunged Johnson into distress. Throughout his life he had suffered from a strong depressive tendency, which he described to Boswell as "a vile melancholy which made him mad all his life, at least not sober."[13] The loss of his wife triggered black moods of despair and self-reproach. This was another failure to add to all the others. He became an isolated figure, avoiding his friends. "When he felt the pressure of time become insupportable," wrote William Shaw, "the only expedient he had was to walk the streets of London. This for many a lonesome night was his constant substitute for sleep."[14] More than two years later, Johnson wrote that ever since Tetty's death he had seemed to himself "a kind of solitary wanderer in the wild of life . . . a gloomy gazer on a world to which I have little relation."[15] This was the unpromising background to Francis Barber's arrival at Gough Square.

It was early April 1752 when Barber arrived at Johnson's home. In her *Anecdotes of the Late Samuel Johnson, LL.D.*, published in 1786, Hester Thrale Piozzi stated that when Tetty Johnson died, Francis Barber ran in the middle of the night to fetch Johnson's friend the Revd. John Taylor. But Piozzi was mistaken, as Barber had not at that date joined the household. Boswell asked Barber about this story and recorded that "Mrs. Johnson was dead a fortnight or three weeks before [Barber] came to the Dr."[16]

What prompted Dr. Bathurst to suggest that Barber might become part of Johnson's household? He was certainly aware that Johnson would willingly agree to such a proposal, as he was well known for his charity to those in need. "He loved the poor as I never yet saw any one else do, with an earnest desire to make them happy," recalled Mrs. Piozzi.[17] Barber had needs, and neither of the Bathursts, father or son, was in a strong financial position to supply them.

Another motive was suggested by John Hawkins in his *Life of Samuel Johnson*, where he wrote that Johnson's earnings at this time had "exalted him to such a state of comparative affluence, as, in his judgment, made a manservant necessary."[18] It is an improbable scenario, the habitually slovenly Johnson regarding a manservant as a necessity. Johnson's recurrent financial difficulties had certainly eased, at least for a while: on the day before Tetty died he sent a draft for £100 towards paying off the mortgage on his mother's house in Lichfield. (He had probably raised the money by selling the rights to the series of *Rambler* essays which he had published between March 1750 and March 1752.) But Hawkins was mistaken about the general extent of Johnson's affluence, wrongly imagining that he had earnings from other work.

However, there was more to the situation than Johnson's benevolence, real though that was. The fact that Tetty's death and Barber's arrival occurred so close together suggests that they were linked. Dr. Bathurst could not have failed to be aware of the depth of Johnson's misery; perhaps he calculated that Johnson might be stirred from his depression by the company of a young boy in his cheerless household.

Whatever the reason, it was an astute move on Bathurst's part and showed a perceptive understanding of Johnson's character. There were many Johnsons, and in some guises—as moralist, satirist, and controversialist—Johnson was capable of high seriousness. But those who knew him best recognised that he also had a certain childlike quality. In spite of (or perhaps because of) his general awkwardness and lack of coordination, there was an intense physicality about him, of a kind which appeals to children. There are many stories of him walking great distances, running races, climbing trees, jumping fences, and rolling down hills, even into old age. It was an aspect which was highlighted in some recollections published in the *European Magazine* in 1798:

> It is a well known fact that [Johnson] would frequently descend from the contemplation of subjects the most profound imaginable to the most childish playfulness. It was no uncommon thing to see him hop, step, and jump; he would often seat himself on the back of his chair, and more than once has been known to propose a race on some grassplat adapted to the purpose.[19]

It is a striking fact about Johnson that many of his friends in his middle and later years were much younger than himself—James Boswell, Hester Thrale, Bennet Langton, and Topham Beauclerk were all some thirty years younger, and his great friend Frances Burney was more than forty years younger. He also had a genuine liking for children, enjoyed their company, and could be playful and entertaining. Frances Burney wrote that

"Dr. Johnson has more *fun* and comical humour, & Laughable & nonsense about him, than almost any body I ever saw."[20]

No one was in a better position to observe Johnson's response to children than Hester Thrale. Over the course of her marriage to the brewer and Member of Parliament Henry Thrale, she gave birth to twelve children, only four of whom survived into adulthood. Johnson took a great interest in them, and visited them at school. He wrote affectionate letters to the eldest daughter, Hester Maria ("Queeney") Thrale, writing to her for the first time when she was seven years old:

> My sweet, dear, pretty, little Miss:
>
> Please to tell little Mama, that I am glad to hear, that she is well, and that I am going to Lichfield, and shall come soon to London. Desire her to make haste and be quite well, for, You know, that You and I are to tye her to the tree, but we will not do it while she is weak . . . tell Harry [her younger brother] that you have got my heart, and will keep it, and that I am, Dearest Miss, your most obedient servant.[21]

Mrs. Thrale recorded that "Mr. Johnson was himself exceedingly disposed to the general indulgence of children, and was even scrupulously and ceremoniously attentive not to offend them."[22]

For Barber a place in Johnson's Gough Square household had much to offer: in a city where many children lived and died on the streets, Johnson provided him with a home and an occupation. But it would be wrong to see Barber as the sole beneficiary of the arrangement—the solitary childless widower would find much to enjoy in the company of his young servant.

There was perhaps another aspect of Johnson's life which aroused his sympathies towards the young Barber. Johnson's strange looks and manner were often the subject of ridicule, and the terms of such comments are revealing of how he was perceived: he was "monstrous," "barbarous," "a savage." This was exactly the language used by many travel writers at the time to characterise the inhabitants of countries which were not "civilised," particularly people of African origins—such as Barber. On some occasions the comparison was expressly made. In 1779 one critic wrote:

> No man has ever yet seen Dr Johnson in the act of *feeding*, or beheld the inside of his *cell* in *Fleet-Street*, but would think the *feasts* of *Esquimeaux* or the *cottages* of *Hottentots* injured by a comparison.[23]

It would be ridiculous to suggest that Johnson's journey from Lichfield to London was comparable with Barber's voyage from Jamaica. But there was a sense in which Johnson was treated as an exotic oddity because of his appearance, and this was an experience he shared with Francis Barber.

Any such sympathy was not a one-sided affair. In Barber's first days and weeks in Gough Square Johnson was overwhelmed by his recent loss, and his sufferings did not go unnoticed by his young attendant. Their relationship might be that of master and servant, but Barber, in spite of his youth, was capable of recognising and sympathizing with Johnson's distress. Many years later he recalled that at this time his master had been "in great affliction."[24] As a domestic servant Barber was well placed to notice his master's moods. Living in the same house, he attended upon Johnson at all times, whenever called upon to do so, observing him at work, in the company of visitors, and in his dealings with Barber's fellow-residents. (As we shall see, this last was no straightforward matter.)

Barber's new home was a substantial house which had been built in 1700 by a wool merchant, Sir Richard Gough.[25] Each of the four floors had just two rooms on either side of a steeply winding staircase, up and down which Francis had to run to carry out his duties. At the very top of the house was the garret, running the full width of the building, the largest room in the house and the one with the best light. In most such houses this space would have been the servants' quarters, or perhaps a nursery. But here it served a different purpose: it was the workroom where Johnson had been labouring on his dictionary for six years by the time Barber joined the household. It was equipped with high desks which could be worked at while standing up, so that Boswell described it as "fitted up like a counting house."[26] There was other furniture too, all in some disorder. Visitors commented on the books, all covered with dust, an old deal writing-desk, and a chair with only three legs.

The garret room was not only a place of work for Johnson, but also a place of refuge. Every other room had strong associations with his wife, especially the bedroom where she had died, but not the garret. When asked why he did not use any other room for study, he replied: "Because in that room only I never saw Mrs. Johnson."[27]

Johnson did not work there alone. Barber soon became used to the presence of the small team of clerks who assisted Johnson (or, to use Barber's phrase as recorded by Boswell, "wrote to him"). They had various roles, one of which was to act as amanuenses. From a vast range of books Johnson would select quotations which illustrated the use of a particular word, and would mark them for an amanuensis to copy out onto a slip of paper. (This was no mean task, as when the *Dictionary* finally appeared in 1755, it contained 113,000 such quotations.) These copyists assisted in other ways as well, some providing administrative help in dealing with the printers and booksellers, and some making minor decisions about the content of the *Dictionary*. They seem to have been as much friends as they were employees, and several of them continued to drop in to see Johnson from time to time, even after they had ceased to work on the project. Barber gave to Boswell in 1786 an impression of the busy garret at this time:

> The younger Macbean brother of the Duke of Argyll's Librarian and Mr. Peyton a linguist who taught foreigners . . . then wrote to him [Johnson]. The elder Macbean and Mr. Maitland, Mr. Stewart and Mr. Shiels who had all written to him before used to come about him.[28]

The whole group was typical of many who formed part of Johnson's shifting household—they were dependent upon Johnson, and he in turn regarded them as his responsibility and did all he could for them. Alexander Macbean, his brother William Macbean, V. J. Peyton, Maitland, Francis Stewart, and Robert Shiels were all men who had some kind of connection with the world of print—Stewart was the son of a bookseller, Shiels had been a journeyman printer and was an author, and Alexander Macbean had assisted Ephraim Chambers with work on his *Cyclopedia*. All eked out a living on the fringes of Grub Street by working on various literary projects. They probably did not all work for Johnson at the same time while Barber was living there; in fact, two of them (Peyton and William Macbean) were probably hired to replace Stewart and Shiels after their deaths.

One of Barber's early tasks was to take money to the struggling Shiels, who died of consumption in December 1753. It meant that from the very beginning of their relationship the young boy recognised Johnson's readiness to help those in need, in spite of the fact that he was far from well off himself. Barber told Boswell, "Though the Dr. had then little to himself Francis frequently carried money from him to Shiels when in distress."[29] Over twenty years later, Johnson was still looking out for his associates. When Peyton fell ill in 1775, Johnson wrote to ask a friend for money, "I have an old Amanuensis in great distress. I have given what I think I can give, and begged till I cannot tell where to beg again."[30] It was a pattern in Johnson's life which Barber was to see over and over again—and from which he too was to benefit.

The garret was awash with paper in one form or another: books being consulted, notes being made, and slips on which quotations were written. Paper was expensive and not to be wasted, and Johnson accumulated large quantities of scrap for reuse at a later date. It is to this cluttered workshop that we owe the survival of a remarkable glimpse of Barber's early life in Gough Square, a clue which lay buried for almost two hundred years. While Johnson and his assistants were toiling away, Francis Barber was present as well—and he too was writing. What he wrote could easily have been lost, but it survived amongst the mass of other materials because of the enormous interest generated in Johnson's manuscripts after his death in 1784.

When Johnson's library was sold at auction in 1785, the sale catalogue included the enigmatically described "13, of Dr. Johnson's dictionary, with MSS. notes." What this actually consisted of was some printed parts from the first edition of Johnson's *Dictionary*, with 1,842 interleaved papers on which notes had been written by the amanuenses. The papers passed through the hands of various collectors and dealers until they were eventually presented to Yale University in 1973. But the significance of these materials for the life of Francis Barber was not recognised until the Johnson scholar Allen Reddick carried out work on them, the results of which were published in 1990.[31] What Reddick discovered, bound into the volumes, were several slips of paper on which Francis Barber had practised his handwriting. The paper had been preserved because the other side had been used for writing new material for the fourth edition (1773) of Johnson's *Dictionary*. Some of the writing consists of repeated letters, and some is complete words. On one slip of paper appears "antigue / an," while on another appear the words "England England." They offer tiny windows into the mind of a small boy, about twelve years old, sitting in a Gough Square garret in the 1750s. Something is making him think of the West Indies, and also of the country which is now, for better or worse, his home.

But the most evocative of all the slips is the one on which is written "Francis Barber / Francis Barber." Like many young children who learn to write, he is practising writing his own name. Anyone who has handled an old manuscript, especially when it is of historic importance, knows the powerful sense of being in touch with the past. To view that scrap of paper nowadays in the Beinecke Rare Book and Manuscript Library at Yale is, in however small a way, to make contact over the gap of 250 years with a young child, struggling to come to terms with a new identity, a new home, and an unknown future.

This writing obviously demonstrates that Barber was by this point literate. It is a striking fact that, at a time when about 40 percent of adult males in Britain were illiterate in the sense that they were unable to sign their own name, this young servant and former slave was learning to read and write.[32] He owed this ability, of course, to the education he received—and to those who paid for it.

There were several stages to Barber's somewhat irregular schooling. Many a master would have thought that the two years at the school in Barton was quite enough for a servant. It was common for boys to receive nothing more than an elementary education from their mothers or perhaps at a dame school run by a widow or spinster who earned a few pennies each week by

Francis Barber's handwriting practice, probably written between 1755 and 1756. On the reverse of the slips of paper is material intended for the fourth edition of Johnson's *Dictionary of the English Language*. (Reproduced courtesy Beinecke Rare Book and Manuscript Library, Yale University)

teaching the alphabet and basic writing skills. But Johnson had a profound belief in the value of education, derived from his own experience, and was determined to do better than that for Barber. "Those who communicate literature to the son of a poor man," he wrote, "consider him as one not born to poverty, but to the necessity of deriving a better fortune from himself."[33]

It had been Johnson's good fortune to be born and brought up in Lichfield, which boasted a famous Grammar School. As a local boy Johnson was entitled to free education there, but the reputation of the school was such that day students and boarders came from much farther away, in spite of the fact that such nonlocals had to pay fees. Their parents thought it worth the money to obtain a Lichfield School education. Judging by the results, they were right, as the school had a level of success out of all proportion to its size, producing not only Samuel Johnson and the great actor and theatre manager David Garrick, but also writers, bishops, and scientists. At one time no fewer than five of the judges sitting in Westminster Hall had been educated at the school.[34]

But how was Johnson, living in some penury in the heart of London, to provide an education for Barber? Fortunately, it turned out that the answer was almost on his doorstep. Almost forty years earlier a merchant named Peter Joye had established a charity school in Blackfriars, intended for the poor children of the parishes of St. Anne, Blackfriars, and St. Andrew by the Wardrobe. (These parishes lay just to the south of Ludgate Hill, and the school itself was in Church Entry, a very short walk from Johnson's home in Gough Square.) The school provided a sound basic education for forty boys and thirty girls. The boys were to be taught "to read English, to write and to cast accounts and also (if the Trustees think fit) to learn some useful work or employment." The boys were usually between six and twelve years old, and most of them went into some form of domestic service after leaving the school.[35]

Not only was the school nearby, but it had another advantage for a child such as Barber. Peter Joye was of Dutch descent, and the school's admissions policy was that preference should be given to the children of foreigners or of foreign extraction. Barber was certainly poor, and was the child of foreigners. The only difficulty was that the school gave priority first to children who were resident in the parish of St. Anne or St. Andrew, and then to those living in neighbouring parishes. Johnson's house in Gough Square was in the parish of St. Dunstan in the West. Its seems that the solution which Johnson found to the problem was that Barber should board near the school: Barber told Boswell that "the Dr. first put him to board at Mrs. Coxeter's that he might go to Blackfriars school."[36] The identity of Mrs. Coxeter is not certainly established, but there is a Coxeter family which was closely connected to St. Anne, Blackfriars. The parish records show that three children of Thomas and Elizabeth Coxeter were baptised there in 1739, 1741, and 1744, respectively. There may be some link to the family of Johnson's friend, the literary scholar Thomas Coxeter, who died in 1747, leaving a daughter and a son with little money. Johnson assisted the family from time to time.[37]

The plan promised to work well for all concerned, providing an education for Barber, and some income for Mrs. Coxeter. But it came to nothing: after only one day at the school Barber fell ill, and smallpox was diagnosed. There could hardly have been a worse outcome for Johnson's careful planning. Smallpox was rampant in London at the time and was the cause of almost 10 percent of the deaths in the city. To many who survived, it brought disfigurement and blindness.[38] (Just the previous year Johnson had devoted two issues of his *Rambler* essays to the story of how Victoria, a beautiful young woman, comes to terms with being robbed of her looks by smallpox.) Barber was one of the lucky ones: he recovered but, like many others, carried the scars on his face for the rest of his life.

When Barber was well again, he stayed with Johnson for a while, until Johnson once more turned his thoughts to Barber's schooling. This time he decided against Blackfriars School following the disastrous experience there. Instead, he sent him to be taught by Jacob Desmoulins (pronounced "Demullins"), a twenty-eight-year-old writing-master. Desmoulins had very recently acquired a connection with Johnson: in May 1752 he married Elizabeth Swynfen, who was the daughter of Johnson's godfather and had been a friend of Johnson's wife in the 1740s. Jacob and Elizabeth had set up their home in Orange Court, Castle Street, Leicester Fields, within walking distance of Gough Square, and it was there that Barber continued his schooling.[39]

How long Barber continued with Desmoulins is not known, but at some point that stage of his education came to an end, and he took up his role as Johnson's household servant.

5. Servant or Slave?

Barber was one of many thousands of people who worked in domestic service in mid eighteenth-century England. London teemed with servants—some 50,000 of them, about a thirteenth of the population of the city.[1] Johnson's friend Henry Thrale, a wealthy brewer, had between eighteen and twenty servants at any one time at his country retreat in Streatham.[2] But servants were by no means confined to the mansions of the gentry, with their retinues of thirty to forty, and the vast majority worked in households where there were only one, two, or three people in service.[3] Compared with Thrale, Johnson was much lower down the financial scale, but his wife, Tetty, had kept a maidservant, even in the days of their worst money difficulties.

The idea of the famously unkempt Johnson taking on a servant seems to have caused his friends some amusement. The biographer John Hawkins wrote:

> The uses for which [Barber] was intended to serve this his last master were not very apparent, for Diogenes himself never wanted a servant less than he seemed to do: the great bushy wig, which throughout his life he affected to wear, by that closeness of texture which it had contracted and been suffered to retain, was ever nearly as impenetrable by a comb as a quick-set hedge; and little of the dust that had once settled on his outer garments was ever known to have been disturbed by the brush. In short, his garb and the whole of his appearance was, not to say negligent, but slovenly, and even squalid.[4]

Hawkins's readers would have understood the reference to the Greek philosopher Diogenes the Cynic, who lived in poverty in a tub in the Athens marketplace, existing on a diet of onions. Johnson's lifestyle was somewhat less extreme, and his diet was a little better.

Barber's duties in the household were not very taxing: as he later remarked, Johnson "required very small attention."[5] He appears in memoirs of Johnson and in his letters, fetching and carrying, bringing a message, a cup of coffee, or a clean shirt, buying food, waiting at table, accompanying Johnson on his occasional jaunts outside London, and opening the door to a stream of visitors. Barber recalled two friends in particular who regularly called at the house in the early 1750s, both of them medical men: Dr. Richard Bathurst (who had placed him with Johnson) and William Deyman, an apothecary who lived in Cork Street, Burlington Gardens. Deyman seems to have been a particularly close friend of Johnson at this time. They dined together every Sunday and made plans for a visit to Iceland, though the trip never took place. (Barber was later to work for an apothecary, and it may have been through Deyman that this connection was made.) Other visitors whom Barber remembered meeting at this time included Joshua Reynolds and David Garrick, the writer Elizabeth Carter, the historian Catherine Macaulay, and many other figures from the worlds of writing, printing, and bookselling. Some of those who arrived at the house were less welcome— Barber remembered that Johnson "used to be disturbed by people calling frequently for money which he could not pay."[6]

Barber was just one of a number of permanent or semipermanent residents who would be part of Johnson's various households over the years. Some were servants while others had more of the status of companions, but what all had in common was that they were needy and Johnson provided a home for them (and in most cases money as well). The house in Gough Square was a busy place, and inevitably some friction would develop between those who lived there. It is not certain who else was there at the same time as Barber, but there seems to have been another servant: when Bishop Percy called on Johnson in the summer of 1756 the door was answered by a maid-servant whose nose had been eaten away by venereal disease.[7] The two residents who lived with Johnson for the longest period of time (in each case, over twenty-five years), and with whom Barber had most to do, were Robert Levett and Anna Williams.[8]

Levett had been a friend of Johnson's since 1746 and had joined the Gough Square household sometime before July 1756. He was a medical practitioner of sorts, though he had no formal training or qualifications. He made an extremely modest living providing services to those who were too poor to pay for an apothecary or physician. They usually paid him in the only way they could, in gin or brandy, and he was often drunk. Johnson loyally explained that Levett accepted payment in this form rather than have his skills go unrewarded. He was, Johnson added, "perhaps the only man who ever became intoxicated through motives of prudence."[9]

In 1762, in curious circumstances, Levett contracted a short-lived marriage to a woman named Margaret Wilbraham. Wilbraham was under the impression that Levett was a physician with a considerable practice, while Levett believed Wilbraham to be entitled to a large sum of money which was wrongfully kept from her by a relative. Perhaps each should have been alerted to the improbability of these claims by the fact that the couple exchanged their confidences while engaged in a business transaction in a small coal shed in Fetter Lane.[10]

The marriage collapsed, and Levett found himself sued for his wife's debts. Shortly afterwards Wilbraham, who was in fact a prostitute, was tried for theft at the Old Bailey. Levett was only with some difficulty restrained from attending in the hope that he would see her sentenced to be hanged. She was acquitted and vanished, and Levett resumed his old place in Johnson's house and affections. Johnson was in fact very attached to Levett, with whom he often shared breakfast around noon in companionable silence, but he had no illusions about him: "Levat is a brutal fellow," he told Hester Thrale, "but I have a good regard for him; for his brutality is in his manners, not his mind."[11]

Levett was gloomy and withdrawn, scarcely congenial company for the young Barber, but his presence in the house was not likely to trouble him much. The focus of Barber's discontents became the dependant who was to stay the longest and to establish herself most firmly at the heart of the household, Anna Williams.

Williams was a woman of considerable talents whose habitual bad temper in later life had its origins in a series of misfortunes. Born in 1706, she was aged forty-six when Barber joined the household. She was the daughter of Zachariah Williams, an amateur scientist who was an inmate of the Charterhouse, a charitable institution in Smithfield which provided a home for impoverished gentlemen. He lived there for many years but often clashed with the authorities and was eventually forcibly evicted in 1748, leaving him and his daughter homeless. (He died in 1755.)

Anna Williams (undated), by Frances Reynolds. (Reproduced courtesy Trustees of Dr. Johnson's House)

The woes of both father and daughter were substantially increased by the fact that by 1740 Anna was completely blind. In this grim predicament they came to know Johnson, who shared Zachariah's interest in scientific and technical matters. Like many others before and after, they became beneficiaries of Johnson's charitable impulses towards anyone who was in need: he was determined to ascertain whether Anna's eyesight could be restored.

It was established that the problem was caused by cataracts, which were sometimes treatable, although only by a painful operation. Johnson arranged for this to be performed at his home in Gough Square by the surgeon Samuel Sharp. The operation took place just after the death of Johnson's wife—in other words, at exactly the time when Barber joined the household. It must have been a brief moment of high hopes, not least because Williams was a gifted poet and a linguist, and could dream of taking up her pen again. In the event the operation failed, and Williams remained blind. The only consolation to be derived from this episode—and it was a considerable one—was that she had found a permanent home. She remained in the Gough Square household and was to stay with Johnson, with short intervals, for over thirty years.[12] For much of that time Barber was also present.

Williams gradually took over the running of the Gough Square establishment. It was a role which was made much more difficult by her blindness, and some visitors were shocked by her habit of handling the food and eating with her fingers. Johnson's friend Giuseppe Baretti avoided dining with him, writing that "I hated to see the victuals paw'd by poor Mrs. Williams, that would often carve, though stone blind."[13] Barber did not appreciate Mrs. Williams taking command, and their clashes became a common event, the inevitable result of a high-spirited young boy being ordered about by a domineering figure. He was not the only one who found Williams difficult. John Hawkins, who knew her for thirty years, recognised that she was "a woman of enlightened understanding" who was possessed of "excellent moral qualities," but also that she was "easily provoked to anger," and he noted "the constitutional asperity of her temper."[14] As Hawkins recorded, Johnson found himself caught between Barber and Williams, and came to dread these conflicts,

> having his ears filled with the complaints of Mrs. Williams of Frank's neglect of his duty and inattention to the interests of his master, and of Frank against Mrs. Williams, for the authority she assumed over him, and exercised with an unwarrantable severity . . . Mrs. Williams, in her paroxysms of rage, has been known to drive [Johnson] from her presence.[15]

Anna Williams was in charge of the domestic arrangements, but both she and Levett also provided company for Johnson, who seems to have enjoyed Williams's conversation as much as he did Levett's silence. Barber was in a different position: we know the kind of tasks he was required to perform in the house, but his exact status is less clear. Writing seven years after Barber's arrival at Gough Square, Johnson recalled, "I had a Negro Boy named Francis Barber, given me by a Friend." Many an eighteenth-century man would have referred to an apprentice or a servant in the way Johnson referred to Barber, but there is another possible way of understanding this turn of phrase: could it be that Barber remained—in spite of his baptism—a slave?

Barber's standing was clear while he remained in Jamaica. The laws of Jamaica declared him to be a slave, and the customs and practices of the planters left no room for any doubt at all about the matter. But things were very different when he arrived in England in 1750. Unlike the position in Jamaica, there was no formal regulation of slavery, no slave code laid down in Acts of Parliament. The statute law had nothing whatever to say about slavery in England. The reason for this was simple: there had been no need for Parliament to address the issue. Between about 1661 and 1711 there were several attempts at introducing legislation in Parliament to regulate slavery in the colonies, but significantly it does not seem to have even occurred to those who promoted the legislation to make provision governing slaves in England.[16]

Nor had the judiciary provided any clear guidance in the handful of court cases which concerned slavery. Some very old decisions dealt with the ancient status of villeinage, a form of bondage which in some ways resembled slavery as practised in the colonies, although the parallel was not exact. A villein, who inherited his status from his father, was tied to working on a particular piece of land and could not work away from it without his lord's consent. If the land was sold, the villein could be sold with it. He could own property, but whatever he owned could be seized by his lord. The lord could exercise corporal punishment such as putting the villein in the stocks, but he could not maim or kill and the villein could bring an action for unreasonable treatment. Villeinage was certainly a kind of unfree status, but it had died out by the seventeenth century.[17] In the eighteenth century, however, a trickle of disputes started to reach the courts, forcing the judges to answer questions which had not been asked before. The cases arose because of slave-owners returning to Britain, bringing with them individuals like Barber who had been slaves in the colonies.

As early as 1569, slavery in England had been successfully challenged in the courts. The terse report of the case stated in full:

> One *Cartwright* brought a slave from *Russia*, and would scourge him, for which he was questioned; and it was resolved, That *England* was too pure an Air for Slaves to breathe in.[18]

It was a grand statement of principle, but it proved overoptimistic when the courts came to reexamine the matter in the eighteenth century. In 1708 a case called *Smith v. Browne and Cooper* came before Lord Holt, the Lord Chief

Justice. Smith sued Browne for debt, claiming that he had sold a negro to Browne in London, and Browne had not paid the £20 due. Judgment was given for Smith, but Lord Holt refused to allow it to be enforced against the defendant. The reason he gave was that the claim stated that the negro had been in England at the time of the sale, and "as soon as a negro comes into England, he becomes free."[19]

In 1749 Lord Hardwicke, the Lord Chancellor, disagreed, in the case of *Pearne v. Lisle*. (This was the case in which, as noted in chapter 3, Lord Hardwicke approved the Yorke-Talbot opinion, to the effect that baptism did not change a slave's status.) Pearne owned fourteen negroes in Antigua and had hired them out to Lisle for £100 a year in Antiguan money. Lisle refused to pay two years' hire, or to give the negroes back, so Pearne asked the court for an order preventing Lisle from leaving England until the matter was resolved. The court refused to make the order, but this was not because there was anything objectionable about treating slaves as objects to be hired out, Lord Hardwicke declaring that "a Negro slave . . . is as much property as any other thing." The reason for refusing to make the order was that Lisle was going to Antigua, and the plaintiff could get justice from the courts there.[20]

The decision of Lord Holt in *Smith v. Browne and Cooper* was of little relevance to the case then before the court, but Lord Hardwicke nevertheless took the opportunity to dismiss it in a few words:

> The reason said at the bar to have been given by Lord Chief Justice
> Holt, in that case, as the cause of his doubt, viz. that the moment a
> slave sets foot in England he becomes free, has no weight with it.

Thirteen years after *Pearne v. Lisle*, the judicial pendulum swung back again in favour of the slave in the case of *Shanley v. Harvey*. Edward Shanley brought a slave to England in about 1740 and gave him to his niece, Margaret Hamilton, who had him baptised and renamed Joseph Harvey. Harvey remained with Hamilton for twelve years, until her death in 1752. When Hamilton was on her deathbed, she gave him a purse containing at least £700, saying to him, "God bless you, make a good use of it." Shanley was the administrator of Hamilton's estate, and in that capacity he applied to the court for an account of the money, clearly intending to challenge the validity of the gift.

The arguments in the case are not recorded but it is apparent from the judgment that Shanley argued that a gift could not be binding if the recipient was a slave. Lord Northington, then the Lord Chancellor, dismissed the argument, holding that Harvey was a servant, not a slave:

> As soon as a man sets foot on English ground he is free: a negro may maintain an action against his master for ill usage, and may have a Habeas Corpus if restrained of his liberty.[21]

In the face of decisions such as these, Barber's status, so far as the law was concerned, was extremely uncertain, and no lawyer could have advised on the subject with any confidence.

Of course, what the law said was one thing, but what people believed and how they acted was quite another. It was clear that in practice full-blown chattel slavery in the Jamaican form did not exist in England; in particular, slave status could not be inherited, and there was nothing like the level of violence and extreme punishment which occurred in the colonies. But a form of servitude did exist, and this status exhibited many of the features of slavery: there were people in England who were compelled to remain in unfree service which was lifelong and unpaid, and with the possibility of being transferred from one master to another. Moreover, this status was racially based: only black people were subject to it. Such servitude had no formal official status or sanction, but equally no one was prepared to contest its legality until 1765, when the abolitionist Granville Sharp commenced the series of legal challenges which were to lead to the *Somerset* case in 1772. If it was not slavery as that was practised in Jamaica it was nonetheless slavery. Barber had experienced Jamaican slavery, and now he could see slaves on the streets of London, on the Strand, Fleet Street, and Cheapside.

In some cases, the signs of slave status were all too visible. The following announcement appeared in the *London Gazette* in 1694:

> A black boy, an Indian, about thirteen years old run away the 8th inst. from Putney, with a collar about his neck with this inscription: "My Lady Bromfield's black, in Lincoln's Inn Fields." Whoever brings him to Sir Edward Bromfield's at Putney, shall have a guinea reward.[22]

The wearing of slave collars continued into the eighteenth century, although they seem to have become less common. They can be seen in caricatures and portraits of the time: in Plate 2 of Hogarth's *A Harlot's Progress* (1732), Moll, the country girl who has become a rich man's mistress, possesses both

Plate 2 of *A Harlot's Progress* (1732), by William Hogarth. Moll's young black attendant appears to wear a slave collar. (Image ID lwlpr22338, reproduced courtesy Lewis Walpole Library, Yale University)

a pet monkey and a small black page boy, complete with turban and what appears to be a slave collar. Such collars were still in existence when Barber arrived in England. In 1756 a goldsmith called Matthew Dyer advertised in the *London Advertiser* that he would make "silver padlocks for blacks or dogs; collars, &c."[23]

There was also visible evidence in the newspapers of slavery in England. Some of this took the form of announcements like Edward Bromfield's concerning runaway black men or boys, usually offering a reward for their return (and often a threat to anyone who might assist them). But there were also "For sale" advertisements. In 1756, when Barber was about fourteen years old (by which time he had four years' experience as a house servant), he could have read this advertisement in the *London Advertiser*: "To be sold, a Negro Boy, about fourteen years old, warranted free from any distemper, and has had those fatal to that colour; has been used two years to all kinds of household work, and to wait at table; his price is £25."[24]

In the period between 1709 and 1792 forty similar advertisements for the sale of young black men or women are known to have been published in England (and a further eight in Scotland), and there must have been other instances for which the records do not survive, or have yet to be discovered.[25] Lord Stowell, a judge who was a member of Johnson's Club and one of his executors, recalled in 1827:

> The personal traffic in slaves resident in England had been as public and as authorised as in any of our West Indian islands. They were sold on the Exchange and other places of public resort by parties themselves resident in London, and with as little reserve as they have been in our West Indian possessions. Such a state of things continued without impeachment from a very early period up to nearly the end of the last century.[26]

As if to emphasise the fact that slaves were items of property, they were sometimes transferred from one owner to another by bequest. In 1701 a Londoner called Thomas Papillon made a will which bequeathed to his son a slave "whom I take to be in the nature of my goods and chattels."[27]

It would be wrong to assume, however, that all blacks in England were kept in this form of servitude. Without knowing the details of any particular person's circumstances, it is difficult to tell whether he or she was a slave or a servant. One factor which pointed to servant status rather than slavery was the payment of wages. This is an area where we know something about Barber's experience, but only at a much later stage of his life. There are entries in Johnson's diaries which indicate that he paid Barber 7s each week. However, Johnson's journal-keeping was sporadic, and in any event not all his diaries have survived, so it is difficult to know when such payments began. The earliest surviving entry of this kind is a payment of 7s on 18 March 1765 (when Barber was probably aged about twenty-four). In surviving diaries for 1782 Johnson records that he paid Frank 7s on 13 August, 24 August, 8 September, 14 September, and 25 September. On 5 October he paid Barber £2 2s, noting "6 weeks to Francis," apparently wages paid in advance. On 1 October he had paid £2 10s "to Frank for wages," suggesting that Frank was responsible for paying other household members.[28] It seems likely that Frank was paid 7s per week from (at the latest) March 1765 until Johnson's death in 1784, but it is not clear how old he was when this wage was first paid.

If objective evidence of Barber's status is lacking, what about the views of those who knew him, and, above all, what did Barber himself think? Colonel Richard Bathurst, who had been Barber's slave-owner in Jamaica, had no doubt at all about the matter. When he made his will in April 1754, he declared: "I give to Francis Barber a Negroe whom I brought from Jamaica aforesaid into England his freedom."[29] It is a striking phrase, because it makes it absolutely clear that Colonel Bathurst considered that Barber's freedom was his to give or to withhold. In spite of the fact that they were now in England—and that Barber had not been a part of Bathurst's household for the two years preceding the date the will was drawn up—Bathurst still regarded Barber as his property, his slave.

It was perhaps to be expected that an old plantation owner would cling to views which were universal in Jamaica. What is much more surprising is that Francis Barber clearly shared this belief, as he told Boswell in 1786 that Colonel Bathurst "made him free" in his will. The young boy *felt* that he was a slave from the time when he joined Johnson's household in the spring of 1752 until Bathurst's will took effect in 1756. He saw himself as still owned by Colonel Bathurst during that period and so must have thought that he was in some sense on loan to Samuel Johnson. Nor did Barber's views about his situation change later on, as thirty years had passed when he told Boswell that Colonel Bathurst had given him his freedom by his will.

Johnson certainly did not believe that Barber was a slave. He was an opponent of slavery, whether in the colonies or at home, and would not have countenanced the transfer of Barber to any other master against his wishes. So how did he and Barber understand the nature of their relationship? The key to the answer to this question is Johnson's role in his Gough Square residence. At that time there was a widely recognised pattern of relationships within the home, in which the ultimate authority over all the residents rested with the (usually male) head of the household.[30] This extended beyond blood relations to include apprentices, servants, and others—all those who were resident under the one roof. The central notion was the idea that the head of the household was a father figure, and that the residents were his "family." As one manual of domestic government put it, "The householder is called *Pater familias,* that is father of a family, because he should have a fatherly care over his servants as if they were his children." Another very popular conduct guide, which went through numerous editions in the first half of the eighteenth century, instructed that "your care must not stop at your Children, let it reach your menial Servants; though you are their Master, you are also their Father."[31] When the word "family" was used in the eighteenth century it often referred to this wider group, in contrast to the narrower modern meaning of the nuclear family.

The historian Naomi Tadmor uses the term "household-family" to capture this meaning of a group of people who were resident in the same house and subject to the same authority.[32] Johnson used the word "family" in this way, defining it in his *Dictionary* as "those who live in the same house." In July 1755 he had no blood relations living with him (his household being made up entirely of servants and unrelated dependants), but he recorded in his diary his resolution, "To instruct my family."[33]

This understanding of the role of the father figure had consequences for both parties, and there were obligations on each side. So far as a servant was concerned, he was obliged to obey his master in all things. As one cleric preached in 1750 to those in domestic service, "Your time and strength are no longer your own, when you are hired; they are your master's, and to be employed in his service . . . a servant is supposed to have no will of his own, where his master is concerned; but to submit himself intirely to the will of his master, and obey all his lawful commands."[34] The servant was expected to give to his master that same support and loyalty which he would give to a parent.

The master, for his part, had the same authority over his servants as he did over his children, but he also owed them the same obligations. He had the right (and the duty) to discipline them, chastising them with reasonable punishment. But he was also responsible for his servants' well-being, both spiritual and material. He was obliged to give guidance concerning the Christian faith, to provide for the servants' daily needs, and to support them when they were ill or otherwise in trouble. This obligation was more than lifelong: a master should provide for a faithful servant in his will, so that he would still be looked after once his master was no longer there to take care of him.

All this, of course, sounds impossibly idealistic, and it is safe to assume that what was written in the numerous conduct books, sermons, and guides to master-servant relations was not necessarily reflected in the behaviour of either masters or servants behind the closed doors of their homes. But there were clearly many households in which at least some attempt was made to follow the precepts which were so widely laid down.

In the case of Barber and Johnson, this notion of the *pater familias* is central to understanding their relationship, from its beginning in 1752 right up until Johnson's death in 1784 (and beyond). Barber regarded Johnson as his father figure and thought of himself as a member of his household family, and Johnson entirely shared these attitudes. Again and again through their lives together, this shared understanding was to be at the heart of their actions.

Johnson gave some thought to the matter of master-servant relationships, and contributed to public discussion of the subject. The best measure of a man's character, he declared, was how he behaved not in his public life but in his family. In his *Rambler* essay No. 68, published in 1750, he wrote:

> It is, indeed, at home that every man must be known by those who would make a just estimate either of his virtue or felicity . . . Every man must have found some whose lives, in every house but their own, was a continual series of hypocrisy, and who concealed under fair appearances bad qualities . . . And there are others who, without any show of general goodness, and without the attractions by which popularity is conciliated, are received among their own families as bestowers of happiness, and reverenced as instructors, guardians, and benefactors.

So the most reliable testimony of a man's character is from those who see him at home:

> The most authentick witnesses of any man's character are those who know him in his own family, and see him without any restraint, or rule of conduct, but such as he voluntarily prescribes to himself. If a man carries virtue with him into his private apartments, and takes no advantage of unlimited power, or probable secresy; if we trace him through the round of his time, and find that his character, with those allowances which mortal frailty must always want, is uniform and regular, we have all the evidence of his sincerity, that one man can have with regard to another; and, indeed, as hypocrisy cannot be its own reward, we may, without hesitation, determine that his heart is pure.

As a result, it was servants who were best placed to judge the character of their master:

The highest panegyrick, therefore, that private virtue can receive, is the praise of servants . . . it very seldom happens that they commend or blame without justice . . . There are very few faults to be committed in solitude, or without some agents, partners, confederates, or witnesses; and, therefore, the servant must commonly know the secrets of a master, who has any secrets to entrust . . . the testimony of a menial domestick can seldom be considered as defective for want of knowledge.[35]

In Johnson's case there was another driving force at work, one which informed all his relationships, including that with Francis Barber. It was his profound, and sometimes troubled, sense of Christian duty. Johnson was a convinced Christian believer, with a deep belief in damnation and salvation, but it was an important aspect of his thought that salvation was conditional upon what a person did. It could not be attained by works, but faith on its own was insufficient: how people lived determined their eternal destiny. So charity was of crucial importance, and it was vital for Johnson that he should regularly examine himself and his way of life, since he could never be sure about his own spiritual state. "We have hopes given us," he declared a few days before his death, "but they are conditional, and I know not how far I have fulfilled those conditions."[36]

For Johnson there was nothing in the slightest remote or merely theoretical about this way of thinking: to read his private record of his self-examination is to realise how deeply he felt about such matters. At Easter 1779 he recorded:

I am now to review the last year, and find little but dismal vacuity, neither business nor pleasure; much intended and little done. . . . Last week I published the lives of the poets written I hope in such a manner, as may tend to the promotion of Piety. . . . I maintain Mrs. Desmoulins and her daughter, other good of myself I know not where to find, except a little Charity.[37]

Johnson's estimate of his work and his charity is revealing about his scale of values. The "little done" during the period he was reviewing included publication of the first instalment (Volumes I–IV) of the *Lives of the Poets*, containing twenty-two lives. In addition to Elizabeth Desmoulins and her daughter, Johnson was supporting at this time Robert Levett, Anna Williams, and at least three other dependants. Johnson's Christian faith was at the heart of his response to anyone who was in need.

For Barber the year 1756 marked a turning point in his relationship with Johnson. It was during that year that Barber ceased to think of himself as a slave, and this transformation in his self-understanding resulted in the first important decision of his life. By then he was thirteen or fourteen years old and had lived in Johnson's Gough Square home for over four years, and become accustomed to its ways. But one day in the autumn of that year Barber walked out of the house, taking £12 with him, and did not come back.

6. An Apothecary in Cheapside

Barber's sudden departure from the household left Johnson at a loss: "You will think I forget you," he wrote to his friend Lewis Paul in the autumn of 1756, "but my Boy is run away, and I know not whom to send."[1] Johnson's dismay and surprise were understandable. The house in Gough Square had offered Barber security and shelter: it was his home. It was also a household of morose, taciturn, argumentative individuals who got up late, ate at strange times, and dressed badly, and whose table manners left a great deal to be desired—in short, the perfect home for a teenage boy. What could have made him leave?

Perhaps one of his frequent disagreements with Anna Williams had sparked a spirit of revolt. When describing his departure to Boswell many years later, Barber said that he left the house "upon some difference." Johnson put it more strongly when he wrote that Barber had left because he was "disgusted in the house."[2] But if we consider the timetable of events it becomes clear that there were also other factors at work.

In April 1755, Colonel Bathurst, who had been living in the Cathedral close in Lincoln, died and was buried in the churchyard of St. Mary Magdalene.[3] In his will he had written,

> I give to Francis Barber a Negroe whom I brought from Jamaica . . .
> into England his freedom and twelve Pounds in Money.[4]

This bequest did not have any immediate effect on Barber, because the will had to go through the necessary legal formalities before he could derive any benefit from it. In this case things did not go smoothly, and there was a lengthy delay in giving effect to the will. The person whom Colonel Bathurst had named as his sole executor, Peter Lely, renounced the office. An alternative had to be found, and this took some time. Eventually, on 14 August 1756, letters of administration to the estate were granted to the Colonel's son, Dr. Richard Bathurst. Until then, the business of gathering in the assets and then distributing them in accordance with the will could not begin. It was not until, at the earliest, August 1756 that Barber could lay his hands on the £12 legacy.[5] Just a few months later, he left Johnson's household.

These events were obviously linked: Bathurst's will sowed the seeds of Barber's departure from Gough Square. Whether or not the will did, in fact, give Barber his freedom remains unclear, but what was much more important was that Barber believed that it did; as he stated, it was Colonel Bathurst who had "made him free."[6] Not only that, he now had money. Twelve pounds was a substantial sum—as Barber was later to discover, it was equivalent to fourteen months' pay for a novice in the navy. For the first time in his life he had both the knowledge that he was free and the means to take advantage of that freedom. In leaving Johnson's household, Barber did exactly that.

Barber was far from being the only Londoner to quit his home that year. To judge from the newspapers of the day, the streets of the city must have been teeming with runaways—apprentices who had tired of their years of training, servants who were being mistreated, bored wives, and faithless husbands.[7] A search for such a person was likely to be exhausting and pointless, as the streets, alleys, and courtyards of the city provided countless hiding places, and there was little chance of finding anyone who did not want to be found. The best hope was to place an advertisement in one of the growing number of newspapers in the hope that someone might have spotted the individual. (Even this was likely to prove a waste of money except for one kind of runaway, one with a distinctive appearance.) A notice which appeared in the *Public Advertiser* in 1761 was typical:

> Whereas James Teernon a Negro Man, belonging to Captain Terrence Teernon, aged 21 years, about five Feet five Inches, with a Scar on his Forehead, speaks good English, did in November 1760, run away from his said Master: This is to give notice, that whoever shall harbour or employ the said Negro Man, will be prosecuted as the Law directs; and whoever will give Notice to his Master where the said Negro may be found, shall immediately after his being secured, receive Five Guineas Reward.[8]

Johnson would have seen such advertisements almost every day. Several months passed, and there was no sign of Barber, and no word from him. Johnson became anxious. London was no place for a young boy who had cash in his pocket but little experience of the city, and who presumably was known to very few people. Then, in early 1757, a report reached Johnson that Barber had been spotted in Wapping, a riverside district just a couple of miles from Gough Square, and much frequented by sailors. Johnson determined to search him out.

On 14 February, and again on the following day, Johnson placed an advertisement in the *Daily Advertiser:*

> Whereas Francis Barber, a black Boy, has been for some Months absent from his Master, and has been said to have lived lately in Wapping, or near it: This is to give him Notice, that if he will come to his Master, or apply to any of his Master's Friends, he will be kindly received.[9]

Johnson's notice stood out from those such as the one for James Teernon, as it made no threat and offered no reward. The words "kindly received" were not a common feature of runaway advertisements.

Barber was, in fact, living much closer than Wapping. He was in Cheapside, just the far side of St. Paul's Cathedral, fifteen minutes' walk from Gough Square. Many years later Barber told James Boswell that "he lived with Dr. Johnson from 1752 to about 1757—when upon some difference he left him and served a Mr. Farren Apothecary in Cheapside for about two years."[10]

The man whose service he entered was in fact Edward Ferrand and not, as Boswell wrote it down, "Farren."[11] Either Barber was very lucky or he made a wise choice when he ended up with this particular master. Ferrand, born in 1691, was sixty-five when Barber joined his household, and by this

Johnson placed this notice for Barber in the *Daily Advertiser* for 14 and 15 February 1757. (LC-sn 88063120, reproduced courtesy Library of Congress)

time hard work and ambition had made him a successful apothecary. His practice was thriving, and the shop in Cheapside must have been a very busy place. For most ordinary London citizens, the apothecary was likely to be the first port of call in the event of an illness. The business was described in 1763 by Thomas Mortimer in his *Universal Director:*

> It was formerly the custom to consider them [the Apothecaries] as the servants of the Physicians, to whom no more was confided than faithfully to make up the medicine ordered by the Doctor; and whose skill was supposed to extend no farther than to an accurate knowledge of the goodness of Drugs: at present the case is reversed; and the Apothecary is so far from being the humble servant of the Physician, that the latter, especially in the early part of life, is obliged to the former for his recommendation and introduction; the Apothecary being, in most families, the first person called upon to visit the sick; and when he does not think proper to take upon himself the entire management of the patient, it is often left to him to determine what Physician is to be sent for.[12]

As this account suggests, the business of the apothecary included making up and supplying medicines, but it had expanded beyond that into diagnosis and prescription. It was a demanding trade, and Ferrand needed assistance. Over the years he had a series of apprentices, including two during Barber's time. John Hingeston (like many apothecaries, including Ferrand, the son of a clergyman) was apprenticed from 1752 to 1760, and Samuel Spalding was apprenticed from 1754 until 1762.[13]

The usual arrangement in London at this time was for the master and his family to live above the shop, and for apprentices and servants to occupy garret rooms, so Barber probably shared with Hingeston and Spalding as well as other servants. They were by no means the only people in the house: Ferrand and his wife Anne had three unmarried daughters, Anne, Elizabeth, and Barbara.

Ferrand ran his business with considerable success, enabling him in the late 1760s to move from Cheapside to the newly developed Southampton-row, and when he died in 1769 he left a substantial estate.[14] The Society of Apothecaries controlled every aspect of the profession, and Ferrand was deeply involved in its activities. He took part in the training of apprentices in the medicinal properties of plants, and was involved in the management of the Society's famous Physic Garden in Chelsea, being appointed to the Garden Committee in 1758.[15] He was to rise almost to the very top, a climb which required both diligence and money.

Barber's decision to leave Gough Square and to join the apothecary's household was the first significant decision of his life. It seems to have been a sign of an increasing sense of independence, and it must have had the effect of greatly expanding his horizons. The difference between Johnson's and Ferrand's households was neatly captured by their locations. Johnson's house was in a small, gloomy, enclosed courtyard, up a narrow alley off Fleet Street, while Ferrand's home was on Cheapside, a broad, light, bustling street lined on both sides by shops and tradesmen's establishments. It was a place where people would come just to stare at the astonishing range of goods on display.

The Cheapside household which Barber joined was also in marked contrast to Johnson's home. Ferrand was eighteen years older than Johnson, but he was in many ways a much more vigorous figure. He was self-confident, wealthy, and successful, an increasingly important figure in the city of London, and he had a flourishing business. The year after Barber joined the

A view of the Church of St Mary-le-bow in Cheapside London (1757), by Thomas Bowles. Barber lived and worked on Cheapside from 1756 to 1758. The busy street is lined with shop signs. (London Metropolitan Archives, City of London (http://collage.cityoflondon.gov.uk) image 4490)

household Ferrand was appointed to the Court of Assistants, an élite group of about twenty-five members who had almost complete control over the activities of the Society of Apothecaries.[16] Only the offices of Renter Warden, Upper Warden, and Master were more prestigious. Ferrand would go on to hold the first of these posts in 1765 and the second in 1766, but he died in 1769 without having held the highest office of Master.[17]

The Ferrand household was full of activity, with a regular stream of customers at the shop. Upstairs were the three Ferrand daughters, all of them (like the apprentices Hingeston and Spalding) only a few years older than Barber. When Barber arrived in the Cheapside household, Barbara was seventeen, Elizabeth was nineteen, and Anne had just celebrated her twenty-first birthday.[18] It was very different from Johnson's household of infirm dependants, all much older than himself. The business of grinding, mixing, and making up intriguing potions was one in which Barber could take some part, and it was much more interesting than dictionary making. Johnson famously described a lexicographer as "a harmless drudge"; as a spectator sport, lexicography lacked appeal.

The attraction to Barber of the apothecary's home and business is not difficult to see, but what was the motivation of Ferrand in taking on the young runaway? One reason may well have been charitable: Ferrand was active in several charities, providing his services gratis to St. Luke's Hospital for Lunaticks, serving as a Governor of the Bridewell and Bethlem hospitals, and also of St. Bartholomew's Hospital, and being a member of the Court of Assistants of the Corporation for the Relief of Poor Widows and Children of Clergymen.[19] However, Barber must have proved his worth to Ferrand: charity might have helped Barber to find a place, but he would have had to demonstrate his value once he got it.

One other factor may have influenced Ferrand in his decision to employ Barber. The conflict with France and, later, Spain which was to become the Seven Years' War had broken out in 1756, and in times of war the apothecaries found it very hard to find journeymen or apprentices, because so many young men were in the army or navy. The city of London authorities prohibited the employment of "foreigners" (journeymen who had not been made free of the city by their guild) which, the apothecaries complained, "put them in great difficulties in carrying out their business."[20] In 1758 Ferrand was a member of a committee which petitioned the Lord Mayor and Common Council of the city of London about the matter.[21] The petition was granted and legislation passed to allow apothecaries to employ journeymen not free of the city "during the Continuance of the present War.[22]

Such a demand for employees could only help Barber's prospects. Ferrand was, as noted, a successful and increasingly wealthy apothecary, and for anyone apprenticed to him the future looked promising. (John Hingeston, Barber's contemporary, served out his apprenticeship with Ferrand and became a Freeman in 1764. Nineteen years later, he was called to the livery.)[23] Barber was the right age to commence an apprenticeship, which usually started at about fourteen years old. What was to stop Barber from becoming Ferrand's apprentice?

For a young boy like Barber, apprenticeship to Ferrand would have been an extraordinary piece of good fortune. In eighteenth-century England most boys started out their working lives as apprentices, but this term covered an enormous range of trades and skills. At the bottom end of the scale were parish apprentices (often foundlings or illegitimate children), who usually worked in an unskilled trade or domestic service. Their apprenticeships were arranged by the parish overseer of the poor and approved by magistrates, with neither the child nor the parents having any say in the matter. A fee of about £5 would be paid to the master. In return, the master had few obligations, so many such cases were simply cheap labour.[24]

At the other end of the scale was apprenticeship in one of the skilled crafts or trades which were regulated by the livery companies of the city of London. The Worshipful Society of Apothecaries of London (incorporated in 1617) was one such company. The apprentice to such a craft was more a pupil than a labourer. At the end of a seven-year apprenticeship, Barber would have been "made free," a Freeman of the city of London, with the right to set up on his own as an apothecary within the city. Only those who had served their time within the city (or had served their time elsewhere, and paid a fee) were allowed to practise their craft in the city. Those who practised there made a good living, and it had become an increasingly respectable and popular profession: in 1747 the *General Description of All Trades* commented that the apothecary's "is a very genteel Business and has been in great Vogue of late years."[25]

It has been said that Barber did indeed become Ferrand's apprentice, thanks to Johnson's intervention. Walter Jackson Bate wrote in his 1978 biography of Samuel Johnson that "Frank . . . wanted to become an apprentice to an apothecary, a Mr. Farren . . . Money was needed to article Frank as an apprentice. Later in 1756 Johnson arranged this."[26] But in fact Johnson knew nothing about Barber joining the apothecary's service. As for money, Barber would certainly have needed some, and his £12 would have been nowhere near enough: anyone entering into an apprenticeship had to pay a premium, and most of Ferrand's apprentices paid sums between £100 and £150. (Ferrand's last apprentice, Samuel Spalding, paid Ferrand a premium of £100 on 7 July 1754.)[27] Even if he had possessed the money, however, any aspirations Barber may have had to join the other apprentices would soon have been dashed. The Society of Apothecaries placed great emphasis on the selection and education of apprentices: they had to attend the Society's Hall to be examined on general knowledge and, in particular, their knowledge of Latin.[28] At this stage Barber knew no Latin.

But there was another, much more serious, obstacle which prevented Barber from becoming an apothecary, one which he could never have overcome. The colour of his skin prevented him by law from becoming an apprentice. This had been established as a result of the experience of John Satia, who, like Barber, had been born into slavery. Satia was brought from Barbados when he was aged about two by a merchant called Gerrard, who was his master and possibly his father. He was baptised in 1716 and apprenticed to a joiner in the city of London in 1718. (Gerrard paid for the apprenticeship.) In September 1731, Satia became entitled to become a Freeman of the city of London, with all the attendant privileges. But the question arose whether Satia was a British subject. It was a crucial question, as a person born in Britain or a country under the dominion of the king was a subject, but anyone born elsewhere was an alien and therefore subject to many constraints. One of these was that neither aliens nor their children could be apprenticed.[29]

Barbados was part of the king's dominions, but in truth the objection to Satia was not his allegiance but his colour. The Aldermen of the city decided that Satia should be granted his freedom, but there then followed a debate about whether in future a black person should be allowed to become a Freeman. It was eventually decided that the fact that Satia had been made free should not be "for the future drawn into precedent and that no Nigros or other Blacks be at any time hereafter admitted into the freedom of this City." Accordingly, on 14 September 1731 a proclamation was issued by the Lord Mayor of London:

It is Ordered by this Court, That for the future no *Negroes* or other *Blacks* to be suffered to be bound Apprentices at any of the Companies of this City to any Freeman thereof.[30]

The guilds had a complete monopoly on the practice of their trades within the city, and they enforced it strictly. (Ferrand was involved in this, on several occasions taking part in raids on people running a business dispensing medicines in the city who were not Freemen of the Society of Apothecaries.) Even those who had served a full apprenticeship outside the city (referred to as "foreigners") had to become Freemen of the city of London—which involved paying a premium—if they wished to ply their trade there. The city also jealously guarded its privileges against all foreign nationals, and the ban joined others already in existence. Jews were barred from being apprenticed, and Huguenots had been prevented from becoming Freemen. From 1731 on, any black person, whether slave or free, subject or alien, could never be apprenticed, could never become a Freeman, and was prevented from practising within the city of London any of the skilled trades.

By the summer of 1758 Barber had been with Ferrand for almost two years, but he had not completely broken with his earlier life and connections. It may be that the advertisement which Johnson had placed in the papers in February 1757 had achieved its end. In any event, Barber later told Boswell that he served Ferrand "for about two years during which he called some times on his master [Johnson] and was well received."[31] Clearly Johnson had been as good as his word in promising that Barber would be "kindly received," to such an extent that at some point in 1758 it was agreed that Barber would return to Gough Square. But Johnson waited in vain: Barber never arrived.

7. The *Stag*

Barber had changed his mind and chosen something rather more exciting than life with a lexicographer or an apothecary. On 7 July 1758 he went to sea.

Barber's decision to join the Royal Navy left Samuel Johnson bereft. He had lost Barber once when he went to work for Ferrand, but now he had lost him for a second time, and this occasion was much worse. Johnson was probably more distressed that Barber had chosen to join the navy than he was that Barber had abruptly turned down his old employer (though that would have been bad enough). This time there would be no wealthy apothecary to look after Barber, and no casual calls at Gough Square. Barber would be going as far away from London—and from Johnson—as it was possible to get. He was also, to Johnson's way of thinking, making a dreadful mistake. "Men go to sea," Johnson once declared, "before they know the unhappiness of that way of life; and when they have come to know it, they cannot escape from it, because it is then too late to choose another profession."[1] But Barber either did not know or did not care what Johnson thought.

There is something puzzling about the level of Johnson's hostility towards the seagoing life. It was a subject to which he returned over and over again, and in the strongest terms. "His abhorrence of the profession of a sailor," wrote Boswell, "was uniformly violent." That phrase "uniformly violent" leaps out at the reader: Johnson's notion of seafaring clearly touched something deep-seated in him. "As to the sailor," said Johnson, "when you look down from the quarter-deck to the space below, you see the utmost extremity of human misery: such crouding, such filth, such stench!" This could easily be a description of a slave ship. "A ship is worse than a gaol," Johnson told Boswell. "There is, in a gaol, better air, better company, better conveniency of every kind; and a ship has the additional disadvantage of being in danger."[2]

Johnson was not talking from experience; he did not travel by ship until his trips around the Hebrides in 1773 and to France in 1775. However, he must have seen the numerous merchant and Royal Navy vessels which thronged the Thames during his lifetime, and perhaps his curiosity had led him to go on board one of them. Whatever his state of knowledge or ignorance, nothing prevented him from being singularly confident in the correctness of his views: his remark about a ship being worse than a jail was made in the presence of James Boswell's cousin Bruce Boswell, who was a sea captain in the service of the East India Company, and might have been thought better qualified to know.[3]

Johnson's views were trenchant and quotable, and were written down and in due course published by several of his friends and acquaintances. What Barber thought was recorded by no one. The result has been that numerous accounts of the life of Johnson have viewed Barber's decision to go to sea through Johnson's eyes, not through Barber's. In Johnson's words, Barber "ran away to sea." John Wain wrote in his biography of Johnson that "Johnson's time and energy went on helping those about him who got themselves into scrapes. Frank Barber was a worry; he ran away and joined the navy." The *Oxford Dictionary of National Biography* records that "Barber . . . ran away again, this time to join the navy."[4] It is a well-used form of words and it has overtones of immature and irresponsible action. "Running away" is the whim of a child, not the considered action of a mature person. An adult decides to join the navy; an adolescent runs away to sea. But Barber's perspective was very different from Johnson's—and much better-informed about the navy. We need to think again about what really motivated Barber.

Not long after Barber had joined the navy, a rumour started to circulate about the circumstances in which he had gone to sea. In March 1759 the novelist Tobias Smollett wrote to the politician John Wilkes (in a letter to which we will return) that Barber had been "pressed on board the Stag frigate."[5] The phrase immediately brings to mind a scene familiar from numerous films and novels: a gang of thugs wielding belaying pins, led by an officer with cutlass in hand, rushing through the streets of some port town or other, seizing the hapless young Barber, and dragging him away from his life of relative ease to one which would alternate between brutality and drudgery—in short, something like the life he would have had in Jamaica.

Impressment was the nearest thing to legalised slavery which existed in England, and its opponents often made the comparison. Granville Sharp, the leading campaigner against slavery, was also a bitter opponent of the press gang. On the one recorded occasion when Sharp met Samuel Johnson, on 20 May 1779, these two opponents of slavery had a long debate about the legality of impressment. Johnson argued forcefully that "it was a condition necessarily attending that way of life; and when they entered into it, they must take it with all its circumstances; and, knowing this, it must be considered as voluntary service." Sharp was no match for Johnson in debate, but he was entirely unconvinced, recording that "all this has been urged to me with such plausible sophistry, and important self-sufficiency of the speaker, as if he supposed that the mere sound of words was capable of altering the nature of things."[6]

However, the main targets of the press gangs were men who were already seamen; indeed, many sailors were pressed into the king's ships as soon as they arrived back in England on merchant vessels, so that their feet never touched the shore.[7] It is true that "seamen" was interpreted liberally by the press gangs to include many people whose occupations involved them in contact with the sea, and gangs were often happy to seize able-bodied men with little or no such connection. Nicholas Rogers, the historian of the press gang, notes that those seized included lamplighters, brass founders, tailors, and tavern servants. But a complete novice was not regarded as a great catch, and both ships' captains and the Admiralty were likely to complain about the quality of such "recruits." "The sending such men," ran one complaint, "is aggrieving the subject, embarrassing me to dispose of them, of no use to the public, a great expense to the government, and tends to no other purpose than to make their numbers raised appear considerable to their Lordships."[8]

The Thames-side inns of places such as Wapping, Limehouse, and Poplar were often frequented by seamen and so were frequently targeted by the press gangs. Barber's supposed connection with Wapping may therefore have been the basis for the story that he had been taken by a press gang. In any event, the gangs also operated farther from the Thames, including in the city and the Strand, where Barber might well have been. There are records of their operations in the parish of St. Clement Danes, the church which

Johnson was accustomed to attend. So it was possible, if unlikely, that Barber had been seized.

Support for this version of events is also provided by the common perception that serving on a British warship in the eighteenth century was not much above being on a slave ship, with every captain a sadistic brute and flogging a daily event, making it impossible that anyone would have willingly joined up. But the popular image of the eighteenth-century navy as an institution so unappealing that it was totally dependent upon the press gang is mistaken. It is true that finding sufficient numbers for the navy was always a problem, but many of those who did serve had joined up willingly. In the period 1755–57 (which covered the beginning of the Seven Years' War), out of a total of 30,323 men recruited ashore, 20,370 were volunteers.[9]

The fact is that Francis Barber was one such volunteer. All naval ships conducted a muster each week, when a record was made of every man who was on board. There are thousands of these muster books in the National Archives, a testimony to the remarkably efficient record-keeping of the Georgian navy. The surviving ships' muster books include those which recorded Barber's naval history. The standard form of these records included a column headed "whether prest or not." The entry against Barber's name in this column reads "Vol," meaning "volunteer."[10] This description is not absolutely conclusive, because some men who had been seized by the press gang promptly (and very sensibly) decided to volunteer, thus qualifying for the bounty which was payable only to those who volunteered in wartime—in 1759 it was £5. But the matter is put beyond all doubt by Barber himself, who told Boswell almost thirty years later that he joined the navy "having an inclination to go to sea."[11]

Why might Barber have taken such a step? He had, in fact, good reasons for doing so, some specific to his situation and some which would have applied to any young black man at that time. There were aspects of his life at Gough Square which made it less appealing than it might have seemed to Johnson. Barber's duties may have been undemanding, but, as we have seen, the fellow members of Johnson's household (especially Anna Williams) were certainly irksome. Living in the same house, Barber had no easy escape route. Mrs. Williams was fifty-eight years old, blind, and irritable, and Johnson was fifty and depressive. In contrast was the camaraderie on board ship, where there would be many boys of Barber's own age, and the majority of the crew would be under twenty-five years old.

There was also the issue of the colour of his skin. It is not known whether at this period in his life Barber encountered prejudice or hostility on this account, but it would not be surprising—he certainly did in later years. We do know that in the navy, where blacks were more common, Barber would not have stood out as much as he did on the streets of London, and this may have influenced his decision to go to sea. The question which Barber faced was one which all black people had to deal with in eighteenth-century London: how could a black person survive in a white society? The chief occupations which enabled them to do so were as a servant or as a sailor.[12] Barber had been one, and now he became the other.

Historians have debated the number of black sailors in the Royal Navy in this period. Establishing reliable figures is very difficult, as the naval records are not helpful in this respect. In Barber's day there was no entry for a man's nationality, colour, or country of origin, so one has to rely on occasional references, such as "discharged, being a slave," or giveaway names, such as Scipio or Quash. It was at one time believed that roughly a quarter of the Royal Navy was black, a very high figure given the number of black people in the population at large. However, most scholars now regard this figure as inaccurate.[13]

The most detailed analysis has been conducted by Charles R. Foy, who carried out painstaking research into the muster records and was able to create a database of black mariners. He concluded that between 1713 and 1725 blacks made up less than 1.5 percent of Royal Navy crews. The number of black sailors increased over the eighteenth century, but during the period 1713–83 it never exceeded 6 percent. At no time during the eighteenth century did black sailors constitute more than 10 percent.[14] (From 1765 onwards muster lists had to include place of origin; applying this information to some figures for 1808—fifty years after Barber's time—suggests that up to 8 percent of Royal Navy crew members were black.)[15] The general picture is that the proportion of blacks in the mid and late eighteenth-century navy, while certainly below the 25 percent once believed, was significantly higher than in the British population at large.

The navy, therefore, offered Barber the possibility that he would not be isolated as a black sailor, and it offered more, too, in the form of a degree of equality. "Black sailors," writes Vincent Carretta in his account of the seaman and former slave Olaudah Equiano, "ate the same food as their white counterparts, wore the same clothes, shared the same quarters, received the same pay, benefits and health care, undertook the same duties, and had the same opportunities for advancement."[16] There are also some signs that Barber would have found in the navy an attitude towards black sailors which was at least relatively liberal. In 1761, two white sailors were court-martialled for sodomy (a capital offence). The principal prosecution witness was a black seaman, and the accused objected that it was unheard of for a black to give evidence against a Christian. The court-martial rejected the objection, convicted the men, and sentenced them to death—on the word of a black man.[17]

Further evidence of the attitude of the Admiralty comes from the story of William Castillo, a black man who was bought by a navy officer, James Jones, in Boston in 1751. He was brought to England the following year and baptised in Plymouth, which, he wrote, "I most humbly Conceive intitiles me to the previllege of a free Subject." At some point he left Jones and went to London, but in 1758 he was spotted there and sent in chains to Portsmouth, under threat of being sent back into slavery in Barbados. Castillo petitioned the prime minister, William Pitt, that he was now being held on board HMS *Neptune* "with a Collar on my Neck in Day and in Irons att night." The petition had the desired effect, and an enquiry was carried out by Admiral Holburne, the Portsmouth harbour-master, who reported back to the Admiralty. The Lords of the Admiralty took a very dim view of Jones's action and responded:

> Acquaint Admiral Holburne that the laws of this country admit of
> no badges of slavery, therefore the Lords hope and expect whenever
> he discovers any attempt of this kind he should prevent it.[18]

The appeal to Barber of a society where he might be treated more equally is apparent. "It is easy," writes the naval historian N. A. M. Rodger, "to see the attractions of a world in which a man's professional skill mattered more than his colour."[19]

Another obviously attractive feature of the navy was the guarantee of a steady income. Barber earned, throughout his naval career, 18s a month. From this was deducted fourpence for the chaplain, twopence for the surgeon, sixpence for Greenwich Hospital (which granted pensions and other provision for seamen), and sixpence for the Chatham Chest (a fund which provided pensions to service widows), leaving him with 16s 6d.[20] A London unskilled labourer's wage was approximately 10s a week, but the labourer would also have had to pay for food and accommodation—and of course the 10s could be earned only if he could find work to do.[21] Barber could rely on having hot food every day, clothes, and, if necessary, medical care. A landman like Barber could also hope to rise to ordinary seaman (earning 19s a month) and then able seaman (£1 4s a month). In addition, there was the tantalising possibility of prize money: if a vessel was captured, her value would be divided among the officers and crew of the vessel effecting the capture. In 1764 George Harford, a black sailor serving on the *Stag*, received £40 in prize money.[22] (This apparent good fortune proved to be something of a mixed blessing, as he was later murdered for the cash.)

Barber's perspective on going to sea, then, was very different from Johnson's. But there was another factor which should not be overlooked: the navy which Barber joined was a navy at war. From 1756 until 1763 Britain was engaged in the Seven Years' War (known in its American theatre as the French and Indian War), the conflict with France, and later Spain, from which Britain was to emerge as the leading European imperial power. For a sixteen-year-old it might well have been an exciting prospect.

Barber also had the advantage—like many other black sailors—of at least having been at sea before, on the voyage from Jamaica to England. But there were also great dangers in a seagoing career. That voyage was a reminder that a black man who chose to go to sea ran a risk that no white man ever did, because in some British territories he would be subject to the constant threat of reenslavement. The risks and rewards of naval service for a black man are well illustrated by the career of Barber's near-exact contemporary, Olaudah Equiano. More is known of Equiano's life than of the life of any other black person in eighteenth-century Britain. We owe this knowledge to his autobiographical account, *The Interesting Narrative of the Life of Olaudah Equiano*, published in 1789, one of very few memoirs written by a black Briton of this period, and also to the extensive research of Vincent Carretta.[23] The *Interesting Narrative* includes a long and detailed account of Equiano's naval service, which offers some parallels with Barber's experience.

Equiano was born around 1745 (within a few years of Francis Barber). How he spent his early years is not clear, but what is certain is that in the summer of 1754 in Virginia he was sold as a slave to Michael Pascal, a lieutenant in the British navy who was on extended leave, serving on merchant vessels. Pascal took him to England, arriving in December 1754, four years

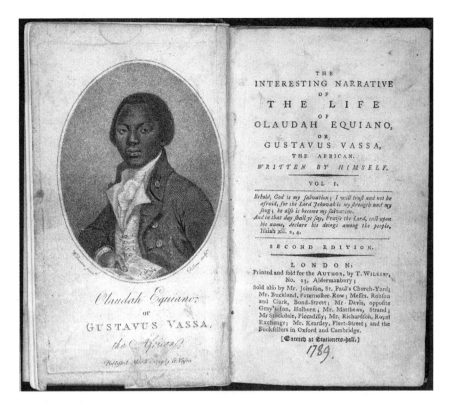

Title page of *The Interesting Narrative of the Life of Olaudah Equiano, or Gustavus Vassa, the African* (1789). (British Library Board/© The Bridgeman Art Library)

after Barber's arrival. From 1755 until 1762, Pascal served on various Royal Navy vessels, and Equiano served with him, seeing action during the Seven Years' War. (His period of service included the years when Barber was also serving in the navy.) Equiano remained a slave in Pascal's eyes, but the navy did not recognize the existence of slavery on board its ships, so Equiano appeared in the muster records of the vessels as a servant (effectively a naval apprentice). On 9 February 1759, while he was onshore for an extended period, he was baptised in St. Margaret's, Westminster. As was so often the case, his master had at first refused to allow the baptism to take place, but he ultimately was persuaded by friends to give his consent.

Equiano remained in the service of Pascal, in whom he placed enormous trust, but believed himself to have been freed by his baptism. When, in August 1759, Pascal was appointed captain of the fire-ship *Aetna,* Equiano went with him, acting as the captain's steward. By December 1762, Equiano had served through much of the war, and Pascal had recently promoted him to able seaman. Equiano was expecting to be discharged when they arrived at Deptford but was horrified when instead Pascal forced him from the *Aetna* on board a barge and hawked him for sale around various ships moored on the Thames. Pascal found a buyer in James Doran, captain of the merchant ship *Charming Sally*. Doran took Equiano on board and soon afterwards sailed for the West Indies, arriving in Montserrat in February 1763. Equiano's hopes of a speedy return to England on the *Charming Sally* were dashed in May of that year when, shortly before the vessel was to sail, Doran sold Equiano to Robert King, a Quaker who was a leading merchant in Montserrat. In addition to the seamanship he had acquired in the navy, Equiano had many more skills than most slaves, and he worked as a shipping clerk as well as on board King's ships, transporting goods between the islands. He himself began to trade in goods in a small way, enabling him to save some money. Equiano had become a trusted and valuable servant, and after three years he had saved enough to be able to buy his freedom from King. In 1766 he was manumitted (formally set free), paying King seventy Montserrat pounds for the privilege, but he continued to work on King's ships, although no longer as a slave but as an employee.

But freedom for a black man in the West Indies was not the same thing at all as freedom for a white: in a slave society any black man was in danger. A month after his manumission, while his ship was in Savannah, Georgia, Equiano got into a fight with a slave and beat him up. The slave's owner was determined to have Equiano flogged, and he went for constables to bring Equiano ashore. Equiano was forced to go into hiding for five days to save his skin, and possibly his life. As Equiano observed, there was "little or no law for a free negro."[24] On another occasion, also in Savannah, he was seized by watchmen who demanded that he give them money or they would flog him for supposed breach of a regulation which forbade a negro from having a light in his house after nine o'clock. He was saved by the intervention of a friendly doctor. Not long afterwards, Equiano talked his way out of trouble when two white men threatened to claim him as a runaway slave.[25]

In addition to the constant risk to his safety and freedom, there were limits too on what he was permitted to achieve in such a society. His seafaring skills were proven, but a free black man would not be allowed to become the captain of a merchant vessel. In 1767, Equiano determined to leave the West Indies, and he sailed for England, bidding "adieu to the sound of the cruel whip, and all other dreadful instruments of torture!"[26] Equiano's experiences amply demonstrate the kinds of risks Barber was taking in joining the navy, as this might well involve sailing to regions where slavery prevailed. Barber judged them to be risks worth taking.

The standard practise was for press gangs to set up a base (known as the "rendezvous") at a riverside inn, and there to try to persuade volunteers to join up, and also to plan raiding expeditions in search of the less willing. Barber signed up on 7 July 1758, presumably at one such London rendezvous, and was paid his volunteer's bounty. (The fact that the rendezvous dealt with both volunteers and pressed men may have contributed to the contemporary misunderstanding that Barber had been impressed.) He was quickly taken on board the *Golden Fleece,* a small tender vessel manned by eight sailors. Volunteers and pressed men alike were usually kept on such a tender to prevent any changes of heart or escapes. Three days later Barber arrived on board HMS *Princess Royal,* which was moored at the Nore, an important navy anchorage off Sheerness in the Thames estuary.[27]

After the excitement of signing up and the nervous tension of the three-day wait, what Barber experienced next was inevitably something of an anticlimax. At first sight the *Princess Royal* was a very impressive vessel. Naval ships were classified using a system which had been standardised by Samuel Pepys, as Secretary to the Admiralty, in 1685. They were divided into six Rates, according to the number of guns they carried, from First Rate (100 guns) down to Sixth Rate (20 and 24). First to Fourth Rate ships were the so-called ships of the line, the vessels which took their place in the line of battle. First and Second Rates had three gun decks.[28] The *Princess Royal* had at one time been one of the largest vessels in the fleet, a 162-foot, ninety-gun three-decker, Second Rate, with a complement of 700.[29] But she had been launched in 1711 and was now old and permanently moored at the Nore as a receiving vessel. (She was in fact to be broken up in 1763.) She provided accommodation for men who were waiting to be assigned to other ships— and also a form of detention for pressed men, who might be looking for opportunities to desert.

If Barber had been expecting to see action soon or to visit exotic places, he was disappointed. He spent the next five months on board the *Princess Royal,* seeing nothing more striking than the Kent coast. When Barber joined, the complement of the ship was 450. Barber was among the "supernumaries," those on board in addition to the authorised complement of officers, ratings (broadly speaking, nonofficers), and marines (nonseamen who were expected to fight ashore, if necessary). Like many others, he was awaiting transfer to another ship. At last, on 20 December 1758, he was formally discharged from the *Princess Royal,* and the following day he joined HMS *Stag,* the ship which was to be his home for two years.[30]

Joining the *Stag* was a piece of good fortune for Barber. She was brand-new, having been launched just a few weeks earlier on 29 November, and was a new type of vessel, a Fifth Rate frigate, lighter and faster than the traditional ships of the line like the *Princess Royal,* and more lightly armed. We know exactly what the *Stag* looked like, because the plans to which she was built survive in the archives of the National Maritime Museum at Greenwich, and there is a contemporary painting of the *Stag*'s identical sister ship, the *Alarm,* launched just two weeks after the *Stag.* She was 125 feet long, with thirty-two guns (twenty-six of which were twelve-pounders) and a complement of 200, and was designed for patrolling, escorting convoys, and cruising in search of privateers—purposes which made her a desirable berth because of the possibility of acquiring prize money.[31]

Her Majesty's ship the Alarm, *a fifth rate . . . conducting a Spanish prize into Gibraltar* (1781). The *Alarm* was identical to the *Stag,* on which Barber served. The vessels were launched two weeks apart in 1758. (PAG8857 © National Maritime Museum, Greenwich, London)

Barber appears in the muster books of the *Stag* as a "landman."[32] The crew was made up of idlers, seamen, and officers. The idlers were specialist non-seamen: the carpenter, purser, chaplain, surgeon, and their subordinates. Seamen could be divided into able seamen, ordinary seaman, and landmen. Generally speaking, one year at sea was required to become an ordinary seaman, and two years at sea to be an able seaman. The rule of thumb in wartime was that a ship needed one-third able seamen, one-third ordinary seamen, and one-third landmen. Another numerically significant group was the "servants." These were not domestic servants but rather boys, some as young as six, who were being trained and brought up for naval service. They were effectively apprentice seamen; indeed some were formally apprenticed. Each officer was allowed one servant, while the captain of a large ship could have many. (Equiano had served Michael Pascal in this capacity.) It meant that quite a number of boys who were younger than Barber were on board.

What was life on board like for Barber and his comrades, and how exactly did he spend his time? It is important to appreciate that "on board" did not necessarily mean being at sea. During his period of service on the *Stag*, Barber was on the high seas for only a little more than half the time. It was perfectly normal for naval vessels to spend much of their time in harbour or at secure moorings. But whether in port or at sea, by day or at night, Barber was always in company. In Johnson's household Barber had been solitary, isolated by his age from the other members of the household. In the navy, he was always part of a group, large or small. At mealtime he messed with five others, eating at a table on the gun deck, which was effectively his home when he was not actually working. He berthed there, along with all the other members of his watch, his hammock occupying the regulation space of twenty-eight inches wide, and head to toe. The ship's crew was split into two watches, which alternated over the seven watches into which the day was divided, five lasting four hours, and two of two hours. One consequence was that catching some sleep whenever possible became a high priority.

When he was on watch, Barber's time was divided between training, working the ship, and maintenance. Life on board was extremely demanding, especially for someone who, like Barber, was short and slightly built.[33] The manoeuvres of the ship involved heavy physical labour; straining around the capstan to weigh anchor could take hours and might involve large numbers of men. The maintenance of the ship was a never-ending task, in port or at sea, the main responsibility of the seamen being the sails and rigging. As a landman, Barber was a novice who had to take part in formal instruction and exercise—rope work, handling the guns, and the difficult and dangerous work on the sails, much of it aloft. In wartime there was no time to lose in turning a landman into a skilful seaman: in 1758 the Admiralty ordered that landmen should be exercised "at the Great Guns, and small arms" and taught "to reef and furl the sails of the ships that lie at anchor."[34] For Barber, learning to load, run out, and fire the guns was crucial, as when the ship saw action it would be his role, along with most other landmen and seamen, to man the guns.

The *Stag* was at first captained by George Tindal, but then Captain Harry Angel, a rising star in the navy, took over command in February 1759. (His promise was to be unfulfilled: his career ended in personal disaster in 1762 when he was court-martialled for indecency. He was acquitted, but suspicions lingered and he resigned his commission.)[35] The captain's log for the *Stag* gives some flavour of the routine nature of the life, broken by the occasional dramatic event:

> 24th December [1758]. The articles of War was Read and the Abstracts of the late Act of Parliament. Employed in Tarring the Bottom to the Water Line.

> 5th January [1759]. Fell overboard and was drowned Christian Flanagan Seaman. Emply'd cleaning the ship & co.

> 8th January. The people employ'd setting up the Rigging & co.

> 13th January. Exercis'd Great Guns and small Arms.

Contrary to popular belief, it was rare for officers to be brutal, and men like the notorious Captain Bligh were few and far between. The simple reason for this was that cruelty did not create an efficient fighting ship. "A brutal officer," writes N. A. M. Rodger, "was, of necessity, an inefficient officer, distrusted by the Service for reasons both moral and practical."[36] However, physical violence was more acceptable in society at large then than it is now, and in a world where children, servants, and apprentices could all be beaten, seamen did not escape from corporal punishment, a fact of which Barber was well aware. On 9 February 1759, he witnessed the most severe punishment short of execution which the navy could impose. The entry in the captain's log records: "His Majesty's ship Torrington made a signal for a Court Marshall. A man flogged from ship to ship for Mutiny."[37] The brief entry gives no indication of the appalling suffering inflicted. The victim was strapped to a scaffold on a boat which went from ship to ship around the whole fleet. At each ship, the whole crew was paraded to watch while a fresh bosun's mate would flog him, the total sometimes reaching 100 lashes. What happened to the victim in this case is unknown; most men who suffered this punishment were left permanently maimed.[38]

It was a common practice to "lend" seamen to other vessels while keeping them on the muster books of their home ship. In March 1759 Barber was lent until 15 July.[39] The ship on which Barber served during this period was HMS *Raven*, a 110-man, ten-gun, ninety-one-foot sloop. She was a smaller vessel than the *Stag*, and while Barber was serving with her was engaged around the British coast, off Yarmouth, Cromer, Lowestoft, and Hull, protecting fishing vessels from enemy attack.[40] It was a disappointing move for Barber, as serving on board the *Raven* was much less desirable than being on the *Stag*. This became clear two months after his departure for the *Raven*. On 31 May, the *Stag* chased and captured the *Dunkerquois*, a French cutter privateer, with a crew of fifty-two men. The prize money was divided among the crew of the *Stag*, but since Barber was no longer part of that crew he missed out on the division of the spoils.[41]

Johnson kept in touch with Barber during this period, or at least was aware of his movements. He knew of his transfer from the *Stag* to the *Raven*: on 16 March 1759 Johnson told Tobias Smollett that Barber was on the *Stag*, while in a letter of 9 November of that year Johnson wrote that Barber was "in the Summer on board the Ship stationed at Yarmouth to protect the fishery"—clearly a reference to the fact that Barber was now serving on the *Raven*.[42]

Life on board the *Raven* was not packed with incident, except for a seaman with an interest in watching fishermen at work. Entry after entry in the captain's log reports on the fishing: "22 of the fishery in sight," "seven smacks in sight," "18 of the fishery in sight." It was probably a great relief to Barber when, in July 1759, he left the *Raven* and was transferred back to the *Stag*. His "loan" appears to have had at least one effect on him: after his return, the records show him buying tobacco for the first time. The sums he spent on it are surprisingly large, sometimes amounting to a twelfth of his wages.[43]

Having spent five months in a naval backwater, he rejoined the *Stag* on 14 or 15 July 1759, just in time to take part in his first major naval operation.[44] The French had devised a plan for the invasion of Britain. One force was to land on the west coast of Scotland, and another in Essex. A diversionary force, under Commodore François Thurot, would sail from Dunkirk to Ireland. However, the British discovered the plan and put blockades of Dunkirk into place.[45] For much of July beginning on the eighteenth, and for the whole of August and September, the *Stag* was off Dunkirk, taking part in the blockade of Thurot's force under Commodore William Boys. (Commodore Boys had a well-deserved reputation for hardiness: years earlier, when adrift in an open boat, he had survived by eating the flesh of his dead comrades.)[46]

The blockade was at first effective, but, unfortunately for the British fleet, in mid-October there was a period of bad weather, and for two days the log of Captain Angel of the *Stag* recorded "strong gales and cloudy."[47] On 18 October the log recorded bad news:

> At 1 pm the *Aurora*, *Tweed* and our Signal was made to Chace to SW.
> The Chace proved to be the *Argo* and *Solebay* who bro[ught]
> Account of the French squadron having sailed from Dunkirk.[48]

The blockade had been broken and Thurot had escaped, along with his force of 1,500 men.[49] But the blockade had been maintained for some four months, and the threat of invasion was to vanish in November after the victory of the British fleet at Quiberon. For the rest of the war, British command of the sea was never again challenged.[50]

The siege was the most eventful period of Barber's naval service. His only other extended voyage was from the end of September 1759 to March 1760, when the *Stag* sailed to Scotland, spending lengthy periods moored at Leith, but also sailing around the eastern coast via Aberdeen to Cromarty on the Black Isle, not far from Inverness. (Thirteen years later, Johnson was to visit Inverness with Boswell, on the travels recorded in two celebrated accounts, Johnson's *Journey to the Western Islands of Scotland* and Boswell's *Journal of a Tour to the Hebrides*. Barber had been there before him.) The Cromarty Firth is best known today as a base for repairing the oil rigs which operate in the North Sea. In the eighteenth century it must have been idyllic in good weather, but perhaps less so when Barber was there in November 1759, the captain recording in his log, "gales and squally with snow and rain." The *Stag* returned south in March 1760.

Barber had served for two years when, on 8 August 1760, his service was abruptly terminated and he was discharged from the navy. The entry in the muster book gives an unusual reason for his discharge: "Admiralty Order."[51] On the same day the captain of the *Stag*, Harry Angel, wrote to John Clevland, Secretary to the Admiralty, from the navy anchorage in the Hamoaze at Plymouth:

> At my arrival here I found Their Lordships order of 27th of June last, and agreeable thereunto have this day discharged Francis Barber the Negroe, and given him the Certification as directed.[52]

The "certification" was a Pay Office certificate showing the time Barber had served, to enable him to claim his wages. It was Barber's final contact with the *Stag*, and the end of his chosen way of life.

The sudden termination of Barber's naval service had been brought about by Johnson. In fact, he had been agitating for it for almost eighteen months. Early in 1759 Johnson had raised the matter with Tobias Smollett, who in turn wrote to John Wilkes on 16 March:

> I am again your Petitioner in behalf of that great Cham of Literature, Samuel Johnson. His Black Servant, whose name is Francis Barber, has been pressed on board the Stag Frigate, Capt. Angel, and our Lexicographer is in great Distress. He says the Boy is a sickly Lad of a delicate frame, and particularly subject to a malady in his Throat which renders him very unfit for his majesty's Service . . . I gave him to understand that I would make application to my Friend Mr. Wilkes who perhaps by his interest with Dr. Hay and Mr. Elliot might be able to procure the Discharge of his Lacquey.[53]

This is, in several respects, a revealing letter. Smollett had served one voyage as a surgeon's mate, so he had at least some knowledge of the ways of the navy, and he clearly believed that Barber had been "pressed." He may simply have assumed that this was the case, but it seems more likely that it reflects Johnson's own belief. If Johnson genuinely believed that Barber had been a victim of the press gang, that presumption would cast a more favourable light on Johnson's attempts to get Barber out of the navy. The letter is also of interest in that it tells us a little about Barber's physical appearance and health, which appears to have been poor. But what is most astonishing about this letter is Johnson's willingness to use first Smollett and then Wilkes as intermediaries to influence George Hay or Gilbert Elliot, two of the Lords of the Admiralty.

Johnson barely knew Smollett, who told Wilkes in the same letter, "[Johnson] was humble enough to desire my assistance on this occasion, though he and I were never cater-cousins." Cater-cousins were next cousins—that is, good friends. Johnson's relationship with Wilkes, on the other hand, could scarcely have been worse. Johnson was a Tory and a Christian moralist; Wilkes was a Whig with a reputation as a gambler and a rake. The two men had nothing in common except their dislike of each other. Just four years earlier, Wilkes had very publicly demonstrated his wit at Johnson's expense. In "A Grammar of the English Tongue," which appeared as a preface to his *Dictionary,* Johnson had carelessly stated that "H seldom, perhaps never, begins any but the first syllable." Wilkes pounced, publishing a letter in the press:

> The authour of this remark must be a man of quick *appre-hension,* and *compre-hensive* genius; but I can never forgive his *un-handsome be-haviour* to the poor *knight-hood, priest-hood* and *widow-hood . . .* I do not wonder at so great a Scholar's disregarding a *maiden-head,* but should he dare to treat the *God-head* with neglect?

For Wilkes, Johnson was "an impudent pretender to literature," while for Johnson, Wilkes was "an abusive scoundrel."[54]

Smollett was well aware of this mutual hostility and played on the fact craftily in his letter to Wilkes, writing, "You know what matter of animosity the said Johnson has against you, and I dare say you desire no other opportunity of resenting it, than that of laying him under an obligation." Wilkes took the bait, and immediately intervened on Johnson's behalf. On 24 March, just eight days after his first letter to Wilkes on the subject, Smollett wrote again, this time to thank him. "Your generosity with respect for Johnson shall be the theme of our applause and thanksgiving."[55]

Johnson, however, seems to have been less appreciative. On 1 April, Smollett wrote again to Wilkes:

> As for Johnson, I wish you may find him sensible of the obligation he owes you. I desired my Printer to tell him what you had done with respect to his black servant; but I heard nothing of his acknowledgement. On the Contrary I saw a very petulant Card which he had sent to the Printer concerning an Article in the last Review.[56]

Johnson was in no mood to express thanks or any other positive sentiment to the printer, Archibald Hamilton. Hamilton had just printed in the *Critical Review* a hostile review of Johnson's fable *Rasselas*, stinging Johnson into writing to him to complain.

Johnson believed that Barber's discharge had been ordered in response to Wilkes's intervention, although there is no evidence of any such order in the naval records. (The letter from Captain Angel of 8 August 1760, quoted above, makes it clear that Barber's discharge had been ordered on 27 June 1760.) When the hoped-for discharge had not taken place by November 1759, Johnson himself wrote to George Hay (in a letter quoted in an earlier chapter):

> I had a Negro Boy named Francis Barber, given me by a Friend whom I much respect, and treated by me for some years with great tenderness. Being disgusted in the house he ran away to Sea, and was in the Summer on board the Ship stationed at Yarmouth to protect the fishery.
>
> It [would] be a great pleasure, and some convenience to me, if the Lords of the Admiralty would be pleased to discharge him, which as he is no seaman, may be done with little injury to the King's Service.[57]

This letter seems eventually to have had the desired effect—that is, the effect desired by Johnson. But it was not what Barber wanted.

By the time of his discharge, Barber had spent five months becalmed on an aged ship of the line, and then served for nineteen months aboard two very different vessels, experiencing daily routine and a major naval action, and seeing the worst that the navy had to offer by way of brutal treatment. He was therefore in a good position—much better placed than Johnson—to make up his mind whether the navy was for him or not. The muster books show that he had not progressed beyond the rank of landman (as many men did after about a year), which suggests that he was perhaps lacking in the necessary strength or skill. In spite of this, however, he had no wish to leave: he told Boswell that he had been "discharged thro' Dr. Johnson's application, without any wish of his own."[58] When Boswell came to publish his *Life of Johnson*, he carefully repeated Barber's statement, also pointing out that Barber was "not pressed as had been supposed, but with his own consent."[59] Nevertheless, modern studies of Johnson often ignore Barber's perspective and cite Johnson's actions as an example of his charity and his support for his improvident household. John Wain wrote that "Johnson had to write a letter . . . begging for [Barber's] discharge," and the *Oxford Dictionary of National Biography* claims that Barber "had to be rescued when he ran away to sea."[60]

Johnson's concern for Barber's welfare was certainly genuine, and his willingness to use the loathed Wilkes as an intermediary was admirable. And his fears about the navy were no irrational prejudice: during the first three years of the Seven Years' War, only 143 men were killed in combat, but a startling 13,000 died of disease and 12,000 deserted.[61] It is also true that Johnson was, as Smollett wrote, in great distress.

In January 1759, just two months before Smollett wrote his letter to Wilkes, Johnson's mother had died at her home in Lichfield. It had been a troubled relationship, and Johnson had not visited her for almost twenty years. Even once she was on her deathbed, Johnson had put off making the journey. Now it was too late, and any possibility of repairing their relationship was gone forever. Seven months after the death he still felt his loss keenly, writing to Lucy Porter ("Tetty" Johnson's daughter and Samuel Johnson's stepdaughter), "I have no great pleasure in any place."[62] Barber had entered Johnson's life immediately after the death of Johnson's wife in March 1752 and had been a source of solace to him then; it seems that on his mother's death Johnson wanted Barber's company again.

The death of Johnson's mother was followed in March 1759 by a loss of a different kind. Johnson's money was running out and he was forced to move out of Gough Square, his home of ten years. He had known since September of the previous year that he could not continue the lease, but now he had to make the move from his substantial house to temporary lodgings in Staple Inn. It was a sharp reminder that all his years of labour on the *Dictionary of the English Language* had not provided him with financial security.

But however deep Johnson's distress may have been, it was *his* distress, not Barber's. Barber had no desire to leave the navy, but so far as we know Johnson made no attempt to ascertain his wishes in the matter. Johnson's interference was the heavy-handed act of a father figure who thinks he knows best—and doubtless was as unwelcome as such actions usually are.

With his naval career snatched away from him—and with it his regular income—Barber urgently needed to find a new way of making a living. The choices open to him were no greater than they had been when he had joined the navy two years earlier. In reality Barber had little option but to return to domestic service with Johnson. But it was not to be in the setting of old in Gough Square.

8. "A Race Naturally Inferior"

When Barber arrived back in London in the autumn of 1760 he found Johnson living in a gloomy set of rooms on the first floor at No. 1, Inner Temple Lane, a home which the playwright Arthur Murphy described as "the abode of wretchedness," where Johnson "lived in poverty, total idleness and the pride of literature."[1] The household was diminished, too: old Levett was still with Johnson, but there was no room for Anna Williams, who had moved into lodgings in Bolt Court, on the other side of Fleet Street, just a few minutes' walk away.

Frank took up his old tasks, running errands, taking messages, fetching, and carrying. On Tuesday, 24 May 1763, he opened the door to a young Scotsman, only a little older than himself, eager to visit Johnson at his home for the very first time. The visitor, James Boswell, recorded the event in his journal:

> I went & waited upon Mr. Samuel Johnson, who received me very courteously. He has chambers in the Inner Temple where he lives in Literary state, very solemn and very slovenly. He had some people with him, & when they left him, I rose too. But he cried "No—Don't go away." Sir (said I)—I am affraid that I intrude upon you. It is benevolent to allow me to sit & hear you. He was pleased with this Compliment which I sincerely pay'd him, and he said he was obliged to any Man who visited him. I was proud to sit in such Company.[2]

It was the beginning of a friendship that was to last until Johnson's death over twenty years later, and to result in Boswell's *Life of Johnson*. When he started to draft the manuscript of the *Life,* Boswell recorded another detail of this visit: "I was shewn in by Francis Barber his faithful black servant."[3] The two men came to be on good terms.

At about the same time, Johnson had another young visitor, on this occasion a Cambridge undergraduate called Baptist Noel Turner. He had obtained an introduction to Johnson from Robert Levett, in order to obtain Johnson's advice concerning a proposed translation of *Plutarch's Lives.* Johnson had taken a liking to Turner, as he often did with young people, and he became a regular visitor. Turner climbed the stairs to the door of the lodgings, which opened into a dingy wainscotted anteroom leading to Johnson's study. But Johnson was not in, and Turner was startled by the sight that met his eyes:

> The Doctor was absent, and when Francis Barber, his black servant, opened the door to tell me so, a group of his African countrymen were sitting round a fire in the gloomy anti-room; and on their all turning their sooty faces at once to stare at me, they presented a curious spectacle.[4]

For the first time we get a glimpse of Barber in company of his own choosing. The job advertisements and conduct books of the day make it clear that many masters did not permit their servants to have visitors. Horace Walpole, looking for a steward-butler in 1762, wrote that "one condition will be, that he is not to have friends coming to my house after him."[5] This was not the case with Johnson. Barber had his own circle of friends, and Johnson allowed him to entertain them at home. His choice of company is revealing: he was no longer isolated in a white society but was part of the wider black community which existed in London at the time.

There were occasions when that community gathered together. In February 1764 the *London Chronicle* reported a social event:

> Among the sundry fashionable routs or clubs that are held in town, that of the Blacks or Negro servants is not the least. On Wednesday night last no less than fifty-seven of them, men and women, supped, drank and entertained themselves with dancing and music, consisting of violins, French horns, and other instruments, at a public-house in Fleet Street, till four in the morning. No Whites were allowed to be present, for all the performers were Blacks.[6]

It is a striking account: a gathering exclusively for black people, involving dancing and making music until the small hours at a pub in the heart of London. The tone of the report is jocular but favourable, and the wording of the news item suggests that such gatherings were regular events. Barber's home in Inner Temple Lane was just off Fleet Street, and it hardly seems to be stretching the bounds of possibility to suggest that such an evening's entertainment, taking place about a hundred yards from his home, would have been an irresistible attraction.

On another occasion in the 1760s, John Baker, Solicitor-General for St. Kitts, returned to his London house late one night and found his black servant, Jack Beef, was still out. Baker recorded in his diary, "Came away between 10 and 11—walk'd home thro' Smithfield and Snow Hill, Fleet Market, Fleet Street and Strand; (found Jack Beef gone out to a Ball of Blacks)."[7]

In 1778 the writer Philip Thicknesse recorded that "London abounds with an incredible number of these black men, who have clubs to support those who are out of place."[8] The suggestion that blacks did not just meet on a casual basis, but that there was a degree of organisation for mutual support, was also made by the magistrate Sir John Fielding, who wrote:

> There are already a great number of black men and women who have made themselves so troublesome and dangerous to the families who brought them over as to get themselves discharged, these enter into societies and make it their business to corrupt and dissatisfy the mind of every black servant that comes to England.[9]

On the day when Baptist Noel Turner called at Johnson's home, the sight of a group of black men clearly surprised him: perhaps he had only ever seen individual blacks before. A black servant opening a door was one thing, but a group of black men at leisure, seated comfortably round a fire, chatting and enjoying each other's company, was quite another. Who were Barber's guests, the members of that group which so startled Turner?

Johnson knew a number of people who had black servants, so Barber probably was acquainted with some of them. In 1764 Joshua Reynolds founded the famous Literary Club, mainly for Johnson's benefit. At least two of the nine founder-members—one of them being the statesman Edmund Burke—had black servants. In 1774 Johnson's friend Hester Thrale paid a visit to Burke at his home in Beaconsfield. She recorded, "The great Orator Mr Edmund

Burke . . . was the first Man I had ever seen drunk, or heard talk Obscaenely—when I lived with him & his Lady at Beaconsfield . . . where Misery & Magnificence reign in all their Splendour, & in perfect Amity. That Mrs Burke drinks as well as her Husband, & that their Black a moor carries Tea about with a cut finger wrapt in Rags, must help to apologize for the Severity with which I have treated so distinguished a character."[10] Unfortunately Mrs. Thrale says no more about the "black a moor," a tantalising glimpse of someone who is clearly a black servant, perhaps brought back from slavery in St. Vincent, where Burke's brother Richard had an interest in a plantation.[11]

Joshua Reynolds himself had a black servant, whose name we do not know. His background was similar to Barber's. He had formerly been the slave of Valentine Morris, a wealthy landowner who had inherited from his father several sugar plantations in Antigua (as well as the beautiful estate at Piercefield House, on the River Wye). At some stage Morris had brought one of his slaves from Antigua to England, and this was the man who became Reynolds's servant, possibly in 1760 when Reynolds acquired a grand house in Leicester Square. In 1813 the painter James Northcote (who knew Reynolds well) recorded that Reynolds painted this servant on several occasions, including in his portrait of the Marquess of Granby, completed in 1766, in which the servant appears holding the Marquess's horse.[12]

It is usually thought to be this servant who is represented in a well-known Victorian picture by James E. Doyle entitled *A Literary Party at Sir Joshua Reynolds's* (c. 1845), which appears in many biographies of Samuel Johnson. The imaginary scene it depicts captures the sense of Johnson's extraordinary circle of friends in the 1760s. Seated around a table are James Boswell, Samuel Johnson, Joshua Reynolds, David Garrick, Edmund Burke, the Corsican leader Pascal Paoli, the musician and historian of music Charles Burney, Oxford poetry professor Thomas Warton, and Oliver Goldsmith. Behind the group, bearing a tray, is a black servant. It may in fact be that the artist had in mind not Reynolds's servant but Francis Barber when he painted the picture; Doyle clearly knew Boswell's *Life of Johnson,* in which Barber appears, and some memoirs of Johnson by Frances Reynolds published in 1831 record that Barber on one occasion waited at table at Reynolds's house.[13]

There is a curious story (which Northcote claimed he knew to be authentic) involving Reynolds's servant, one which is significant for the questions it raises about issues concerning colour in the eighteenth century.[14] One day in 1769, while reading an account of trials at the Old Bailey in his

John Manners, Marquess of Granby (c. 1766–67), by James Watson (after Joshua Reynolds). The model for the black groom is thought to be Reynolds's own servant. (NPG D34760 © National Portrait Gallery, London)

A Literary Party at Sir Joshua Reynolds's (c. 1845), by James E. Doyle, engraving by William Walker. In this Victorian image, Johnson appears in the left foreground. The black servant in the background represents either Reynolds's servant or Francis Barber. (Reproduced courtesy Trustees of Dr. Johnson's House)

morning paper, Sir Joshua was startled to discover that a prisoner had been condemned to death for a robbery committed on Sir Joshua's own servant. He made enquiries and confirmed that the story was true, whereupon "Sir Joshua reprimanded this black servant for his conduct, and especially for not having informed him of this serious adventure." The servant told him that he had concealed the event, "only to avoid the blame he should have incurred had he told it."

According to Sir Joshua's servant the incident had taken place sometime earlier, on a night when Anna Williams had dined at Sir Joshua's with his sister, Frances. The servant had been sent to see Williams safely home to Bolt Court. On the way back he had met some friends and remained with them so late that when he got home everyone had gone to bed and the doors were locked. He wandered the streets for some time and eventually took refuge in a watch-house, where he stayed for the remainder of the night "amidst this assembly of the wretched."

The black man fell sound asleep, when a poor thief, who had been taken into custody by the constable of the night, perceiving, as the man slept, that he had a watch and money in his pocket (which was seen on his thigh), he seized an opportunity and stole the watch, and with a penknife cut through the pocket, and so possessed himself of the money. When the Black awaked from his nap, he soon discovered what had been done to his cost, and immediately gave the alarm, and a strict search was made through the company; when the various articles which the Black had lost were found in the possession of the unfortunate wretch who had stolen them.

The culprit was seized and was later committed for trial at the Old Bailey. The servant prosecuted (as was the normal procedure), and the thief was convicted and sentenced to death.

When he heard this story Reynolds immediately sent his principal servant, Ralph Kirkly, to make enquiries about the criminal. Kirkly found the prisoner in his cell, "reduced almost to a skeleton by famine and by filth, waiting till the dreadful morning should arrive when he was to be rendered a terrible example by a violent death." Northcote records Reynolds's reaction when Kirkly reported back to him:

> Sir Joshua now ordered fresh cloathing to be sent to [the condemned man], and also that the black servant as a penance, as well as an act of charity should carry to him every day a sufficient supply of food from his own table; and at that time Mr. E. Burke being very luckily in office he applied to him, and by their joint interest they got his sentence changed to transportation; when, after being furnished with all necessaries, he was sent out of the kingdom.

What are we supposed to make of this account? Northcote seems to intend the reader to admire Reynolds's generosity towards the robber, and his successful endeavour, together with Edmund Burke, to have the death sentence commuted. But what strikes us rather more forcefully is Reynolds's determination to humiliate his black servant by forcing the victim of the crime to become the servant of the perpetrator. What impulses are at work here? We are not told, but the implication seems to be that the thief was white. Would the story have been the same if the thief had been black and the servant white? Was there a racial undercurrent to Reynolds's actions, or did they simply reflect the horror of the newly knighted Sir Joshua at having his name dragged into the papers?

The episode illustrates the difficulty in trying to judge, with all the benefits of hindsight, how much issues of colour influenced behaviour towards any individual, a difficulty which also affects our understanding of the life of Francis Barber. How did those who knew him respond to the colour of his skin? In some cases, their hostility was undisguised, but in others we have to make the best estimate we can from their actions or their writings.

So far as Reynolds was concerned, there is a clue to his views in a contribution he made in November 1759 to Johnson's series of *Idler* essays. He had already contributed two essays, both devoted to the subject of painting, and in his third he turned to man's ideas of beauty. Reynolds argued that there are no objective criteria by which we can determine that one species is more beautiful than another: "He who says a swan is more beautiful than a dove, means little more than that he has more pleasure in seeing a swan than a dove." He went on to argue that our preferences are determined principally by familiarity:

"Among the various reasons why we prefer one part of [nature's] works to another, the most general, I believe is habit and custom; custom makes, in a certain sense, white black, and black white; it is custom alone determines our preference of the colour of the Europeans to the Aethiopians, and they, for the same reason, prefer their own colour to ours. . . . We, indeed, say that the form and colour of the European is preferable to that of the Aethiopian; but I know of no other reason we have for it, but that we are more accustomed to it. . . . The black and white nations must, in respect of beauty, be considered as of different kinds, at least a different species of the same kind; from one of which to the other, as I observed, no inference can be drawn."[15]

For Reynolds, later to be a supporter of the movement for the abolition of the slave trade, there was nothing innately superior about white skin: any preference for one colour over another was purely subjective, determined by whatever the person holding that view was most accustomed to seeing.

Reynolds's views, however, were not shared by all members of his family. In 1764 Barber travelled with Johnson and Sir Joshua when they visited Devon, meeting some of Reynolds's family, including his sister, Frances. It seems unlikely that she held any high opinion of Barber. When she published her *Enquiry Concerning the Principles of Taste and of the Origins of Our Ideas of Beauty* in 1785, she wrote:

> It is cultivation that gives birth to beauty as well as to virtue, by calling forth the visible object to correspond with the invisible intellectual object. In the face or form of an idiot, or the lowest rustic, there is no beauty ... The negro-race seems to be the farthest removed from the line of true cultivation of any of the human species; their defect of form and complexion being, I imagine, as strong an obstacle to their acquiring true taste (the produce of mental cultivation) as any natural defect they may have in their intellectual faculties. For if, as I have observed, the total want of cultivation would preclude external beauty, the total want of beauty would preclude the power of cultivation. It appears to me to be inconceivable, that the negro-race supposing their mental powers were on a level with other nations, could ever arrive at true taste, when their eye is accustomed *only* to objects so diametrically opposed to taste as the face and form of negroes are!

Her reasoning is obscure. Johnson commented to Reynolds on a draft of her text, "Many of your notions seem not very clear in your own mind." But there could be no doubt about her verdict on the relative position of blacks in society: "I am induced to believe that they are a lower order of human beings than the Europeans."[16]

Frances Reynolds was writing at a time when there was a ferment of new ideas about nature and society, many of which had implications for the position of blacks in the world. The seventeenth and early eighteenth centuries had seen an outpouring of literature about travel and exploration, subjects which attracted a wide readership. The European authors of such accounts often drew unfavourable comparisons between the populace of the places visited and those of their own countries, their judgments being based on the notion of civilisation. On the one side were countries which were "civilised," a matter which was judged by their political and social structures, their language and education, and their religion. On the other were those which were "savage" or "barbarous." It was a distinction which was very widely applied. The comparison did not turn on skin colour, but the perspective from which these matters were being judged was European, so inevitably Africans and Native Americans came out badly in the contrast.

With the development of natural history, questions began to be asked about the reasons for such differences: why had people developed in different ways, in terms of both their physiognomy and their culture? In Barber's life-time the most widely accepted view was that all men sprang from one act of creation (as recorded in the Bible), but that a process of degeneration had occurred by reason of the effect of climate. This was the cause not only of physical development, including skin colour and stature, but also of civil development.[17]

A number of naturalists began to apply to human beings systems of categorisation which had previously been applied to only flora and fauna. In 1735 Carl Linnaeus published his *Systema Naturae,* in which he divided what he was later to term "homo sapiens" into four groups: European, American, Asian, and African. The French naturalist Comte de Buffon published a multivolume work *Histoire Naturelle* (1749–1804) in which he argued that there had originally been one species which had undergone various changes because of the effect of climate, food, and mode of living, and that those changes were transmitted from generation to generation. The resulting subgroups of the species were "races." The ideal was the European, and the groups which had degenerated furthest from that ideal were the Africans and the Native Americans.

These theoretical matters were not as remote from Barber's life as might be imagined: they certainly influenced one other individual within his acquaintance as well as Frances Reynolds. In 1774 Oliver Goldsmith, an old friend of Johnson's and a founder-member of the Literary Club, published his *History of the Earth and Animated Nature,* a work which was heavily dependent upon Buffon. Goldsmith wrote:

> All the variations in the human figure, as far as they differ from our own, are produced either by the rigour of the climate, the bad quality or the scantiness of the provisions, or by the savage customs of the country. They are actual marks of the degeneracy in the human form; and we may consider the European figure and colour as standards to which to refer all other varieties, and with which to compare them . . . That we have all sprung from one common parent, we are taught, both by reason and religion, to believe; and we have good reason also to think that the Europeans resemble him more than any of the rest of the children . . . All those changes

which the African, the Asiatic, or the American undergo, are but accidental deformities, which a kinder climate, better nourishment, or more civilized manners would, in a course of centuries, very probably remove.

Such departures from the European ideal in physical appearance reflected differences in the character of individuals: "Of all the colours by which mankind is diversified, it is easy to see that ours is not only the most beautiful to the eye, but the most advantageous. The fair complexion seems, if I may so express it; as a transparent covering to the soul." For Goldsmith the "persons of negroes" were "deformed," but black inferiority was not just a matter of aesthetics: their minds were "incapable of strong exertions," and they were in general "stupid, indolent, and mischievous."[18]

Most of those writing about such matters affirmed that blacks and whites shared a common origin in God's creation, but at the same time their work established an apparently objective quasi-scientific hierarchy of "races." Their writings had the potential for creating—or, more commonly, reinforcing—attitudes of white superiority. For those who already felt hostile or superior towards groups who were visibly different from themselves, such ideas provided a justification for their attitudes. It is difficult to believe that such views did not influence attitudes towards individuals, and there is clear evidence that the development of ideas of race impinged on Barber; on at least one occasion such thinking was directly linked to him.

In June 1787 an anonymous correspondent to the *St. James's Chronicle* commented on John Hawkins's recently published *Life of Johnson,* in which Barber was portrayed as undeserving and ungrateful. The newspaper comments had echoes of the work of Edward Long, an extreme pro-slavery propagandist. Long had expressed the view in his *History of Jamaica* (1774) that there was a more radical explanation for human differences than climate or environment, and that different races had sprung from separate acts of creation. He also relied upon the notion of the Great Chain of Being, a permanent hierarchy of the natural world on which the relative positions of blacks and whites were fixed and progress was impossible. These ideas underpinned the comment on Barber in the *St. James's Chronicle.* "I am not surprised," wrote the correspondent, "at the base Ingratitude of Johnson's Black . . . The Truth is, these People are the worst Race of Men on the habitable Globe, and I strongly suspect them to be a lower Link of the human Chain of Beings."[19]

Beliefs about race and colour were further complicated by the issue of slavery. The links between the two were not at all straightforward. There were pro-slavery figures who were on friendly terms with individual blacks, and there were opponents of slavery who believed that blacks constituted a race which was inferior to whites. The *Universal Modern History*, a massive reference work published in 1747–60, condemned the slave trade but displayed an attitude to black people so extreme in its hostility that Anthony J. Barker described it in *The African Link* (his study of attitudes to race and colour in England in the eighteenth century) as "almost hysterical Negrophobia."[20]

James Boswell's friendship with Francis Barber was an example of such complexities. An indication of Boswell's attitude to issues of colour may be gleaned from a passing comment in the original manuscript of his *Journal of a Tour to the Hebrides with Samuel Johnson*. On 21 August 1773, as Boswell and Johnson were leaving the home of the Scottish judge Lord Monboddo for Aberdeen, Monboddo provided his black servant, Gory, as a guide. Boswell observed how curious it was to see "an African in the north of Scotland, with little or no difference of manners." He concluded: "A man is like a bottle, which you may fill with red wine or with white," a view which sounded much like Joshua Reynolds's idea of the essential neutrality of colour.[21]

Throughout Boswell's life, a notable aspect of his character and of his professional work was his sympathy and active support for the oppressed and the poor. In his legal practice he acquired a "distinct reputation as a man who would take on, become ardently concerned in, the causes of common criminals, the unfortunate, the desperate, the clearly guilty and imminently threatened with the pains of law," in spite of the fact that such attitudes were unpopular, and badly damaged his chances of professional advancement.[22] Boswell's support for the underdog was reflected in his actions on behalf of the slave Joseph Knight when he was fighting for his freedom in the Scottish courts in 1777. As we shall see, Boswell elicited Johnson's support, sent him the pleadings in the case, and asked Johnson to provide an argument in favour of Knight.

In the spring of 1787 Boswell attended the dinner which gave rise to the formation of the Society for Effecting the Abolition of the Slave Trade. According to Thomas Clarkson's account of the occasion, Boswell expressed

James Boswell (1785), by Joshua Reynolds. (NPG 4452 © National Portrait Gallery, London)

anti-slavery sentiments which Clarkson described as "strong expressions."[23] But he later changed his mind, perhaps in reaction to the events in revolutionary France. In 1791 he published his poem *No Abolition of Slavery; or The Universal Empire of Love*, a bizarre piece of work which combines crude attacks on individual abolitionists with an absurd and plainly uninformed portrayal of the happy state of the slaves in the colonies:

> The cheerful *gang!*—the negroes see
> Perform the task of industry:
> Ev'n at their labour hear them sing,
> While time flies quick on downy wing;
> Finish'd the bus'ness of the day,
> No human beings are more gay.[24]

The anti-abolitionist sentiment sits oddly with Boswell's frequent endeavours (which continued to the end of his life) on behalf of those who were most downtrodden.[25] Barber would certainly have been in a position to cure Boswell of some of his naïve notions about slave life, but he probably never knew of the poem, which did not achieve wide circulation.

The pro-slavery views which Boswell held in 1791, however, had no effect on his relationship with the former slave Francis Barber, or on his portrayal of Barber in the *Life of Johnson* (also published in 1791). From its beginnings in 1763, it was a friendly and supportive relationship. Boswell's occasional references to Barber in his letters and diaries are genuinely affectionate, and suggest that the good feeling was mutual.[26] In 1786 Boswell presented to Barber a copy of the second edition of his *Journal of a Tour to the Hebrides,* one of only seven known presentation copies. The gift placed Barber in good company. One of the seven copies was given to Boswell's close friend Bennet Langton. Another was to be presented to the King, although it is not known whether he ever received it.[27] Late in Barber's life, when he was sick and impoverished, Boswell loaned him money.[28]

The portrait of the relationship between Barber and Johnson in Boswell's *Life of Johnson* is sympathetic. Barber often appears respectfully as "Mr. Barber," "Mr. Francis Barber," or "good Mr. Francis."[29] Introducing Barber into his narrative, Boswell writes:

> That [Johnson's] sufferings upon the death of his wife were severe, beyond what are commonly endured I have no doubt, from the information of many who were then about him, to none of whom I give more credit than to Mr. Francis Barber, his faithful negro servant, who came into his family about a fortnight after the dismal event.

At this point Boswell adds a note which outlines Barber's life and states that he was in Johnson's service from 1752 till Johnson's death, with the exception of two intervals, "so early and so lasting a connection was there between Dr. Johnson and this humble friend."[30] He is portrayed as a loyal servant, frequently described as "honest" or "faithful," and considered with affection by Johnson. Writing of Johnson's concern, late in his life, to provide financially for Barber, Boswell records that "it had been for some time Johnson's intention to make a liberal provision for his faithful servant, Mr. Francis Barber, whom he looked upon as particularly under his protection, and whom he had all along treated truly as an humble friend."[31]

Samuel Johnson was the most significant presence in Barber's daily life; his views and attitudes on matters of slavery, race, and colour inevitably affected their relationship. It has been known ever since the publication of Boswell's *Life of Johnson* in 1791 that Johnson was fervently opposed to slavery. Boswell leaves the reader in no doubt about the matter, while at the same time recording his own emphatic disagreement:

> [Johnson] had always been very zealous against slavery in every form, in which I with all deference thought that he discovered "a zeal without knowledge." Upon one occasion, when in company with some very grave men at Oxford, his toast was, "Here's to the next insurrection of the negroes in the West Indies." His violent prejudice against our West Indian and American settlers appeared whenever there was an opportunity. Towards the conclusion of his "Taxation no Tyranny," he says, "how is it that we hear the loudest *yelps* for liberty among the drivers of negroes?"[32]

Boswell's *Life* established Johnson's anti-slavery reputation. None of the previous accounts of his life had mentioned his hostility to slavery, but in fact it was an attitude of long standing, going back at least as far as his early writing days. In his "Life of Admiral Drake," published in 1740, Johnson referred to fugitive slaves near Panama who, "having escaped from the Tyranny of their Masters . . . asserted their natural Right to Liberty and Independence."[33]

Johnson returned to the issue of slavery on a number of occasions but the arrival of Barber in his life seems to have given more focus to his attacks.[34] As noted earlier, it was in 1756, four years after Barber became part of Johnson's household, that Johnson excoriated Jamaica as "a place of great wealth and dreadful wickedness, a den of tyrants and a dungeon of slaves."[35] Johnson had read accounts of Jamaica and had often talked to Dr. Bathurst, who could tell him of his own experiences because he had been born and brought up there. But he had a better source of information close by in Francis Barber, who had experienced that wickedness firsthand. It was one thing to read accounts of slaves in the pages of the *Gentleman's Magazine*; it was quite another to hear from the lips of a former slave.

Barber's absence from Johnson's household while he was at sea seems to have particularly focussed Johnson's mind on the subject of slavery and also on the broader issue of the welfare of blacks in the colonies and elsewhere. In November 1759 Johnson had begun his efforts to have Barber discharged from the navy, and these resulted, as we have seen, in his service being brought to an end in August 1760. It was also during this time—in April 1760—that Johnson joined the Associates of Dr. Bray. Thomas Bray was an Anglican clergyman who was deeply troubled by the ineffectiveness of the missionary efforts of the Church of England, especially in the Americas. In 1723 he had been instrumental in founding a trust for the conversion and education of blacks in the colonies, and it continued after his death in 1730 under the name of the Associates of Dr. Bray. It established libraries and schools, provided books, and employed catechists to teach blacks about the Christian faith.[36]

Johnson was committed to the cause of Christian education for blacks, as indeed for all people—he vigorously attacked opposition to the translation of the Bible into Gaelic.[37] He supported the Associates for the rest of his life, donating ten guineas to them in May 1784. On his deathbed he arranged for his prayers to be edited and published by the Revd. George Strahan, and directed that the proceeds of the first edition (which turned out to be £47 7s 2d) should go to the Associates.

The Associates were concerned with the spiritual welfare of the blacks, not with the temporal conditions under which they lived. The trust was not an anti-slavery organisation; its members included some who were convinced that slaveholding was justified by the scriptures as well as others who were to become active in the abolitionist movement. When Johnson was elected as a member, the chairman of the Associates was Benjamin Franklin, who was then living in London with his son William and his slave Peter. (William's slave, King, had run away.) Johnson and Franklin must have met when both men attended the meeting of the Associates on 1 May 1760, as only eight members in total were present.[38]

Significantly, four of the known comments made by Johnson about slavery were published during November and December 1759. On 3 November 1759, in one of his series of *Idler* essays (No. 81), Johnson put into the mouth of a native Canadian chieftain the following words about the colonists:

> When the sword and the mines have destroyed the natives, they supply their place by human beings of different colour, brought from some distant country to perish here under toil and torture.[39]

Less than a week later, on 9 November, Johnson wrote to George Hay, endeavouring to procure Barber's discharge from the navy. On 1 December

Johnson returned to the subject of slavery in an anonymous introduction which he contributed to *The World Displayed*, a collection of travel accounts. Commenting on attacks by Portuguese adventurers on indigenous Africans, Johnson wrote:

> They murdered the negroes in wanton merriment, perhaps only to try how many a volley would destroy, or what would be the consternation of those that should escape. We are openly told, that they had the less scruple concerning their treatment of the savage people, because they scarcely considered them as distinct from beasts; and indeed the practice of all the *European* nations, and among others of the *English* barbarians that cultivate the southern islands of *America* proves, that this opinion, however absurd and foolish, however wicked and injurious, still continues to prevail. Interest and pride harden the heart, and it is vain to dispute against avarice and power.[40]

On 15 December, in *Idler* 87, Johnson remarked, "Of black men the numbers are too great who are now repining under English cruelty."[41] In the same month he published anonymously a review of John Hawkesworth's version of the popular play *Oroonoko*. Slavery is central to the events of the play, but earlier versions of it had been ambiguous in their attitudes to the practice. Hawkesworth had introduced two completely new scenes, one featuring slaves plotting a rebellion and another in which two slaves who are lovers declare that their love cannot survive without their liberty. In his review of the text Johnson focused almost exclusively on these two scenes, and James G. Basker argues that, in doing so, he emphasised the anti-slavery elements in Hawkesworth's revision of the play.[42]

This chronology suggests that there was a connection between Johnson's thinking about Barber and his writing about slavery: his concern for Barber was feeding into, and contributing to, his broader interest in the welfare of blacks and the issue of anti-slavery. At no other time in Johnson's life did he write so much about the subject of slavery.

Yet there remains a puzzle about Johnson's attitude towards slavery and the impact on his thinking of Barber's presence in his life. Barber was with Johnson through most of the time from 1750 until his death in 1784. This was before the beginning of an organised anti-slavery movement (which can be dated to the founding of the Society for Effecting the Abolition of the Slave Trade in 1787), but it was a period when anti-slavery sentiments were circulating widely, and there was much debate about slavery in the press, in pamphlets, and elsewhere. Granville Sharp commenced his one-man campaign against slavery in 1765 and published his *Representation of the Injustice and Dangerous Tendency of Tolerating Slavery* in 1769. He probably discussed the issue with Johnson when they met in 1779. John Wesley published his anti-slavery *Thoughts upon Slavery* in 1774. There were also several much-publicised events which made slavery a talking point: numerous slave rebellions were reported in the *Gentleman's Magazine* during the mid eighteenth century; in 1772 the *Somerset* case (to which we will return) raised questions about the legality of slavery in England; and in 1781 the dreadful voyage of the ship *Zong* took place, during which the captain, becoming concerned about lack of drinking water, threw 130 slaves overboard—and the vessel's owners claimed the loss on their insurance.[43]

It is therefore a striking fact that in spite of all these events—which must have cried out for comment—not one of Johnson's numerous topical essays is a blast against slavery, and he never addressed the subject in print at any length. Many of his comments on slavery occurred in obscure, anonymous, or fugitive pieces—a review, a preface, a letter, or in two instances a remark in a private conversation (later to be published by Boswell), and they were often only a passing reference while addressing another subject.

The oddity of this is the more marked as Johnson was a formidable controversialist, and one who had a ready marketplace for his views. He was certainly not reluctant to discuss social issues in print. He wrote on the criminal law and the use of capital punishment, the position of women in society, the treatment of prisoners of war, and the imprisonment of debtors. Tyranny and the abuse of power are topics to which he returned again and again.

It is not that Johnson's opposition to slavery was not genuine; on the contrary, it was heartfelt. He detested the slave trade and had nothing but contempt for the slave-owning colonists, "a Race of Mortals whom I suppose no other Man wishes to resemble."[44] But the issue of slavery did not dominate Johnson's thinking in the way it did for such campaigners for abolition as Granville Sharp or Thomas Clarkson. His anti-slavery convictions, though passionately held, lay beneath the surface, occasionally bubbling through when prompted by some particular event.

Johnson took an enormous interest in foreign travel, but when it came to attitudes to other cultures he shared the commonly held view of European superiority. According to Boswell, "The truth is, like the ancient Greeks and Romans, he allowed himself to look upon all nations but his own as barbarians."[45] That may have been too sweeping a judgment. Johnson admired aspects of Chinese law, the Confucian code of ethics, and "the Mahometan world," and, as we have seen, was perfectly capable of criticising the "English barbarians." His views were based on civilisation (or the lack of it), not on colour: amongst those he regarded as barbarous were the Highland Scots. Such barbarism, however, was not innate to peoples: "The manners of mountaineers are commonly savage, but they are rather produced by their situation than derived from their ancestors."[46]

To these general views Joshua Reynolds added an important qualification: "The prejudices he had to countries did not extend to individuals. The chief prejudice in which he indulged himself was against Scotland, though he had the most cordial friendship with individuals."[47] Johnson emphatically rejected the "wicked and injurious" notion that nonwhites were somehow less than human and wrote that "wherever human nature is to be found, there is a mixture of vice and virtue, a contest of passion and reason, and . . . the Creator doth not appear partial in his distributions, but has balanced in most countries their particular inconveniences by particular favours."[48]

A different picture of Johnson, however, was painted by Hester Thrale Piozzi. In her *Anecdotes of the Late Samuel Johnson, LL.D.*, published in 1786, she wrote:

> When he spoke of negroes, he always appeared to think them of a race naturally inferior, and made few exceptions in favour of his own; yet whenever disputes arose in his household among the many odd inhabitants of which it consisted, he always sided with Francis against the others, whom he suspected (not unjustly, I believe) of greater malignity.

Elsewhere in her *Anecdotes* Mrs. Piozzi records Johnson as saying that "the natural spendthrift, who grasps his pleasures greedily and coarsely, and cares for nothing but immediate indulgence, is very little to be valued above a negro." This sounds like a stereotypical view of black people as essentially childlike in their demands for immediate gratification of their desires— perhaps with Barber in mind? On another occasion, according to Piozzi, Johnson remarked that nothing promoted happiness so much as conversation, and when a lady's appearance and behaviour were praised, he responded:

"She says nothing Sir . . . a talking blackamoor were better than a white creature who adds nothing to life."[49]

The remarks which Mrs. Piozzi attributes to Johnson do not appear in her *Thraliana*, the journals which she used as her main source for the *Anecdotes*, and it is impossible to know whether she accurately recalled them. But when she wrote that Johnson "spoke of negroes" as "a race naturally inferior," she did so as someone who was well placed to comment on his views, having spent many hours in his company over the years. According to Mrs. Piozzi, Johnson espoused views of black inferiority, treating Barber as an exception in only a few respects. What Johnson thought the nature of that inferiority was—whether cultural, moral, or otherwise—Mrs Piozzi does not say. It is difficult to reconcile this attitude with the views he expressed in writing, but perhaps such contradictions should not surprise us. Johnson himself was acutely aware of his failure to live up to his own standards. "For many reasons," he wrote, "a man writes much better than he lives."[50]

Whatever views Johnson may have held on black people in general, they do not seem to have affected his belief in Barber's capacity, nor his determination that the young man should be as well educated as any white person, let alone a servant. By 1768 Barber had been with Johnson for eight years since his return from the sea. Now there was to be another great change in his circumstances.

9. "This Is Your Scholar!"

Johnson's fortunes had experienced something of an upturn after Barber had rejoined the household from the navy. Somewhat to his embarrassment, in 1762 Johnson had been awarded a royal pension of £300 a year—a rather awkward thing to happen to a lexicographer who had defined "pension" as "pay given to a state hireling for treason to his country." But Johnson was eventually persuaded by Reynolds that the award was in recognition of his literary achievements, not for services rendered or required, and he accepted the pension. This regular income enabled Johnson to become master of a house again, and in August 1765 he moved to the appropriately (but coincidentally) named Johnson's Court. The Court was on the north side of Fleet Street, very close to Gough Square and Bolt Court.

Johnson's new home was a substantial property, and he was able to reassemble his household. Boswell visited for the first time in February 1766:

> I returned to London in February, and found Dr. Johnson in a good house in Johnson's-Court, Fleet-street, in which he had accommodated Miss Williams with an apartment on the ground floor, while Mr. Levett occupied his post in the garret: his faithful Francis was still attending upon him.[1]

The financial stability which made possible the move to Johnson's Court also enabled Johnson to turn his thoughts once more to Barber's education. His choice of school is revealing—he decided to send Barber to the highly regarded Bishop's Stortford Grammar School. "The famous grammar school at Bishop's Stortford," wrote a correspondent to the *Gentleman's Magazine* in 1795, "produced a succession of learned and virtuous men, some of whom adorned elevated status in church and state."[2] Barber's contemporaries there included Robert Fiske, who went up to St. John's College, Cambridge, in 1768, and later became Vicar of All Saint's, Fulbourn, and John Wright King, who went on to become a Fellow of Christ's College, Cambridge.

The school was an ancient foundation—dating from the sixteenth century—which had moved into three purpose-built rooms in a new building in 1709. These consisted of the schoolroom, a writing room, and a room to house the library, all standing on arches beneath which were a market and shops. The collection of books was a particular feature of the school. It had been established in 1621 by the Revd. Thomas Leigh, who donated several hundred volumes, many of them old and rare, and it became the custom for every scholar leaving the school to present a book to the library. The collection grew to over 2,000 books and was very valuable.

The school's reputation was at a high point when Barber first went there. It had been built up by the Revd. Joseph Clapp, a graduate of Christ Church, Oxford, who was appointed Master in 1764, but he died suddenly in November 1767, shortly before Barber started at the school. The trustees placed an advertisement for a replacement in the *St. James's Chronicle*:

> WANTED a School-master for the Grammar School . . . consisting at this time of 28 Boarders, besides Town-Boys. A single Gentleman would be most agreeable, as the Trustees are inclined to favour, in the Article of Boarding, their late deceased worthy Schoolmaster's Widow and Children, who have the Property of the large and commodious Boarding-House, where the young Gentlemen are now accommodated.[3]

The first candidate to be offered the post turned it down because of his concerns about the lack of proper financial provision for the school, a sign of trouble that was to come.[4] On 1 December 1767 the Revd. Robert Fowler, a graduate of Magdalene College, Cambridge, was appointed Master, and the following month he placed an advertisement for the school in the *St. James's Chronicle* in which he declared his "intentions of discharging his duty with the utmost fidelity and attention." To reassure any hesitant parent he added:

> Mrs. Clapp, Widow of the Rev. Mr. Clapp, late Master, continues in the same large, commodious, well-situated Boarding-House where

the young Gentlemen will be under the constant Inspection of the Master, who lives in the same House.

Mons. Gautier, a Native of Lyons, who has resided seven Years in Tuscany, teaches the French and Italian Languages which, with Dancing and Music, are paid for separately.[5]

Mrs. Clapp's boardinghouse was Barber's home for three years. It is not clear how Johnson knew of this particular school, but he had links with two people from Bishop's Stortford, Susannah Smith and Joseph Smith, who may have been related. Susannah Smith was married to Johnson's friend John Hoole. Johnson corresponded with Joseph Smith, who was an iron-monger in Bishop's Stortford, and references in the letters make it clear that Smith also knew John Hoole. Johnson placed some trust in Smith, sending him money to pay Mrs. Clapp's bill, and in several letters to Barber at the school Johnson pays his compliments to Smith.[6]

In any event, the school Johnson chose had the advantage of being reasonably close to London—some thirty miles away. That and the excellent education it offered must have made it seem, at first, a good choice. Barber learnt Latin and Greek there, though whether he benefited from the teaching of Monsieur Gautier, or indeed of the dancing and music master, is not known. He was no great scholar; when Boswell was researching his *Life of Johnson* in 1788 he wrote to Thomas Percy, Bishop of Dromore, enquiring about Johnson's role in sending Barber to the school. Percy replied that "poor Frank, I fear, never got beyond his accidence" (that is, the elements of Latin grammar). But Johnson was proud of his servant's achievements, giving him a "smile of approbation" when he demonstrated his knowledge of Latin vocabulary.[7] In any event, the learning Barber acquired was to prove sufficient for him to make a living, at least for a while, thirty years later.

Johnson used to write letters of encouragement to Barber. On 28 May 1768, Johnson wrote to "Mr. Francis Barber at Mrs. Clap's in Bishop Stortford." (Johnson's spelling alternates between "Clap" and "Clapp.")

Dear Francis:

I have been very much out of order. I am glad to hear that you are well, and design to come soon to see you. I would have you stay at Mrs. Clapp's for the present, till I can determine what we shall do. Be a good Boy.

North West View of the Church at Bishop's Stortford, Hertfordshire (1834), by J. C. Buckler. Windhill House, on the right, next to St. Michael's Church, was Barber's home from c. 1767 to c. June 1771. (DE/Bg/2/9, reproduced courtesy Hertfordshire Archives and Local Studies)

My compliments to Mrs. Clap and to Mr. Fowler. I am, yours affectionately,

Sam. Johnson[8]

The wording of this letter—"stay at Mrs. Clapp's for the present, till I can determine what we shall do"—suggests some problem which had to be addressed. The schoolhouse had not been properly maintained for some time and had fallen into disrepair. In addition there was friction between the trustees and the Master, who had refused to take pupils who boarded elsewhere in the town rather than with him, an issue which clearly affected the financial viability of the school.

These difficulties were not resolved, and in July 1769 the trustees called a meeting of interested people to discuss the "decay'd condition of the High School, which . . . is not only unsafe for present use, but is likewise incapable of being repaired." They also wrote to the Master, demanding that he inform them whether he would take as pupils boys who boarded with other inhabitants of the town; otherwise it would be peremptorily determined at the next meeting whether the school should be taken down. They presumably did not obtain the assurances they wanted, and a month later the trustees ordered that the grammar school, writing school, and library should be demolished and that the books should be properly secured. On 26 December Fowler suddenly resigned, and Mrs. Clapp agreed that the school should have the use of the schoolroom in her house until a new school could be built.[9] The trustees were forced to advertise for an urgent replacement for the Master:

> WANTED, a Schoolmaster, at Bishop's Stortford, Herts, the late Master having quitted the School. Candidates are desired to apply to Mrs. Clapp, at her House in Bishops-Stortford, immediately.[10]

The trustees were anxious to point out the financial attractions of the post: "The yearly Income of the late Master, including a Curacy, was upwards of £200, and there is little Doubt but that a Curacy may be obtained for a future Master in the Neighbourhood." This is a notably high salary at a time when grammar school Masters usually earned £30-£40 a year (though a few earned £100), to which might be added the income from a local benefice.[11]

The advertisement achieved its effect, as the Revd. William Ellis was appointed Master from January 1770. Johnson paid his respects to Ellis in his next surviving letter to Barber, which is dated 25 September 1770:

> Dear Francis:
>
> I am at last sat down to write to you, and should very much blame myself for having neglected you so long, if I did not impute that and many other of my failures to want of health. I hope not to be so long silent again. I am very well satisfied with your progress, if you can

really perform the exercises which you are set, and I hope Mr. Ellis does not suffer you to impose on him or on yourself.

Make my compliments to Mr. Ellis and to Mrs. Clapp, and Mr. Smith.

Let me know what English books you read for your entertainment. You can never be wise unless you love reading.

Do not imagine that I shall forget or forsake you, for if when I examine you, I find that you have not lost your time, you shall want no encouragement, from, yours affectionately,

Sam Johnson[12]

Johnson's interest in what Barber read for pleasure sprang from his belief that this was the best way to learn: "I would let [a boy] at first read *any* English book which happens to engage his attention; because you have done a great deal when you have brought him to have entertainment from a book. He'll get better books afterwards."[13] His wish that Barber should "read for your entertainment" and "love reading" seems to have been satisfied, judging by some later correspondence—though there is a hint that this was an unexpected outcome. In January 1778 the young Frances Burney (daughter of Johnson's friend Charles Burney) published anonymously her first novel *Evelina*. It was a great success, and Johnson was delighted when he discovered the identity of the author. In November of the same year Johnson mentioned the book in a letter to Mrs. Thrale, remarking:

> Murphy told me that you wrote to him about Evelina. *Francis* wants to read it.[14]

Johnson thought Barber's desire to read the book sufficiently noteworthy to tell Mrs. Thrale, but the tone of his comment is unclear. The emphasis on "*Francis*" is Johnson's, and it is ambiguous: is it surprise, pleasure, or something else?

The last of the surviving letters which Johnson wrote to Barber at the school is dated 7 December 1770:

Dear Francis:

I hope you mind your business. I design you shall stay with Mrs. Clapp these Holydays. If you are invited out you may go if Mr. Ellis gives leave. I have ordered you some cloaths which you will receive,

I believe next week. My compliments to Mrs. Clapp and to Mr. Ellis, and Mr. Smith etc. I am your affectionate,

Sam Johnson[15]

The phrase "If you are invited out" indicates that Barber had some kind of social circle apart from the school. Clearly he needed to look respectable for any such visits, so acceptable clothing was important. It was not the first time Johnson had bought clothes for Barber. On 16 June 1769, a local hatter, John Phillips, recorded in his order book a hat for "Mr Barber at Mrs Clapes."[16] The cost was 8s 6d. On the same date are records of orders for hats for "Master James Wathen and Master George Wathen at Mrs Clapes." In this case the cost was 7s 9d each; obviously a child's hat was cheaper than an adult's. The hatter was clearly aware of the distinction between "Mr" Barber (now aged about twenty-seven) and "Master" Wathen, and the title applied to Barber shows a degree of courtesy towards him.

From December 1769 there is a continuing sense in the surviving records that the school was going rapidly downhill. For a while pupils continued to board with Mrs. Clapp, but she advertised her house to let in the *Public Advertiser* for 27 May 1771. A few weeks later the trustees agreed to rent the house for nine years, but nothing came of that plan. At some point, probably in the summer of 1771, Barber left the school and returned to Johnson. The last we hear of the school is in October 1772, when various fixtures, together with the famous library, were removed from Mrs. Clapp's house.

Johnson's decision to send Barber to the grammar school remains something of a puzzle. It was not completely unknown for a master to pay for a servant's education: in 1776 the Revd. James Woodforde (author of the *Diary of a Country Parson*) paid 4s 6d per quarter to have his footman taught to read and write.[17] But provision of this kind remained exceptional, and in any event there was a considerable difference between such elementary teaching and the grammar school education which Johnson provided.

There is no doubt that Johnson was deeply committed to the value of education. This extended to the education of black children and, as we have seen, was reflected in his membership of the Associates of Dr. Bray.[18] Then, too, he remembered his own experience of a grammar school with great pleasure: "The time, till I had computed it, appeared much longer by the multitude of novelties which it supplied, and of incidents, then in my thoughts important, it produced. Perhaps it is not possible that any other period can make the same impression on the memory."[19] But why did Johnson send Barber at that particular point in his life? When Barber went to the school in 1768, he was about twenty-six years old; when he left, he was about twenty-nine. He spent his time there living at Mrs. Clapp's house with some twenty-eight schoolboys, to whom a man in his twenties must have seemed an impossibly ancient figure. In many schools the Master had a paid assistant (known as an usher) who could assist with teaching the lower school, and it has been suggested that Barber might have occupied this role. But this is very unlikely; an usher was usually a university graduate, or at the least had a grammar school education, and in any event would require licensing by the Bishop.[20]

According to one early biographer, Johnson had some idea of making a Christian missionary of Barber. In his life of Johnson, published in 1785, William Cooke wrote:

> [Johnson] had the noblest motive for this extraordinary care in [Barber's] education, intending to make him a *missionary* in order to instruct his countrymen in the principles of the Christian religion. His parts, however, after repeated and extraordinary trials, not admitting this cultivation, he took him into his service, where he experienced in the Doctor rather the friend than the master.[21]

This account gets the order of events confused: Barber had entered Johnson's service long before being sent away to school. But there may be something in the suggestion that Johnson had hopes that Barber would become a missionary. The conversion of slaves was one of the aims of the Associates of Dr. Bray, and shortly before Barber started at the school an example of a black missionary going to Africa attracted much publicity. The Revd. Philip Quaque was sent to England in 1754 from Cape Coast (modern-day Ghana) to be educated; in 1765 he became the first African ordained in the Church of England. The following year he returned to Cape Coast as a minister and teacher.[22] He was not alone: in July of the same year the *London Chronicle* reported that "there are no less than nine Indians and Blacks lately admitted to Holy Orders, who are preparing to embark for their respective missions to America and the coast of Guinea."[23] In fact there were hundreds of African, Afro-American, and Native American missionaries who were sent out to the colonies during the seventeenth and eighteenth centuries.[24]

The decision to send Barber away to school may also have been affected by changes in Johnson's way of life in the early 1760s. As we have seen, from 1762 Johnson's financial situation became stable, so he was more easily able to afford the fees. There were also significant developments in Johnson's social life. His hunger for company was always great, but a number of important new relationships had gone some way to meeting his needs. In 1763 his long friendship with James Boswell began, and the following year Reynolds formed the Club, principally for Johnson's benefit. It met weekly for food, drink, and conversation, and its formidably gifted founder-members included Edmund Burke, Oliver Goldsmith, and Johnson's biographer John Hawkins (who resigned after a few years). Edward Gibbon, Charles James Fox, and Adam Smith joined later. In 1765 Johnson met Henry Thrale, a wealthy brewer and Member of Parliament, and his wife, Hester, a lively and intelligent hostess. They owned both a house in Southwark and an estate in rural Streatham; Johnson was so frequent a visitor that these almost became his second and third homes. Hester Thrale (later Piozzi) remained a central figure in Johnson's life until almost its end. With this growing circle of friends and acquaintances, Johnson may have felt less in need of Barber's company.

Johnson's action in sending Barber to school exemplified his attitude towards his now not-so-young servant. Like the intervention which terminated Barber's naval career, it was an act which displayed Johnson's characteristic mix of authority and affection where Barber was concerned. It was, after all, Johnson who had made the decision that Barber should attend the school—possibly with the intention of making a missionary of him—although it seems unlikely that Barber would have acceded if he had been completely opposed to the idea. The risks to be run in going to Bishop's Stortford were rather smaller than in going to sea, but teenage boys are not known for their sympathetic treatment of anyone who does not conform to their group—and how could a black twenty-six-year-old have been at home amongst white teenagers? What might Barber's fellow pupils have made of him being publicly described as "sickly" and "delicate" when Smollett's letter to Wilkes attempting to get Barber out of the navy was published in full in the *St. James's Chronicle* in July 1769?[25] (It was one of a collection of letters from Smollett to Wilkes which the newspaper printed.) On the other hand, Johnson's choice of school clearly demonstrated his determination that Barber should have the best education Johnson could afford—significantly, one which closely resembled Johnson's own at Lichfield Grammar School—and also that the cost would not be an obstacle.

Johnson's correspondence with Barber during this period illustrates these two aspects of his character. He is glad Barber is well, plans to visit him, is happy with his progress, tells him that he will neither forget nor forsake him. But he would have him stay till "I" can determine what "we" shall do, tells him to "be a good Boy," and to "mind your business." Johnson promises that "if when I examine you, I find that you have not lost your time, you shall want no encouragement." As encouragement goes, this is distinctly double-edged, the unspoken question being what happens if Johnson finds that he *has* lost his time. Each of the letters to Barber, however, contains a small but telling indication of Johnson's true feelings: the subscription is always "yours affectionately" or "your affectionate Sam. Johnson." There are many hundreds of surviving letters from Johnson to his numerous correspondents, and this form of subscription is particularly frequent in his letters to the two male correspondents to whom Johnson was closest, and with whom he corresponded most frequently, James Boswell and Johnson's lifelong friend, John Taylor.[26]

There were those in Johnson's circle who regarded his provision of an education for Barber as an absurd folly. Foremost among these was John Hawkins. He was one of Johnson's oldest friends, having known him since the early 1740s, and became one of his executors and his first major biographer. From modest origins, and without the advantage of a university education, Hawkins became a man of many accomplishments: a successful lawyer and magistrate, editor of *The Compleat Angler*, and a historian of music. His achievements were rewarded with a knighthood in 1772. But Johnson famously characterised him as "unclubbable," whilst Boswell attacked the "dark, uncharitable cast" of his biography of Johnson.[27]

There was a side of Hawkins which was captured in Johnson's half-joking comment to Frances Burney: "As to Sir John: why really I believe him to be an honest man at the *bottom*,—but to be sure he is penurious; & he is mean;—& it must be owned he has a degree of brutality, & a tendency to savageness, that cannot easily be defended."[28] In his *Life of Samuel Johnson* Hawkins wrote of Barber:

> Of this negro-servant much has been said, by those who knew little
> or nothing of him, in justification of that partiality which Johnson

shewed for him . . . [Johnson], for no assignable reason, nay, rather in despite of nature, and to unfit him for being useful according to his capacity, determined to make him a scholar.[29]

Hawkins's views on this subject were entirely shared by Johnson's dependant Anna Williams, who would frequently reproach Johnson for his idiocy in spending so much money (according to Hawkins, £300) on Barber's schooling. Hawkins lined Williams up as another witness against Barber:

Mrs. Williams, who, with a view to the interest of her friend, was very attentive to the conduct of this his favourite, when she took occasion to complain to his master of his misbehaviour, would do it in such terms as these: "This is your scholar! Your philosopher! Upon whom you have spent so many hundred pounds!"[30]

As for the cost of "so many hundred pounds," the figure of £300 which Hawkins cites for Barber's three years at school is probably an exaggeration. In January 1770 the trustees decided that boys who were not inhabitants of Bishop's Stortford, wherever boarded, should pay £4 a year for their education, and local boys should pay £2 a year. The entrance money from each inhabitant was 10s 6d. (There is no mention of any entrance money for those boys who did not live locally.) In addition, every scholar who chose to learn to write was to pay £1 a year.[31] The only known payment Johnson made was in March 1770 when he sent £50 to Joseph Smith "to satisfy Mrs. Clapp's account."[32] It is not clear whether this was to cover just board and lodging or whether it included the school fees.

By June 1771 Barber's time in Bishop's Stortford had come to an end.[33] If Hawkins and Williams did not welcome Barber's return from the school, there were others who were glad to see him again. On 21 March 1772, James Boswell visited Johnson for the first time in several years. (He had been busily pursuing his career as an advocate in Scotland and had not been in London since November 1769.) He recorded in his journal, "I went to Johnson's Court, Fleet Street, and was happy enough to find Mr. Johnson at home. Frank, his black, who had left him for some years, was returned to him, and showed me up to his study. Frank and I were pleased to renew our old acquaintance."[34]

10. Slavery on Trial

In the years while Barber had been away, Johnson had become firmly established as a celebrity. His fame had been steadily increasing over the seventeen years since he had published his *Dictionary of the English Language* in 1755, and now almost his every movement or saying was likely to be published in the London press and then repeated a few days later in the provincial papers. Dr. Johnson makes a funny remark, Dr. Johnson is unwell, Dr. Johnson goes out, Dr. Johnson stays at home. The scholar Helen Louise McGuffie drew up a checklist of Johnson's appearances in the British press between 1749 and 1784: it fills 348 pages.[1] Now a little of this fame started to rub off on Barber.

In April 1771 an anecdote appeared in the *Town and Country Magazine:*

> Dr. Goldsmith, meeting Dr. Johnson with his little lacquey behind him, for whom he has a sort of parental affection, asked his learned friend if he intended to bring him up a scholar? "Yes," replied Dr. Johnson, with his usual roughness, "I intend to make him scholar enough to write a *bailiff scene* in a comedy."[2]

The joke is at Goldsmith's expense, as he had written just such a scene in his comedy *The Good-Natur'd Man.* The description of Johnson's attitude towards Barber as "a sort of parental affection" is particularly telling. It suggests that the public perception of their relationship confirmed Johnson's own claim to have treated Barber "with great tenderness."[3]

As was the usual way, many of the other papers reprinted the squib over the following few weeks. When *The London Packet, or New Evening Post* published it in July, it was slightly altered:

> Dr. Goldsmith, meeting Dr. Johnson with a young Negro at his
> Heels, asked, "What do you intend to do with that Boy, Doctor? Do
> you mean to make him a Scholar?" "Yes, yes (replied surly Samuel)
> I shall make him Scholar enough to write a Bailiff Scene in a
> Comedy."[4]

In this version, the "little lacquey" had been more closely identified as "a
young Negro," an obvious reference to Francis Barber.

The joke was regarded as entertaining enough to appear in book form,
as it was published in 1773 in John Cooke's snappily titled collection, *The
macaroni jester, and pantheon of wit; containing all that has lately transpired in
the regions of politeness, whim, and novelty. Including A singular Variety of
Jests, Witticisms, Bon-Mots, Conundrums, Toasts, Acrosticks, &c. with Epigrams
and Epitaphs, of the laughable Kind, and Strokes of Humour hitherto unequalled;
which have never appeared in a Book of the Kind.* It is apparent that Johnson's
determined efforts to ensure that Barber was educated had become public
knowledge.

Johnson was happy to have "his favourite" back again. On 20 June
1771, he wrote to his friend Hester Thrale:

> This Night at nine o'clock Sam. Johnson and Francis Barber
> Esquires set out in the Lichfield stage. Francis is indeed rather upon
> it. What adventures we may meet with who can tell?[5]

It was one of several occasions on which Barber accompanied Johnson to
Lichfield, and this time they spent almost four weeks there. Everything about
the note which Johnson sent to Mrs. Thrale concerning their trip suggests the
friendly nature of relations between Johnson and Barber; the tone is light-
hearted and the pair are both portrayed as "Esquires," setting forth in search
of adventure.

It is an attractive glimpse of their relationship—especially given a very
different perspective of white–black interaction which could also be seen in
Lichfield. Shortly after the visit of Barber and Johnson an auction took place
in the city. The commodity for sale was "A Negroe Boy, from Affrica,
supposed to be about ten or eleven Years of Age . . . well proportioned,
speaks tolerable good English . . . sound, healthy, fond of Labour, and for
Colour an excellent fine Black."[6] The fact that such a sale could take place
was a stark reminder of the unresolved issues around the subject of slavery.

Slaves advertised for sale in *Aris's Birmingham Gazette*, 11 November 1771.
(Reproduced with permission of Library of Birmingham)

The threat of being reenslaved and sent back into colonial slavery had hung over Barber (as it hung over all former slaves) when he arrived in Britain in 1750, and it had remained a dreadful possibility throughout the twenty-one years which had passed since. Faced with the prospect of being dragged back into colonial slavery, some blacks took the only way out. As late as 1773, an item appeared in the newspapers:

A black servant to Capt. Ordington, who a few days ago ran away from his master and got himself christened, with the intent to marry his fellow-servant, a white woman, being taken and sent on board the captain's ship in the Thames, took an opportunity of shooting himself through the head.[7]

But the very legality of slavery in England was about to be challenged, largely as a result of the strenuous efforts of just one man, Granville Sharp.

Sharp was a devout lay Anglican, from a family of prominent clergymen, who was employed as a clerk in the ordnance office. He was intense and studious, and once his convictions were engaged by an issue he was extraordinarily tenacious in pursuing it. (On one occasion he found himself bested in debate about Christ's atonement and Old Testament prophecies because of his lack of knowledge of the original texts, so he quickly taught himself Greek and Hebrew.) The incident which turned Sharp into a committed anti-slavery campaigner was his encounter with Jonathan Strong, a former slave.[8]

Strong's history was in some ways similar to that of Francis Barber. His owner was a barrister named David Lisle, who had attempted to set up practice in Barbados. The venture was not a success, and sometime after 1757 he returned to England, bringing with him Strong, who was then about ten years old. Lisle had a violent temper, and Strong was often on the receiving end of his outbursts. As a result of the repeated assaults and ill treatment, Strong was in chronically poor health. Then, in 1765—possibly provoked by the fact that Strong had recently been baptised—Lisle attacked him again, this time using a pistol as a club to beat him badly around the head. The beating, coming on top of Strong's already frail health, affected his sight and left him so debilitated as to be of no further value to Lisle, who threw him out into the street.

Strong was in desperate need of medical care, and fortunately he met someone who told him of a free clinic for poor people in Mincing Lane, run by the surgeon William Sharp. He was barely able to walk or to see where he was going, but he made his way there. As he approached the door, he was spotted by the doctor's brother, Granville.

The two Sharp brothers arranged for Strong to be admitted to St. Bartholomew's hospital, where he received treatment for the next four months. Upon his discharge, Granville Sharp found him work with an apothecary in Fenchurch Street and thought no more about the black youth. But two years later, on 12 September 1767, he received a letter from Strong, who was in the Poultry Compter (the jail) and was begging for his help. Strong's former owner, David Lisle, had spotted him in the street and, seeing that Strong was once again healthy and of value, had him seized and thrown into prison.

Sharp immediately went to the Lord Mayor, who summoned those who had detained Strong to appear before him. On the appointed day, two men appeared. One was a notary public, who produced a bill of sale which showed that Lisle had sold Strong to James Kerr, a Jamaican planter, for the sum of £30. The other was a ship's captain, who was waiting to take Strong to slavery in Jamaica. When the facts were set before the Lord Mayor, he pronounced that Strong had committed no offence and was therefore free to go. The captain immediately seized Strong, telling the Mayor that he was the property of the Jamaican planter to whom he had been sold. Sharp angrily exclaimed: "Sir, I charge you for an assault." The captain let go, and Strong went free.

If Sharp thought that was the end of the matter, he was soon proved quite wrong. A few days later Kerr issued a writ against Sharp, alleging that he had robbed him of his slave and claiming £200 in damages. Lisle attempted a more direct method of revenging himself upon Sharp, by challenging him to a duel. Sharp recorded in his diary what occurred:

> Oct. 1, 1767. David Lisle, Esq. (a man of the law) called on me in Mincing Lane, to demand *gentlemanlike satisfaction*, because I had procured the liberty of his slave, Jonathan Strong. I told him, that, "as he had studied the law so many years, he should want no satisfaction that the law could give him."[9]

Sharp's legal advisors were pessimistic and urged him to settle before the matter came to trial. Sharp was astonished to discover that the law might not be on his side. In his own words, he "could not believe that the Laws of England were really so *injurious* to *Natural Rights*."[10] Having been failed by his lawyers, Sharp took matters into his own hands. He had never previously opened a law book in his life, yet he searched through the indexes of a law library, looking for ammunition to use against Lisle. For the next two years he continued his research, which culminated in a memorandum entitled, "A Representation of the Injustice and dangerous Tendency of tolerating Slavery, or even of admitting the least Claim to private Property in the Persons of Men, in England." He circulated numerous copies, especially among the lawyers in the Inns of Court.

The memorandum would have been impressive if it had been written by a trained lawyer—formidable research combined with detailed analysis, running to 167 pages in Sharp's printed version. But the fact that it originated from someone who had until recently known nothing at all about the subject made it a particularly remarkable achievement. As it turned out, Sharp's arguments were not to be tested in court in this particular case. During the two years in which Sharp had been preparing his memorandum, Kerr had taken no steps at all in his action, with the result that the case was struck out, and Kerr was ordered to pay Sharp's costs. In 1769 Sharp published his memorandum, the first major anti-slavery work to be published in Britain.[11] Over the next few years Sharp took on several cases where slavery was in issue. They culminated in the *Somerset* case, decided in June 1772, which marked the beginning of the end of slavery in England.[12]

The events which led James Somerset to the Court of King's Bench began in 1769 when Charles Steuart, a Scot working as a customs official in Virginia, came to England for an extended visit, bringing with him a young slave. In August 1771, that slave was baptised "James Summersett [*sic*]" at St. Andrew's, Holborn. Somerset may have believed that baptism freed him, as in October he ran away from his owner. But his freedom was short-lived: he was recaptured by Steuart the following month, and put on board a ship bound for Jamaica, to be sold as a slave.

Fortunately for Somerset, his godparents intervened and obtained a writ of habeas corpus, which was served on the ship's captain, John Knowles, ordering him to produce the captive and justify his actions. The captain freed Somerset, but Steuart determined to fight the matter, encouraged by West Indian slave-owning interests, and it soon became apparent that this would be a test case.

The case was fought over four months and attracted enormous press attention. The principal judge was Lord Mansfield, the Lord Chief Justice, by common consent the greatest judge of the eighteenth century. Mansfield had some personal knowledge of the position of blacks in England; at the time of the case he had a young black girl, Dido Elizabeth Belle, living in his household. She was the illegitimate daughter of Mansfield's nephew Sir John Lindsay, a navy captain who had taken prisoner her mother (who was probably a slave) from a Spanish vessel. Dido was taken into Lord Mansfield's household at Kenwood, where she seems to have been part servant and part companion for Mansfield's great-niece and adoptive daughter, Lady

William Murray, 1st Earl of Mansfield (1786), by Francesco Bartolozzi (after Sir Joshua Reynolds). Lord Mansfield, Lord Chief Justice, delivered the judgment in the *Somerset* case. (NPG D32121 © National Portrait Gallery, London)

Lady Elizabeth Murray and Dido Elizabeth Belle (c. 1780), unknown artist. Lady Elizabeth Murray was Lord Mansfield's great-niece; Dido Elizabeth Belle was her half-cousin and companion. Both lived in Mansfield's household at the time of the *Somerset* judgment. (Reproduced with permission from the collection of the Earls of Mansfield, Scone Palace, Perth, Scotland)

Elizabeth Murray. Mansfield's affection for Dido was a cause of concern to those who did not want to see Somerset's freedom confirmed. One Jamaican planter commented, "No doubt he will be set free, for Lord Mansfield keeps a Black in his house which governs him and the whole family."[13] (This attributed to Dido a somewhat improbable level of influence, as she was only ten or eleven years old when the case was heard.)

The trial opened in Westminster Hall on 26 January 1772. It began with the reading of the "return," the formal explanation by captain Knowles of why Somerset had been in his custody. He stated that a trade in slaves from Africa to the colonies had long existed for the necessary supplying of the colonies and plantations, and such slaves were saleable as goods and chattels under the laws of the colonies. Somerset had been bought by Steuart and had never been set free. He had run away and was recaptured and placed on Knowles's ship to be taken to Jamaica and sold as the property of Charles Steuart. So the reason he was being held was simple: Somerset was Steuart's slave and his property, and Steuart had decided to sell him.

At the request of Somerset's lawyers the case was adjourned for twelve days to allow more time to prepare, but it was postponed again when it became apparent that the hearing was likely to be lengthy and could not be completed before the end of that judicial term. It resumed in May. The arguments ranged widely and were unusually lengthy and detailed. Sergeant Davy, one of the barristers appearing for Somerset, opened his case:

> My Lord this is as great a Question and perhaps a Question of as much Consequence as can come before this or any Court of Justice ... The proposition I shall endeavour to maintain before your Lordship upon this occasion is, that no Man at this Day is, or can be a Slave in England.[14]

Both sides quoted extensively from legal writers and philosophers: Grotius and Pufendorf approved of slavery for captives in war; Montesquieu was against, except for purposes of self-preservation; Thomas Rutherforth and John Locke were absolutely against it; Aristotle defended it. There was much discussion too of the positions of other countries, both ancient and modern: Scotland, Holland, Spain, France, America, Africa, Asia, Russia, Poland, Greece, and Rome.

Somerset's lawyers gave both moral and pragmatic reasons for opposing slavery. It corrupts the morals of the master, they argued, giving rise to luxury, pride, and cruelty; it endangers the master, upon whom the slave desires revenge; it debases the mind of the slave, and threatens the state, the destruction of which is the slave's only hope. But much of their argument centred on the law of England. What did it matter, they argued, if Somerset was a slave in Africa or Virginia? "In *England*, where freedom is the grand object of the laws, and dispensed to the meanest individual, shall the laws of an infant colony, *Virginia*, or of a barbarous nation, *Africa*, prevail?"

Moreover, they demanded, could anyone in England tolerate the reality of colonial-style slavery?

> The horrid cruelties, scarce credible in recital, perpetrated in *America*, might, by the allowance of slaves amongst us, be intro-duced here. Could your lordship, could any liberal and ingenuous temper, endure, in the fields bordering on this city, to see a wretch bound for some trivial offence to a tree, torn and agonizing beneath the scourge?

There was also much discussion of villeinage, the ancient unfree status which, in some respects, resembled slavery. But, argued Somerset's lawyers, villeinage was long extinct:

> There is no Law against it—No Act of Parliament against it . . . why should not a man be a villein—where is the law? . . . Shew the Book if you can that forbids it!—No such Book can be found, but there is the Law written in the hearts of Men of this Country—That is the Law—it is the constitution . . . true genuine Liberty is the Birth Right and Inheritance of the People in this Country.[15]

If slavery was not a form of villeinage, how else could the state of slavery arise? It could not be based on contract, said Somerset's lawyers; what power could there be in any man to dispose of the rights vested in him and his descendants by nature and society?

Sergeant Davy closed the case for Somerset by referring to the state-ment (quoted in chapter 5) which the judges had made in 1569 regarding English air and slavery: "It has been asserted, and is now repeated by me, this air is too pure for a slave to breathe in: I trust I shall not quit this court without certain conviction of the truth of that assertion."

Somerset's lawyers rested their case, and it was the turn of Steuart's counsel. They argued from every angle: legal, moral, and practical. Somerset had been a slave according to local law in Africa, and had been sold according to the laws of the colonies. He was therefore a slave both in law and in fact. There was no law against slavery in England: if the air of England was too pure for slavery, how could villeinage ever have existed? "Let me take notice," said John Dunning, counsel for Steuart, "neither the air of *England* is too pure for a slave to breathe in, nor the laws of *England* have rejected servitude."

As to the morality of slavery, the practice was near universal: it "is found in three quarters of the globe, and in part of the fourth." In any event, the worst features of colonial slavery were unknown in England. Particular emphasis was placed on the practical consequences which would arise if slaves were freed:

> The Court must consider the great detriment to proprietors, there being so great a number in the ports of this kingdom, that many thousands of pounds would be lost to the owners, by setting them free.

The hearing lasted four days. Before adjourning to consider his judgment, Lord Mansfield made it clear that he had urged the parties to settle the case. He was anxious about the possible consequences of a judgment in Somerset's favour: "The setting 14,000 or 15,000 men at once free loose by a solemn opinion, is much disagreeable in the effects it threatens." But if the parties were not willing to settle, then so be it: "If the parties will have judgment, *fiat justitia, ruat cœlum;* let justice be done whatever be the consequence."

The parties did not settle, and judgment was handed down on 22 June 1772. Lord Mansfield's exact words have been much debated by scholars, but it seems most probable that he pronounced:

> The only question before us is, whether the cause on the return is sufficient? If it is, the negro must be remanded; if it is not, he must be discharged. Accordingly, the return states, that the slave departed and refused to serve; whereupon he was kept, to be sold abroad. So high an act of dominion must be recognized by the law of the country where it is used. The power of a master over his slave has been extremely different, in different countries. The state of slavery is of such a nature, that it is incapable of being introduced on any reasons, moral or political; but only positive law, which preserves its force long after the reasons, occasion, and time itself from whence it

was created, is erased from memory: it's so odious, that nothing can be suffered to support it, but positive law. Whatever inconveniences, therefore, may follow from a decision, I cannot say this case is allowed or approved by the law of *England;* and therefore the black must be discharged.[16]

Somerset had won, and could go free. But what is striking about the judgment is how narrow the finding is. The judge offered no grand statements of moral principle, no sweeping rhetoric, and nothing about the quality of the air of England. There was simply a finding that slavery can be established only by "positive law"—by which Mansfield meant statute or well-established custom—and there was no power to send a man abroad to be sold.

Mansfield subsequently insisted that nothing had been decided in the *Somerset* case except that a master could not forcibly send a slave abroad.[17] In spite of the narrowness of the judgment, however, he must have been well aware of the implications: if slavery could be established only by positive law, and there was no such positive law in England, then how could slavery continue? Moreover, how could slave-owners prevent their slaves from running away when they had lost their most potent threat, that of sending a slave back into colonial slavery?

Certainly the black community thought the judgment a triumph. On the following day the *Middlesex Journal* recorded that "a great number of Blacks were in Westminster-Hall to hear the determination of the cause and went away greatly pleased." A few days later the *London Packet* reported that "near 200 Blacks, with their ladies" gathered,

> at a public house in Westminster, to celebrate the triumph which their brother Somerset had obtained over Mr. Stuart his master. Lord Mansfield's health was echoed round the room, and the evening was concluded with a ball. The tickets for admittance to this Black assembly were 5s each.[18]

According to the historian Simon Schama, celebrations also took place at "a party at Dr Johnson's house organized by his servant Francis Barber."[19] It is an appealing idea, but sadly there is no evidence that such an event took place. However, Barber could hardly have been unaware of a case which was so widely publicised and which had such momentous implications for the black community, especially as Johnson certainly did know about the judgment. The outcome affected Barber, as it did all other blacks in his position, making his place in society more secure, removing any lingering doubt that his liberty might be provisional and that if circumstances changed he might find himself enslaved once more.

The judgment took on a life of its own. The day after the decision, the *Middlesex Journal* reported that Mansfield had ruled that "every slave brought into this country ought to go free." Numerous other reports in the newspapers and elsewhere gave similar accounts. Edmund Burke wrote that "even a negro slave, who had been sold in the colonies and under an act of parliament, became as free as every other man who breathed the same air with him."[20] The news spread further afield to the colonies. On 30 June 1774, the *Virginia Gazette* carried an advertisement on behalf of one Gabriel Jones, seeking the return of his runaway slave Bacchus. It stated that Bacchus might "attempt to get on Board some Vessel bound for Great Britain, from the Knowledge he has of the late Determination of Somerset's Case."[21]

Johnson had followed the ruling closely and referred back to it a few years later when similar litigation took place in Scotland in the case of *Knight v Wedderburn*.[22] The *Somerset* judgment did not apply there, as the Scottish legal system was (and is) different from the English legal system, and slavery continued to be practised. John Wedderburn, a Jacobite who had fled from Scotland in 1746, returned in 1768, bringing with him Joseph Knight, a slave he had purchased in Jamaica. Knight remained enslaved for several years, but then, in July 1772, he read a report of the *Somerset* case in the *Edinburgh Advertiser* and believed that it meant he was free. However, he chose not to leave Wedderburn at that time, perhaps influenced by the fact that he had formed a relationship with Ann Thomson, a chambermaid in Wedderburn's household at Ballindean. She became pregnant, and Wedderburn seems initially to have been supportive, giving Knight money for Thomson's medical care and, when the child died, paying for the funeral. Knight married Thomson in March 1773, and asked Wedderburn to readmit his wife into the house as a servant, and also to pay him wages instead of his very small allowance. Wedderburn refused both requests. Ann Knight ended up living and working some distance from Ballindean, and Joseph Knight decided to leave Wedderburn and to join her. Wedderburn, however, became aware of Knight's intentions and resolved to take every possible step to prevent his departure. He applied to the Justices of the Peace of Perthshire for a ruling that he was entitled to enforce his slave's services, and the order was duly granted. The decision was perhaps not wholly unexpected, as the hearing took place in Wedderburn's home, and he was related to two of the three Justices. One of them also owned a Jamaican plantation, on which he employed Wedderburn's brother as overseer.

Knight applied to the Sheriff Court at Perth, stating that "the petitioner does not admit that he is a slave," but the Sheriff-Substitute refused to hear the matter on the ground that he had no jurisdiction, the case having already been decided by competent judges. Knight persisted, and his case was heard before the Sheriff-Depute, John Swinton, who, on 20 May 1774, handed down a judgment which left no room for doubt or ambiguity:

> The State of Slavery is not recognized by the Laws of this Kingdom,
> and is inconsistent with the principles thereof . . . the Regulations in
> Jamaica concerning slaves do not extend to this Kingdom.[23]

Wedderburn was determined not to let the matter rest, and the following year he applied to have it reconsidered by the Court of Session, the highest civil court in Scotland. Both parties were ordered to produce printed "Informations" (written statements of their case), which they duly did, and the case came to trial in February 1776. But after several days of argument the matter was adjourned, and the parties were ordered to provide "Additional Informations." These contained extensive further argument: the Additional Information for Wedderburn (prepared by one of his advocates, Robert Cullen) was seventy-eight pages, and that for Knight (prepared by John Maclaurin, one of the lawyers appearing for the slave) took up forty-four pages.

James Boswell, a friend of Maclaurin, took an interest in the case and attended the February hearings. In June of 1776 he sent copies of the Additional Information for Knight to Samuel Johnson. Johnson replied a week later with a reminder of the precedent of the *Somerset* case: "It was last year determined by Lord Mansfield, in the Court of King's Bench, that a negro cannot be taken out of the kingdom without his own consent."[24]

Johnson had the year of the case wrong, but it was an accurate statement of the judgment. Clearly he had not read the Additional Information before replying to Boswell, or he would have known that the reminder of that judgment was unnecessary because Maclaurin had devoted several pages of the document to discussion of the *Somerset* case.[25] However, Johnson subsequently read it and wrote to Boswell with approbation, offering money to support the case:

I have looked over Mr. Maclaurin's plea, and think it excellent. How is the suit carried on? If by subscription, I commission you to contribute, in my name, what is proper. Let nothing be wanting in such a case.[26]

The case still had not come to a hearing when, a year later, Boswell sent to Johnson the Additional Information for Wedderburn. In his reply Johnson wrote, "I long to know how the Negro's cause will be decided."[27] Two months later, Boswell and Johnson were both guests of John Taylor at Ashbourne, and on 23 September Boswell went to Johnson's room at night and requested that Johnson dictate a pleading in favour of Knight. Johnson did so, and Boswell wrote down the text.[28] It was the only occasion on which Johnson set out a sustained argument against slavery. Its existence was unknown to the general public during Johnson's lifetime, and it would probably have remained so had not Boswell—in spite of his by then pro-slavery views—published the document in 1793.

In fact Boswell took some pains to ensure that Johnson's argument became public knowledge. He was unable to include it in the first edition (1791) of the *Life of Johnson*—he had mislaid his copy—but he drew attention to the existence of the argument in the body of the text and, in a footnote, promised to make it available when found.[29] He proved as good as his word. The second edition (1793) of the *Life of Johnson* was issued in a hurry and without adequate preparation, and the resulting text was chaotic. Boswell was already reading the proofs when he located a mass of new material which included the missing argument, so he set it out in a separate section entitled, "Additions to Dr. Johnson's Life recollected, and received after the second edition was printed." He also published it in a separate pamphlet of forty-two pages, *The Principal Corrections and Additions to the First Edition of Mr. Boswell's Life of Dr. Johnson* (1793), which was distributed (at Boswell's own expense) to owners of the first edition.[30]

The heart of Johnson's argument was a general statement of the natural rights of man—a statement which clearly reflected his understanding of Francis Barber's position, and which applied equally to Joseph Knight:

The sum of the argument is this:—No man is by nature the property of another: The defendant is, therefore, by nature free: The rights of nature must be some way forfeited before they can be justly taken away: That the defendant has by any act forfeited the rights of nature we require to be proved; and if no proof of such forfeiture can be given, we doubt not but the justice of the court will declare him free.[31]

On 15 January 1778 the Court of Session in Edinburgh handed down its judgment. The twelve judges expressed a variety of opinions, and reference was made to the *Somerset* case. Some thought that Knight remained a slave, while others decided that he was a servant for life without wages but that Wedderburn's power over him was limited—a subtle distinction, and probably not one likely to appeal to Joseph Knight. Five of the judges were opposed to Knight's being a slave in Scotland, whatever his status in Jamaica. The strongest statement against slavery came from Boswell's father, Lord Auchinleck:

> Although, in the plantations they have laid hold of the poor blacks, and made slaves of them, yet I do not think that *that* is agreeable to humanity, not to say to the Christian religion. Is a man a slave because he is black? No. He is our brother; and he is a man, although he is not our colour; he is in a land of liberty, with his wife and his child: let him remain *there*.[32]

In the end, the judges voted eight to four to adopt the judgment which the Sheriff-Depute, John Swinton, had handed down: the laws of Jamaica had no effect in Scotland, and the institution of slavery was inconsistent with the laws of Scotland. Knight, like Somerset before him, was allowed to go free.

There is no evidence that Knight's advocates made any use of Johnson's argument. In any event it seems unlikely that it would have influenced the outcome of the case, as there was little Johnson could usefully add to the eighty-seven pages of wide-ranging argument already produced by Knight's lawyers. But if nothing else Johnson's involvement did at least supply valuable moral support. It may be that—however indirectly—the presence of Francis Barber in Samuel Johnson's life contributed in some small measure to the ending of slavery in Scotland.

The *Somerset* and *Knight* cases did not bring about a complete end to slavery in England and Scotland, but subsequent instances were rare. In the colonies slavery continued; not until 1807 did legislation abolish the slave trade, and the Slavery Abolition Act was not passed until 1833.

As for Barber, there had been great changes in his life since the *Somerset* judgment in 1772. That case had been followed by an outpouring of comment in broadsheets and in the press. The debate was often bitter, and the most virulent participant by far was Edward Long, who published a pamphlet in August 1772 entitled *Candid Reflections upon the Judgment . . . on what is Commonly Called the Negroe-Cause*. For anyone who, like Long, was familiar with the lifestyles of the plantation owners, it was an irony that one of his principal concerns was the defilement of pure English stock by the birth of mixed-race children:

> The lower class of women in *England*, are remarkably fond of the blacks, for reasons too brutal to mention; they would connect themselves with horses and asses, if the laws permitted them. By these ladies they generally have a numerous brood. Thus, in the course of a few generations more, the English blood will become so contaminated with this mixture . . . This is a venomous and dangerous ulcer, that threatens to disperse its malignancy far and wide, until every family catches infection from it.[33]

Long's views on race were the most extreme published in the eighteenth century, and historians have debated the extent to which they were representative or influential. What is clear, however, is that there was opposition to interracial marriages in some quarters, a fact which Barber was shortly to find out for himself. On Thursday, 28 January 1773, at the Church of St. Dunstan in the West, he married a white woman, Elizabeth Ball.

11. "Nobody but Frank"

Attracting women was an area of life in which Barber was notably successful. Even Johnson's friend Mrs. Thrale—no friend to Barber—could grudgingly concede that "Francis was very well-looking for a Black a moor." Writing in her journal in 1777, she recorded Johnson's response to that remark:

> Oh Madam says he Francis has carried the Empire of Cupid farther than many Men: When he was in Lincolnshire seven Years ago, he made hay as I was informed, with so much Dexterity that a female Hay Maker followed him to London for Love.[1]

Elizabeth Ball was seventeen or eighteen when she married Barber; he was then about thirty-one. Hester Thrale described her as "eminently pretty," and the Revd. Thomas Whalley, a clergyman with literary interests who met her in 1810, recorded that she was "sensible and well-informed." (Perhaps he had in mind James Boswell's comment shortly before his own marriage that to be "sensible and well informed" was a "great advantage" in a wife.)[2] She seems to have been literate, in the sense that she was able to sign the marriage entry in the parish register.[3] Curiously she omitted the letter "t" from her signature, but it is not clear whether this was poor spelling or wedding nerves. Like Barber, she was living in the parish of St. Dunstan in the West at the time of their marriage. She may have been born in a neighbouring parish; an Elizabeth Ball was baptised on 22 May 1755 in the church of St. Andrew, Holborn.[4] It is not certain whether this is Barber's wife, but the age and the location are consistent. Her parents were Benjamin and

Ann Ball, of Cross Street, off Hatton Garden, and the name "Ann" provides another clue: the Barbers' elder daughter was named Elizabeth Ann, and their younger daughter was named Ann, indicating that it was a family name.

The ceremony was in all probability a low-key affair. It was conducted by the Vicar, the Revd. Joseph Williamson. The witnesses were Thomas Twist and John Sales, about whom nothing more is known. Nor do we know whether anyone else attended the wedding service. Samuel Johnson wrote to Hester Thrale two days before the wedding, but he made no reference to it, the principal topic of his letter being his poor health.

The location of the church of St. Dunstan in the West was certainly no idyllic setting. It was on Fleet Street, just to the east of the boundary of the city of London at Temple Bar. The church stood at a particularly busy point, as it stuck out into the thoroughfare, creating a bottleneck through which pedestrians, carriages, and horses had to crowd, with all the associated noise and smell. (The traffic problem became so acute that in 1831 the church was demolished, the road was widened, and St. Dunstan's was rebuilt on its present site, although retaining its original clock.) To add to the general hubbub—the Barbers' wedding took place on a working day—the building was surrounded by shops and businesses. Contemporary prints show numerous stalls hard up against the sides of the church.

As St. Dunstan's was the parish church for both Francis Barber and Elizabeth Ball, it is likely that they would have attended worship there (though Johnson preferred to attend St. Clement Danes, also on Fleet Street but farther to the west). The church was just a few minutes' walk from Johnson's Court. Its best-known feature was—and still is—the great 1671 clock, on either side of which were the figures of two giants holding hammers which struck every quarter. Barber's home was within earshot of the hammers (as was his earlier home in Gough Square).

What would the people going about their daily business on Fleet Street have made of the sight of the black groom and his white bride? That Barber should marry a white woman is hardly surprising, given that there were considerably more black men than black women in London. Kathleen Chater estimates that about 80 percent of the black population of England and Wales was male and that the total black population in the city at that time was probably only a few thousand.[5] Although the marriage of a black man would have been an unusual event in and of itself, it would not have been uncommon for his bride to be white. How were such marriages regarded?

A perspective view of the Temple Barr and St. Dunstans Church (1753), print made by J. Maurer. Barber married Elizabeth Ball at the church of St. Dunstan in the West in 1773. The church clock can still be seen on Fleet Street. (British Museum, Heal, Topography 149 © Trustees of the British Museum)

It is difficult to generalise about the eighteenth-century British attitude towards an interracial marriage. Vincent Carretta, the biographer of Olaudah Equiano, writes that:

> Such couples were occasionally noted but only very rarely condemned. No record exists, for example, that Equiano's marriage in 1792 to an Englishwoman led to any discrimination against him, his wife, or their two daughters.[6]

There may be no record of discrimination against Equiano, but his marriage was, at the very least, an object of curiosity. As Carretta notes elsewhere, when Equiano visited Edinburgh in 1792 with his new bride, Susanna Cullen, the *Gazetteer and New Daily Advertiser* for 30 May recorded that "Gustavus Vasa [Equiano], with his *white* wife, is at Edinburgh."[7] There is no further comment on the subject, and the reader is left to guess at the significance of the use of italic for "white": is it merely marking an unusual event or is it expressing disapproval?

If mild interest was the reaction of some observers, others were bitterly opposed to such unions, and horrified at the thought of mixed race children. Nor was such opposition confined to supporters of the West Indian interest. In 1804 the journalist William Cobbett wrote in his weekly *Political Register:*

> Who, that has any sense or decency, can help being shocked at the familiar intercourse, which has gradually been gaining ground, and which has, at last, got a complete footing between the Negroes and the women of England? No black swain need, in this loving country, hang himself in despair. No inquiry is made whether he be a Pagan or a Christian; if he be not a downright cripple, he will, if he be so disposed, always find a woman, not merely to yield to his filthy embraces, that, amongst the notoriously polluted and abandoned part of the sex, would be less shocking, but to accompany him *to the altar,* to become his wife, to breed English mulattoes, to stamp the mark of Cain upon her family and her country! . . . their own conduct is foul, unnatural and detestable.[8]

Francis Barber experienced contrasting responses to his marriage to Elizabeth Ball. The most hostile recorded reaction was that of Sir John Hawkins, who wrote: "In his search of a wife, he picked up one of those creatures with whom, in the disposal of themselves, no contrariety of colour is an obstacle."[9] This comment was not hidden away in a personal diary or private correspondence. It appeared in Hawkins's biography of Johnson, which was published in February 1787, and he must have known that it would come to the Barbers' notice. (When Hawkins revised the book for a second edition in June 1787, he made some changes to the surrounding text but retained this comment unaltered.)

The attitude of Johnson's friend Hester Thrale (later Piozzi) towards Barber's marriage and towards Elizabeth Barber is more complex; a number of different factors were at work. In her *Anecdotes of the Late Samuel Johnson* (1786), Mrs. Piozzi recounted that when Johnson's cat Hodge had grown old,

> Mr. Johnson always went out himself to buy Hodge's dinner, that Francis the Black's delicacy might not be hurt, at seeing himself employed for the convenience of a quadruped.[10]

The story is intended to be comical in its use of the pseudo-Johnsonian vocabulary "the convenience of a quadruped." It is also intended to show

Johnson in a good light, willing to stoop to menial tasks rather than give offence to his employee. On both these accounts, it succeeds. But it is impossible to miss the sneer at Barber in the phrase "that Francis the Black's delicacy might not be hurt"—there is clearly an implication that he is getting above himself. There were other servants in the household (as Mrs. Piozzi knew), so Barber was not the only one to benefit from Johnson's action, but he alone is the object of Mrs. Piozzi's jibe.[11] It is not just any servant who is giving himself airs; it is a particular black servant. Boswell's version of the story, published in his *Life of Johnson,* provides a revealing contrast:

> I never shall forget the indulgence with which he treated Hodge, his cat: for whom he himself used to go out and buy oysters, lest the servants having that trouble should take a dislike to the poor creature.[12]

In this account the dig at Barber does not appear, and Johnson's actions are for the benefit of all the servants, not just Barber.

Hester Lynch Thrale (1781), by Robert Edge Pine. (Reproduced courtesy of the owners. This image © Christie's Images Limited 2008)

Hester Thrale (as she then was) disapproved of the Barber marriage, but her disapproval was aimed primarily at Elizabeth Barber. Significantly, Mrs. Thrale could never bring herself to use Elizabeth Barber's name: whenever she referred to her, she called her "his wife," or more often (and more tellingly) his "white wife," and on one occasion "his Desdemona."[13]

On 5th February 1774 Elizabeth Barber gave birth to their first child, a boy. It is impossible to miss the significance of the name they chose for him: "Samuel." Sadly, only fourteen months later he died, and was buried in St. Bride's churchyard. It was six years before the Barbers had another child, Elizabeth Ann Barber, who was baptised on 28th November 1781 at St. Andrew's Holborn (the same church where, ten years before, James Somerset had been baptised).[14] Johnson, who was away from London at the time, wrote to Mrs. Thrale on 24th November:

> Frank's wife has brought him a wench; but I cannot yet get intelligence of her colour, and therefore have never told him how much depends upon it.[15]

Two days later, Johnson wrote anxiously, sending instructions for Mrs. Desmoulins (now another member of Johnson's household), "I desire Mrs. Desmoulins to write immediately what she knows. I wish to be told about Frank's wife and child."[16]

What was it that depended so much upon the baby's colour, and which caused Johnson such concern? The answer is suggested by the reaction of others when Elizabeth was born and turned out to be white. Mrs. Thrale and John Hawkins both believed that this proved the father of the child was not Frank, but a white man. Mrs. Thrale called Barber and the child "Black Francis and his White Wife's Bastard." She believed that Barber was ignorant of the fact—as she considered it to be—that he was not the baby's father. (She later described Ann Barber, born in 1786 and also light-skinned, as "Frank's soidisant daughter," and "rather a remarkably fair Girl, & approaching to pretty; but Frank tho' almost 15 years at School, never I supposed learned much of Natural History.")[17]

Whether such beliefs were well-founded, it is impossible to say. The fact that Johnson was already concerned before he knew of the child's colour may suggest that he suspected Elizabeth Barber of having an adulterous relationship. But it may simply reflect his anxiety at the possible disadvantage to a young girl of being visibly the child of a black parent. Whether

Mrs. Thrale's views were correct or not, they were at least confined to her private journal and commonplace book. John Hawkins published his aspersions for all to see in his biography of Johnson:

> It is said that, soon after his marriage, [Barber] became jealous, and it may be supposed, that he continued so, till, by presenting him with a daughter of her own colour, his wife put an end to all his doubts on that score. Notwithstanding which, Johnson, in the excess of indiscriminating benevolence, about a year before his death, took the wife and her two children, into his house, and made them a part of his family.[18]

Johnson's response to the Barber marriage was certainly in marked contrast to those of Thrale and Hawkins. In fact Hawkins was wrong about the date when Francis and Elizabeth Barber joined Johnson's household: they were already living with Johnson when young Elizabeth was born. Mrs. Thrale recorded in her diary in December 1777 that the Barbers were living with Johnson, and William Cooke suggested in his *Life of Johnson LL.D.* that the Barbers always lived with him after their marriage.[19]

From 1776 the home which the Barbers shared with Johnson was at No. 8 Bolt Court, in another of the courts off the north side of Fleet Street which he loved. Johnson was to remain there until his death in 1784. It was a much better house than Johnson's Court, and although it was in a gloomy corner it had a pretty little garden, which even contained a vine which Johnson enjoyed watering. The membership of Johnson's household of the impecunious and the unfortunate had increased. Writing in her journal on 11 December 1777, Mrs. Thrale noted that "Mr Johnson has more Tenderness for Poverty than any other Man I ever knew . . . In consequences of these Principles, he has *now* in his house whole Nests of People who would if he did not support them be starving." She later listed the occupants:

> [Levett] lived with Johnson as a sort of *necessary Man,* or Surgeon to the wretched Household he held in Bolt Court; where Blind Mrs Williams, Dropsical Mrs Desmoulines, Black Francis & his White Wife's Bastard with a wretched Mrs White, and a Thing that he called Poll; shared his Bounty, & increased his Dirt.[20]

Barber's old foe, Anna Williams, who was now aged seventy-one, occupied a ground floor room. Levett was frequently at odds with her and

Dr. Johnson and his servant Francis at Bolt Court, Fleet Street (1801), by Charles Tomkins. A rare representation of Barber and Johnson together. (Private Collection/The Bridgeman Art Library)

also with "dropsical Mrs Desmoulines." Mrs. Desmoulins (whose daughter also lived in the house) had an old connection with Barber: she was the widow of Jacob Desmoulins, the writing-master who had taught Barber over twenty years before. Perhaps more intriguingly for the atmosphere of the household, Desmoulins and Johnson shared a little history. Over thirty years before, at a time when Johnson's wife was insisting that they occupied separate beds, Johnson had fondled and kissed Desmoulins, then a young unmarried woman, although (as she told Boswell in 1783) he "never did anything that was beyond the limits of decency." She recalled, "Such was my high respect for him, such the awe I felt of him, that I could not have had resolution to have resisted him," but he was smitten by an attack of conscience and desisted.[21] By the time when Mrs. Thrale recorded her presence in Bolt Court in 1777, Desmoulins was aged sixty. Whatever Johnson had once felt for her, his feelings had changed, and his opinion was not high when he wrote to his step-daughter in 1779:

> Mrs. Desmoulins Doctor Swinfen's daughter, and her daughter are still with me, but the money which they cost me I should not spend perhaps better. She is agreeable enough but I do not think over well of her, and her Daughter by ill health or ill management is I am afraid what Ladies call a *dawdle*.[22]

By a "dawdle" Johnson meant an indolent person. The "wretched Mrs White" to whom Mrs. Thrale referred in her journal was a servant to whom Johnson was to leave £100 in his will, and the "Thing that he called Poll" was Poll Carmichael, possibly a former prostitute. The novelist Frances Burney recorded in her journal Johnson's memorable characterisation of Carmichael:

> Poll is a stupid slut; I had some hopes of her, at first; but when I talked to her tightly & closely, I could make nothing of her;—she was wiggle waggle,—& I could never persuade her to be categorical.[23]

This mix of personalities made for an interesting household, if not a tranquil one. The occupants were bound together by their dependence on Johnson, and by little else. In a letter to Mrs. Thrale Johnson described the atmosphere in his home:

> We have tolerable concord at home, but no love. Williams hates every body. Levet hates Desmoulins and does not love Williams. Desmoulins hates them both. Poll loves none of them.[24]

Barber's role in Johnson's life had increased in significant but subtle ways, as Boswell observed in a revealing tribute. In a passage intended for use in his *Life of Johnson* Boswell transcribed an extract from Richard Steele's periodical *The Englishman:*

> The Esquire is usually attended from his lodgings . . . by a coeval servant in a dark suit and gray hair who has been to him for forty years that kind of favourite which a learned man is seldom without, to wit one that is very powerful from his wonderful address in ordinary things which his Master does not understand.

Next to this section Boswell wrote, "Similar to Dr. Johnson's Frank."[25] Clearly Barber's role and his standing had changed considerably over the years since he had returned from Bishop's Stortford school. The allusion suggests a growing confidence and capability in Barber, perhaps something which had become more obvious since his marriage.

Elizabeth Barber had some domestic role, judging by the fact that Johnson paid her wages of 5s a week and bought an apron for her in December 1777.[26] (He recorded the cost as 9s.) Mrs. Desmoulins was in charge of the cooking arrangements for the house, at least in so far as anyone was—"a general anarchy prevails in my kitchen," said Johnson.[27] In the evenings the members of the household would gather in a circle around the fire, while Johnson chatted or dictated. He was often prompted to expound on a subject by a question from one or the other, but Barber was reluctant to join in. There was always an element of reserve according to Barber: "I never could take the same liberty with my Master as with another person."[28]

Johnson, for his part, felt great affection towards Barber. "Give my love to Francis" he wrote to Levett while visiting Paris in 1775.[29] It sounds like a casual greeting, such as might appear in any letter, but Johnson's correspondence tells a different story. He wrote large numbers of letters, many hundreds of which survive and are printed in the five volumes of the Hyde edition of *The Letters of Samuel Johnson*. He corresponded with men, women, and children alike. He wrote to his wife (only one letter survives) and to his mother. The numerous close friends to whom he wrote include Hill Boothby, James Boswell, Edmund Hector, Bennet Langton, John Taylor, and Hester Thrale. In all the pages of these letters he addresses only one person, his stepdaughter Lucy Porter, as his "dearest love," and there is only one occasion when Johnson sends his love to anyone: it is to Francis Barber.

These feelings extended to Elizabeth Barber too—Johnson was very happy to have the couple living in his household. "Francis and his Wife have both given great satisfaction by their behaviour," he wrote to Levett in September 1776. A few weeks later, writing to Levett from Brighton, he requested, "Remember me kindly to Francis and Betsy."[30] There are few other references to Elizabeth in Johnson's surviving correspondence and diaries, but there are two pieces of evidence of a different kind which provide eloquent indications of Johnson's affectionate feelings for her.

The first is a copy of *The Book of Common Prayer*. For Johnson, a staunch Church of England Christian, this was a very important book, second only to the Bible in its significance for his spiritual life. He knew most of it by heart, quoted from it, used it in his own prayers, and considered writing a book explaining how best to use it.[31] Johnson owned a number of copies at different times, one of which he bought shortly after it was printed in 1739. The following year, 1740, was the most difficult one in Johnson's sometimes troubled relationship with his wife.

Beginning in August of 1739 Johnson had been absent from London—and from Tetty, his wife. He spent several months in Lichfield, and when Tetty suffered what seems to have been quite a serious leg injury Johnson wrote to her, but he did not return home. Altogether he was away for about seven months. We know nothing of their relationship in the months that followed, but on Christmas Day 1740 Johnson gave Tetty the copy of *The Book of Common Prayer*. He wrote in it, "Eliz. Johnson, Decr 25. 1740." At the close of a turbulent year, on one of the most important days in the Christian calendar, Johnson gave to his wife a copy of a book which he valued above almost all others. It does not seem overspeculative to suggest that in this gift there was an element of both making amends and promise of reform.

The copy must have had great sentimental value to Johnson; after Tetty died in 1752 Johnson kept it for the next twenty-seven years. But then he passed it on again. Thirty-nine years after Johnson had given the book to Tetty, he gave it to Elizabeth Barber, who was by then, along with Francis and their child, part of Johnson's household. Below the name of Elizabeth Johnson is written: "Elizabeth Barber, her Book Dec: 20th779 [*sic*]." The handwriting is probably Elizabeth Barber's, and in a cramped space the figure "1" has been omitted from "1779," in the same way as the letter "t" was omitted from Elizabeth Barber's signature on her wedding day.[32]

The other item which testifies to Johnson's regard for Elizabeth Barber is a miniature painting of Johnson. The miniature was probably based on his earliest known portrait, painted by Joshua Reynolds about 1757. Shortly before his death Samuel Johnson gave it to Elizabeth Barber, and she in turn kept it for twenty-five years, parting with it only towards the end of her life when poverty forced her to sell. (The buyer was the Revd. Thomas Harwood, a clergyman and antiquary who served as headmaster of Johnson's old school in Lichfield. The miniature has survived and is today in the Donald and Mary Hyde Collection in the Houghton Library at Harvard.)[33]

Johnson, then, was happy with the Barbers, but were Francis and Elizabeth happy with each other? Numerous biographers have suggested otherwise: Peter Martin states that "it was not a happy marriage," while

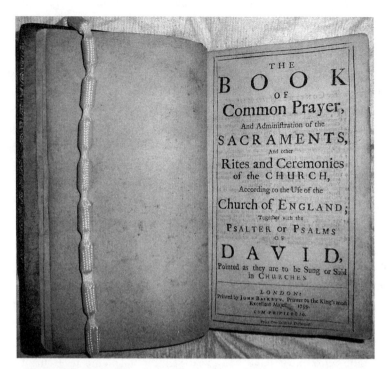

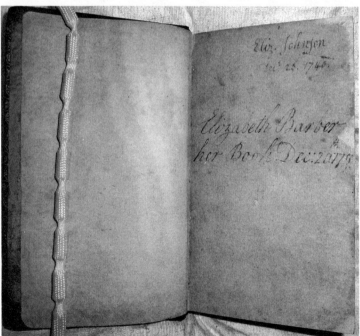

This copy of *The Book of Common Prayer* (1739) was given by Johnson to his wife, Elizabeth, on Christmas Day 1740, and then to Elizabeth Barber on 20 December 1779. (© The Samuel Johnson Birthplace Museum, Lichfield)

according to David Nokes the Barbers lived under Johnson's roof "not very harmoniously." Jeffrey Meyers describes the Barber marriage as "contentious," and the *Oxford Dictionary of National Biography* declares that Barber "made an unhappy marriage."[34]

This negative view of the Barbers' marriage appears largely to be based on an anecdote told by Mrs. Thrale, who recounted that on one occasion Francis and Elizabeth were invited to a dance for the servants at the Thrales's home in Streatham. According to Mrs. Thrale, Elizabeth "was eminently pretty, and he was jealous . . . Frank took offence at some attentions paid his Desdemona, and walked away next morning to London in wrath." Mrs. Thrale continues:

> His master and I driving the same road an hour after, overtook him. "What is the matter, child says Dr. Johnson, that you leave Streatham to-day. *Art sick?*" He is jealous (whispered I). "Are you jealous of your wife, you stupid blockhead (cries out his master in another tone)?" The fellow hesitated; and, *To be sure Sir, I don't quite approve Sir*, was the stammering reply. "Why, what do they *do* to her, man? do the footmen kiss her?" No Sir, no!—Kiss my *wife Sir!*—I hope not Sir. "Why, what *do* they do to her, my lad?" Why nothing Sir, I'm sure Sir. "Why then go back directly and dance you dog, do; and let's hear no more of such empty lamentations."[35]

As evidence of an unhappy marriage, this is strikingly thin. What it does suggest is that Barber felt some insecurity when his wife—young, attractive, and white—was befriended by the other servants (who were presumably also white). It is hard not to see Barber's colour as being at the root of this insecurity. There were certainly occasions when something—or more often someone—drew attention to it. The actor Samuel Foote was once Johnson's guest for dinner, and, observing Barber, he joked that the dinner was to be "black broth."[36] It is unlikely that Barber laughed.

In spite of Barber's status as a married man with a daughter, Johnson remained the father figure he always had been, concerned for Barber's welfare in the broadest sense. The sense of his responsibility for Barber's spiritual well-being emerges clearly from some entries in Johnson's diaries. On Good Friday 1775, "I gave Francis some directions for preparation." On Easter Day 1779, "I have for some nights called Francis to prayers, and last night discoursed with him on the Sacrament." On Sunday, 17 March 1782, "I prayed with Francis, which I now do commonly, and explained to him the Lord's Prayer . . . I made punch for myself and my servant."[37]

As time went on a slight but revealing change of tone started to creep into Johnson's references to Barber: "I am going to dine with Mr. Dyot, and Frank tells sternly, that it is past two o'clock," wrote Johnson to Hester Thrale in September 1777.[38] The Johnson who once thought of Barber as a child is now being addressed by him "sternly." The tone of the comment suggests that Johnson was amused by Barber's attitude, but the fact that Barber could address him in such a manner indicates that the dynamic of their relationship was changing.

Significant changes in the composition of the household contributed to the development of Barber's relationship with Johnson. On 17 January 1782, Robert Levett died. Johnson felt the loss of his old friend keenly, and expressed it in one of the finest elegies in the English language, "On the Death of Dr. Robert Levet":

> His virtues walk'd their narrow round,
> Nor made a pause, nor left a void;
> And sure th'Eternal Master found
> The single talent well employed.[39]

At about this time Barber too fell ill. His health had never been good, and Johnson had at one time arranged for his treatment by John Hunter, the celebrated surgeon. The nature of the problem is unknown.[40]

There was a growing sense of gloom in the Bolt Court household. In March 1782 Johnson wrote to his stepdaughter Lucy Porter, "My dwelling is but melancholy, both Williams and Desmoulins and myself are very sickly; Frank is not well, and poor Levet died in his bed the other day by a sudden stroke. I suppose not one minute passed between health and death. So uncertain are human things."[41] Levett's death was the first of several heavy blows which Johnson was to feel over the succeeding years.

Boswell paid a visit on 17 May 1783. While he was waiting for Johnson to dress, he sat with Anna Williams, who delivered a diatribe against Mrs. Desmoulins. Wearied by the endless clashes with Williams, Desmoulins had left the house. This brought some of the household hostilities to an end, but it increased Johnson's sense of isolation. Writing to Mrs. Thrale to tell her of Desmoulins's departure he added, "Ubi solitudinem faciunt, pacem appellant" (they make a desolation and they call it peace).[42]

A month later, on 17 June 1783, at about three in the morning, Johnson suffered a stroke and discovered that he had lost the power of speech. "I was alarmed," he wrote to Mrs. Thrale two days later, "and prayed God, that however he might afflict my body he would spare my understanding. This prayer, that I might try the integrity of my faculties I made in Latin verse. The lines were not very good, but I knew them not to be very good, I made them easily, and concluded myself to be unimpaired in my faculties." He was still able to write with one hand. When day eventually came, Barber entered Johnson's room as usual but was puzzled when he received no response to his greeting. Instead, Johnson thrust a note into his hands, explaining what had happened, and instructing him to summon medical assistance and a neighbour.[43]

In the event Johnson made a remarkable recovery from the stroke, but he now fell victim to the depression which afflicted him from time to time:

> The black Dog I hope always to resist, and in time to drive though I am deprived of almost all those that used to help me. . . . When I rise my breakfast is solitary, the black dog waits to share it, from breakfast to dinner he continues barking, except that Dr. Brocklesby for a little keeps him at a distance. Dinner with a sick woman You may venture to suppose not much better than solitary. After Dinner what remains but to count the clock, and hope for that sleep which I can scarce expect. Night comes at last, and some hours of restlessness and confusion, bring me again to a day of solitude. What shall exclude the black dog from a habitation like this?[44]

A few months later another blow fell: on 6 September Anna Williams died while Johnson was away in Wiltshire. Johnson wrote to Joshua Reynolds, "My Loss is really great. She had been my domestick companion for more than thirty years, and when I come home I shall return to a desolate habitation."[45] Williams, always irritable, had often been at odds with Barber, but Johnson valued the conversation of intelligent women and it had been his long-standing practice to take tea with her when he returned late at night from an evening at the Club or elsewhere. The day after Williams's death Johnson sent to Barber a letter which is now lost, perhaps concerning the funeral arrangements. Ten days later he wrote to Barber again, this time in a rather more cheerful tone:

> As Thursday is my Birthday, I would have a little dinner got, and would have You invite Mrs. Desmoulins, Mrs. Davis that was about Mrs. Williams, and Mr. Allen, and Mrs. Gardiner.[46]

It seems to have been only a momentary lifting of the clouds. Johnson's letters at this time refer repeatedly to his desolation. Levett and Williams were dead, and Desmoulins was now living elsewhere. The latest of his many ailments was a testicular tumour, for which his doctors had recommended a painful and potentially dangerous operation. His friend the playwright Arthur Murphy wrote:

> By the death of Mrs. Williams [Johnson] was left in a state of destitution, with nobody but Frank, his black servant, to soothe his anxious moments.[47]

Nobody but Frank. Johnson was not, after all, completely isolated. In December 1783 he was taken seriously ill again and was unable to leave the house for three months. He was heavily dependent upon Francis and Elizabeth Barber to look after him and provide for his needs. "Visitors are no proper companions in the chamber of sickness," he wrote to Hester Thrale. "They come when I could sleep, or read, they stay till I am weary, they force me to attend, when my mind calls for relaxation, and to speak when my powers will hardly actuate my tongue." But if visitors were not wanted in a time of illness, there were others who were: "The amusements and consolations of languor and depression are conferred by familiar and domestick companions, which can be visited or called at will, and can occasionally be quitted or dismissed."[48]

Johnson had enjoyed such company in Levett and Williams, but they were gone. His "familiar and domestick companions" were now Francis and Elizabeth Barber. The most enduring image of Johnson is the public figure, the great talker, proclaiming, contradicting, and arguing, always surrounded by people. But as his powers faded, the only company he wished for was that of his manservant and his wife. It was a remarkable reversal of their roles of thirty years earlier: Johnson had in effect become part of the Barber family. That family increased when the Barbers' second son was born on 29 December 1783. On 18 January 1784, he was baptised at St. Dunstan's in the West, the church where the couple had been married.[49] Their choice of name for the child could hardly have been more significant: like their first son he was named Samuel.

Yet the Barber family forms no part of the accepted picture of the last year of Johnson's life. Few of the numerous biographies of Johnson mention the presence in the house in Bolt Court of the toddler Elizabeth Barber and her baby brother Samuel Barber. But they were there and must sometimes have lightened the mood in the house, and eased Johnson's depression.

Johnson rallied once more in an astonishing way, helped, it must be assumed, by the Barbers' care for him. By June of 1784 he was sufficiently recovered to be able to visit Oxford with Boswell. Barber had gone on ahead, and Johnson and Boswell came later by post-coach. As they travelled Johnson told Boswell that he had been giving thought to how he could provide for Barber after he was gone. "I have . . . about the world I think above a thousand pounds," he said, "which I intend shall afford Frank an annuity of seventy pounds a year."[50] Johnson and Barber returned to London after a fortnight, but in July they went on their travels again, this time on a longer trip to Lichfield and Ashbourne, and then on to Oxford once more in November. Elizabeth Barber stayed behind with the children, and Johnson made arrangements for her to be paid via his printer William Strahan, who was also effectively his banker.[51]

Johnson had been ill again while they were in London and continued to be unwell on their travels. As his health problems multiplied, Barber provided the intimate care of a nurse, as he had done for some years. (On one occasion in 1777 Barber had assisted in the middle of the night when Johnson bled himself, an unpleasant treatment which was supposed to relieve his acute breathlessness. As might be expected, neither man was very skilful in carrying out the procedure. Johnson recorded: "I rose and opening the orifice let out about ten ounces more. Frank and I were but awkward.")[52] Johnson now particularly feared what he called "the dropsy": this was oedema, a buildup of fluid which caused his feet and legs to swell. Barber kept a close watch on the progress of this ailment. "My Water has lately run away, my Man tells me that my legs are grown less," wrote Johnson to one of his doctors, and a few months later he recorded in his diary, "The dropsy encroaches by degrees; I felt this and today Frank told me of it."[53]

One great attraction of their visit to Oxford was the prospect of seeing a hot air balloon flight. The Montgolfier brothers had been responsible for the first such flight, which had taken place in France the previous year, and the subject had rapidly captured the public imagination. "All our views are directed to the air," wrote Horace Walpole in December 1783, "*Balloons* occupy senators, philosophers, ladies, everybody."[54] Johnson, who had a long-standing interest in technology, was fascinated, agreeing to subscribe to an experimental balloon and writing a long letter to Mrs. Thrale on the subject. The first ascent in England took place in London on 15 September. Three days later Johnson wrote to Joshua Reynolds, "I have three letters this day, all about the ballon [*sic*]."[55]

The first flight by an Englishman, James Sadler, took place in Oxford on 4 October, and he was due to make another ascent on 12 November. A massive crowd gathered to witness the spectacle as the balloon took off from the University Botanic Gardens. The streets were crammed with people. Some climbed trees, while the luckier ones ascended nearby towers to get a better view. One observer reported:

> A few minutes before one o'clock Mr. Sadler stepped into the car, suspended from the machine by a net work, and constructed in the form of a boat, when the fastenings being loosened, a most beautiful balloon ascended with such wonderful velocity, that in three minutes Mr. Sadler was enveloped in clouds.[56]

The flight was short (just seventeen minutes) but dramatic. The balloon soon lost much of its air, and Sadler was forced to jettison all his ballast, his provisions, and his scientific instruments in a desperate effort to gain some height. But the balloon continued its descent and briefly became entangled in some trees, then dragged along the ground and took off again, before Sadler was able to bring the flight to an abrupt end by throwing an anchor onto a hedge. The balloon was completely destroyed, but Sadler was unhurt. He arrived back in Oxford at seven o'clock, to be hailed by a joyous but unruly mob who pulled his carriage through the streets in riotous (and somewhat inebriated) celebration. The Montgolfier brothers might have got there first, but Sadler was English. The *London Chronicle* proudly declared:

> It may be proper to observe, that our English adventurer is the first person who has been his own architect, engineer, chemist, and projector; that he exhibited wonderful share of genius, intrepidity and cool resolution; and that he justly merits the patronage and liberality of a generous public.[57]

It was a great national moment, and Barber could boast that he had been there. But Johnson, who was increasingly unwell, had missed the occasion and could only learn about it from Barber's report. He wrote disconsolately to his friend Edmund Hector, "I sent Francis to see the Ballon fly, but could not go myself."[58] Four days later, Barber and Johnson travelled back to London. It was to be the last occasion on which they would travel together.

Johnson was now declining fast. On 20 November John Hoole called at Bolt Court and found "my dear friend Dr. Johnson very ill indeed and in great dejection of spirits." Johnson urged Hoole to stay, as "he always went to prayers with his man Francis every night."[59] As their thirty-two years together moved inexorably towards a close, the responsibility for Johnson's physical well-being rested on Barber while Johnson remained as concerned for his servant's spiritual welfare as he always had been. Hoole stayed, and together the three men knelt by Johnson's bed as he repeated several prayers.

Johnson had always been anxious not to give Barber demeaning tasks to perform. In later life Barber recalled one occasion when he had offered to buckle his shoes, and Johnson had replied, "No, Francis; time enough yet. When I can do it no longer, then you may."[60] That time had now come.

12. Hawkins v. Barber

As the end came nearer, Johnson wrote to his old friend John Hawkins, "Let me have the benefit of your advice, and the consolation of your company."[1] Hawkins was better qualified than anyone to advise Johnson. He was both a practically minded lawyer and an intimate of long standing—he had known Johnson for over forty-five years. He knew as well as any man that Johnson was terrified of death and of judgment. Now, as Johnson started to prepare himself spiritually for death, Hawkins repeatedly urged him to make practical preparations as well.

Johnson's thoughts turned once more to making provisions for Francis and Elizabeth Barber, and for the young Elizabeth and Samuel. He asked for advice from his physician Richard Brocklesby, "What would be a proper annuity to bequeath to a favourite servant?" Brocklesby told him that it depended on the circumstances of the master, and that, in the case of a nobleman, £50 a year was deemed an adequate reward for many years' service. Johnson replied, "Then shall I be nobilissimus [most noble]; for, I mean to leave Frank £70 a year, and I desire you to tell him so."[2]

Johnson had made a similar comment to Hawkins over a year earlier, and they had discussed how to organise the provision for Barber, but nothing had been done. Johnson shrank from the implications of such a final step as making a will, and repeatedly put it off. Hawkins even went so far as to draw up a draft will, leaving blanks for the names of the executors, and also a blank space where Johnson would write the name of his choice of residuary legatee—the person who, after specific bequests, would inherit all of Johnson's worldly goods. Hawkins realised that it would be a considerable estate, and he urged Johnson to bequeath it to his relatives. Johnson did nothing.[3]

On 27 November 1784, John Hawkins pressed him once again about the drawing up of the will. Hawkins recorded, "I then began to discourse with him about his will, and the provision for Frank, till he grew angry." Why Johnson was angry is not known; was it his resentment at being badgered into making a will, or was it something in the nature of their discussions about the inheritance for Barber? Whatever the problem, it was overcome, and Hawkins succeeded in persuading Johnson to draw up his last will and testament. It provided for a bequest of £200 to the representatives of a bookseller, William Innys. (Innys, who had given Johnson's father financial assistance, had died many years earlier, but Johnson still wished to show his gratitude to his descendants.) The will also included a provision for the £70 annuity for Barber. So far as the key issue of the identity of the residuary legatee was concerned, the bulk of Johnson's estate, including the proceeds of sale of his house in Lichfield, was left on trust for a religious association (probably the Associates of Dr. Bray). The following day Hawkins reminded Johnson that he had meant to leave a few small gifts to some friends, and proposed that a codicil be added to the will. Johnson irritably dismissed the suggestion.

As the word spread that Johnson was dying, many friends called on him or wrote. On one occasion Barber brought a note to him, and Johnson remarked that an odd thought had struck him: "One should receive no letters in the grave!"[4] Barber later recounted that Johnson took pleasure in talking to him about religious subjects, explaining passages in the Bible and often saying to him, "Attend Francis to the salvation of your soull which is the object of greatest importance."[5] Johnson had made financial provision for Barber's future but still felt responsible for his spiritual state.

As the days wore on, Johnson became deeply concerned about the fate of his private diaries. The reason for his anxiety emerges from subsequent communications between Boswell and Hawkins. In 1785 Boswell recorded a conversation in his journal:

> HAWKINS. "I have read his [Johnson's] diary. I wish I had not read so much. He had strong amorous passions." BOSWELL. "But he did not indulge them?' HAWKINS. "I have said enough."[6]

The entry is enigmatic, but it seems that Johnson's diaries contained references to his youthful sexual experiences, matters which caused him great remorse. In their biographies Boswell and Hawkins both referred to the matter in guarded terms, Boswell recording that "his [Johnson's] amorous inclinations were uncommonly strong and impetuous. . . . it must not be concealed, that . . . Johnson was not free from propensities which were ever 'warring against the law of his mind,'—and that in his combats with them, he was sometimes overcome."[7]

Many years earlier, Boswell had recorded the advice Johnson had given him concerning his journal, "that I should keep it private, and that I might surely have a friend who would burn it in case of my death."[8] Clearly any such friend must be trustworthy. Now that Johnson's death was near, he determined to destroy his own diaries, and the friend whom he called on to assist him was Francis Barber. It was a substantial task: one of his doctors recorded on 13 December that Johnson "has been for a week past doing little else than burning his manuscripts." That may have been an exaggeration, but he certainly burnt many papers at this time, as several friends recorded. Amongst the materials Barber burnt were letters from Johnson to his wife.[9]

But not all the papers went up in flames. Barber preserved some pages, making up a short account of the first ten years of Johnson's life. They were published over twenty years later, and whatever may have been in the burned papers, these are wholly innocuous.[10] It is hard to criticise Barber for keeping these particular fragments. Rather more revealing is the fact that nothing else survived, which indicates that Johnson's faith in Barber's discretion was not misplaced.

On Sunday, 5 December, a group of friends gathered to take Holy Communion with Johnson for what they all knew would be the last occasion. Barber opened the door to the seven visitors, as he had so often done before. John Hawkins and Bennet Langton had been regular callers during the thirty-two years of Barber's life with Johnson, and John Hoole and his wife, Susanna, had first met Johnson in 1761. Ann Gardiner, the wife of a tallow chandler, was an old friend of Johnson; Barber recalled that he had known her when she used to call at the Gough Square household in the 1750s. John Desmoulins was the son of Barber's old fellow resident Mrs. Desmoulins. Johnson welcomed them all, and, as Hoole noted in his journal, the sacrament was administered by the Revd. George Strahan to each in turn, "Frank being of the number."

Before the administration of communion took place, there had been a curious incident when Hawkins put into his pocket two of Johnson's diaries.[11]

He explained to Langton and Strahan that he took the books for safekeeping to prevent them from falling into the hands of George Steevens, a notorious and sometimes malicious prankster who had been known to publish private papers. (Hawkins had been warned by Barber that Steevens had recently insisted on seeing Johnson, even when Barber had told him that he was not receiving visitors.) After the ceremony was over, Langton told Johnson what had happened, and Hawkins repeated his reason for what he had done. The story later became public knowledge, and Hawkins's explanation did not convince everyone. Some accused him of outright theft, and the incident contributed to the generally unfavourable picture of Hawkins which has lasted ever since.

The incident distressed Johnson, and it may also have alerted him to the fact that once he was gone there might well be competing claims to ownership of his goods. What might happen if Barber was found with items in his possession which had once belonged to Johnson? On the following day, Johnson gave to Barber a silver coffee pot, and with it a small card on which he had written, "Dec. 6th. 1784. I gave to My Man Francis Barber, in consideration of his care and trouble, a large Silver Coffee pot."[12] It was signed by Johnson and was clearly intended as proof to all the world that Barber was the rightful owner.

On Tuesday, 7 December, Johnson was visited by William Windham, then a rising politician, and later Secretary at War under Pitt. Johnson was still concerned about Barber's future, and he asked Windham to promise to be Barber's "friend, adviser, and protector in all difficulties which his own weakness and imprudence, or the force or fraud of others, might bring him into." Windham recorded in his diary:

> Having obtained my assent to this, he proposed that Frank should be called in, and desiring me to take him by the hand in token of the promise, repeated before him the recommendation he had just made of him, and the promise I had given to attend to it.[13]

Hawkins arrived at Bolt Court the next day to find that Johnson had just dictated a new will to the clergyman George Strahan, and that he was in time only to assist with the formal execution of the document. (Hawkins later stated that the previous will had been intended only as a temporary provision.) Clearly Johnson was having second thoughts. In this version of the will there was no bequest to the Associates of Dr. Bray, and no provision concerning Johnson's house. It included the £200 bequest to the representatives of William Innys and added a bequest of £100 stock to Mrs. White, Johnson's servant. It did not include the annuity for Barber; instead, all of Johnson's money (£750 held by Bennet Langton, £300 held by the brewers Barclay and Perkins, £150 on loan to Bishop Percy, and £100 in cash), together with his books, plate, and household furniture, was to be held on trust for Barber. It seems that Johnson wished to provide for Barber, but was uncertain how best to do so.

The following evening Hawkins returned to find that Johnson had once again reconsidered the contents of his will and was dictating a codicil to Strahan. (Could it have been that Johnson preferred the advice of the clergyman to that of the lawyer?) The codicil made a number of provisions to which we shall return. Amongst other things it provided once more for the £70 annuity for Barber.

In spite of his worsening condition, Johnson was determined to ensure that this provision was put into effect. At Johnson's request, two days after he had signed the codicil his friend Bennett Langton entered into a deed with Philip Metcalfe, an attorney, and George Stubbs (a Member of Parliament), under which Langton received £750 from Johnson and in return he agreed to provide the annuity of £70 to Barber. (Metcalfe and Stubbs were the trustees of the arrangement and would make the annual payment to Barber.) To make the payment safe against any eventuality, Langton also entered into another deed which secured payment of the annuity against his income from navigation rights of the River Wey. Effectively, Langton was not only agreeing to provide the annuity, he was also providing a mortgage to back it up. If he were to become bankrupt, and therefore unable to make the annual payment, Metcalfe and Stubbs could claim the £70 from the navigation rights so that Barber would still receive his money. As a token of his gratitude, Johnson gave Metcalfe a copy of the Sermons of Robert South. The final step towards making Barber financially secure was taken at one p.m. on 14 December, when a note of the deed was formally lodged at the Chancery Office, as was required by law.[14]

As Johnson continued his slow decline, it was Barber who was in the closest attendance, acting both as nurse and as guardian of the door against the numerous people who wanted to see Johnson. Anyone wishing to call on him had first to persuade Francis Barber. The experience of the author Frances Burney, who called on Sunday, 12 December, was typical of many:

This morning, after Church time, I went,—Frank said he was very ill, & saw nobody; I told him I had understood by my Father the Day before that he meant to see me. He then let me in. I went into his Room up stairs,—he was in his Bed Room. I saw it crowded, & ran hastily down,—Frank told me his master had refused seeing even Mr. Langton, I told him merely to say I had called, but by no means to press my admission.[15]

Burney stayed for several hours, but she never saw Johnson, who was growing steadily weaker. As the day wore on, Johnson took an affectionate farewell of William Windham, then turned to Barber and said, "Before tomorrow at this hour I shall be consumed," a prediction which he later repeated to John Desmoulins. The following day, a Miss Morris, daughter of a particular friend of Johnson, called and begged Barber to permit her to see Johnson and obtain his blessing. Barber led the girl into Johnson's room, and the dying man turned in his bed and said, "God bless you my dear." At about seven in the evening, Johnson died. Keeping him company were Francis Barber and John Desmoulins.[16]

Ten days after Johnson's death, James Boswell wrote to Barber from Edinburgh, asking him to call on his brother, Thomas Boswell, who was in London, to give him an account of Johnson's last days. Barber did so, in spite of his deep distress, Thomas Boswell recording that "the poor man when he related what passed between his Master & Miss Morris cryed bitterly, and could not proceed for some minutes."[17]

Thomas Boswell wrote down Barber's account in a letter which he sent to his brother, and which James Boswell set out in large part in the climax of his monumental *Life of Johnson*, introduced with the words, "Of his last moments, my brother, Thomas David, has furnished me with the following particulars."[18] It has become a classic account, the only narrative of Johnson's last moments from an eyewitness, but few readers realise that its source is Francis Barber.[19] And yet what James Boswell published in his *Life of Johnson* was not entirely accurate. In one respect this was his own fault, as he mistranscribed his brother's handwriting. To this day every edition of the *Life* states that the two people who were with Johnson when he died were Barber and *Mrs.* Desmoulins, not *Mr.* Desmoulins.[20] A second inaccuracy was due to Barber, and it was deliberate.

Barber told Thomas Boswell that "the Doctor from the time that he was certain his death was near, appeared to be perfectly resigned, was seldom

"GOD BLESS YOU, MY DEAR!"

"God bless you, my dear!" by E. H. Shepard, from *Everybody's Boswell* (London: G. Bell, 1930). There are many illustrated editions of Boswell's *Life of Johnson*, but few include representations of Barber. (copyright © The E. H. Shepard Trust, reproduced with permission of Curtis Brown Group Ltd, London)

or ever fretful or out of temper."[21] James Boswell reproduced this verbatim in his *Life of Johnson*. In telling the story this way Barber was displaying enormous loyalty to the memory of Johnson, but he knew that it was far from the whole truth.

What had actually happened on Johnson's last day was dramatically different, as is apparent from Hawkins's published account and from the diaries of John Hoole and William Windham. Johnson's limbs were by this time hugely swollen with dropsy, and his testicle was once again seriously enlarged. In the past he had often obtained relief by having his physicians make incisions to allow the accumulated fluid to drain away. Early on the morning of Monday the thirteenth, when Barber and John Desmoulins were watching over him, Johnson decided to take matters into his own hands. He ordered Barber to give him a particular cabinet drawer, and reaching into it he pulled out a lancet. Realising what he had in mind, Barber and Desmoulins grabbed his hand. Johnson, by now deeply agitated, threatened to stab Desmoulins and shouted at Barber that he was a scoundrel. After a little while, however, he seemed to have calmed down and agreed not to do anything rash, and they released their grip. Immediately they saw his hand move beneath the bedclothes and, pulling them back, discovered blood pouring out. Johnson had cut himself deeply, twice in the legs and once in the scrotum. Barber and Desmoulins staunched the flow and sent for medical help.[22]

It seems unlikely that the bleeding had any positive effect, but the storm was now past, and once the physicians had attended to him and he had settled down, Johnson dozed for most of the day. John Hoole called at about eleven, meeting Miss Morris as she was on her way out, and Barber told him with magnificent understatement that Johnson had "had a restless night."[23] At one point Barber brought a cup of warm milk and placed it in Johnson's hands. As the day wore on, various friends came and went, but none of them disturbed Johnson. At last, only Barber and Desmoulins were left with Johnson when he died.

The events of that day were an appalling end to their thirty-two-year relationship. The following morning Hawkins heard the news of Johnson's death, sent for Barber, and, by his own admission, "interrogated him very strictly" about what had happened.[24] It was a characteristically insensitive way of handling the shocked and bereaved Barber.

Johnson's funeral took place at Westminster Abbey on 20 December. The newspapers published detailed reports. The *Public Advertiser* printed a list of the mourners, beginning with the executors, Sir Joshua Reynolds, Sir John Hawkins, and Dr. William Scott (later Lord Stowell), in a coach and four. Then followed eight more coaches containing twenty-five friends of Johnson's who had been invited by the executors. The list included Dr. Brocklesby, the Revd. George Strahan, Mr. Hoole, and Mr. Desmoulins, and concluded with "other distinguished persons, and the deceased's favourite black servant." After them came two coaches containing the six pallbearers, and then two more coaches with seven mourners.[25]

In his life of Johnson, Hawkins described the ceremony:

On Monday the 20th of December, his funeral was celebrated and honoured by a numerous attendance of his friends, and among them, by particular invitation, of as many of the literary club as were then in town, and not prevented by engagements. The dean of Westminster, upon my application, would gladly have performed the ceremony of his interment, but, at the time, was much indisposed in his health; the office, therefore, devolved upon the senior prebendary, Dr. Taylor, who performed it with becoming gravity and seriousness. All the prebendaries, except such as were absent in the country, attended in their surplices and hoods: they met the corpse at the west door of their church, and performed, in the most respectful manner, all the honours due to the memory of so great a man.[26]

In Hawkins's account the funeral was conducted with all the solemnity and dignity which was due such a person as Johnson. But many who had attended saw it differently. In spite of the numbers who were there and the distinguished names, the funeral was thought to be surprisingly low-key for such a well-known public figure, with no organ and no choir. There was much adverse comment on this in the press, at first directed at the Dean and Chapter of the Abbey. But when it became known that it was Hawkins who had decided on a cheap ceremony, he came in for considerable criticism. Dr. Charles Burney, who had been present, wrote, "The Dean and Chapter of Westminster Abbey lay all the blame on [Hawkins] for suffering Johnson to be so unworthily interred. . . . [Hawkins] determined that, 'as Dr. Johnson had no music in him, he should choose the cheapest manner of interment.' And for this reason there was no organ heard, or burial service sung."[27]

What Hawkins thought about this can be judged by the comments of his daughter on the subject. Laetitia-Matilda Hawkins was a loyal daughter, especially where Francis Barber was concerned, and in her memoirs, published forty years after Johnson's death, Barber appears as "that worthless being." "The immortalised Frank," she wrote, "the *faithful* black servant of Dr. Johnson, could scarcely, I think, less deserve the reflected credit given him." She wanted to shift the blame for the botched funeral arrangements away from her father, and Barber—by that time long dead—was a convenient target:

When the funeral was to be arranged, and a proper person to conduct it, was to be treated with, Francis interposed a low connection of his wife's, and Sir J. H. very wisely gave way, considering perhaps, that he who had lived like Johnson, needed not to be buried with the precision of rank; the numerous attendance of friends spoke sufficiently that it was no common personage whose remains were conveying to the mausoleum of royalty, learning, genius, and wit.[28]

The idea of Johnson's funeral being arranged not by the executors but by some "low connection" of Elizabeth Barber is fanciful. Even if such a person existed and had some role in the funeral, the decision that Johnson did not need to be "buried with the precision of rank" would not have been theirs; the choice was made by Hawkins and by him alone.

But it was Johnson's bequest to Barber which was to be the greatest source of controversy, and the basis for an astonishing attack by Hawkins on Barber. Johnson, both in life and in death, was news. The newspapers had carried frequent reports of his declining health, followed by announcements of his death and tributes to him. There was particular interest in Johnson's legacy to Barber: numerous papers commented on it, including the *Public Advertiser*, the *St. James's Chronicle*, the *Gazetteer*, the *Morning Herald*, and the *General Evening Post*, often in surprisingly well-informed detail. The *Bath Chronicle* for 16 December carried the following account:

> The Doctor asked what he should leave his honest old black servant, that had lived with him about 40 years? He was informed that a man of the first quality usually bequeathed no more to a faithful servant than an annuity of £50. "Why then (said the Doctor) tell Frank (meaning his black) that I will be above a Lord; for I will leave him £70 a year!"

The *Public Advertiser* for 18 December did not merely report the legacy; it went out of its way to defend it and described the relationship between Barber and Johnson in glowing (and possibly ironic) terms:

> It is not at all to be wondered at that Dr. Johnson should have so liberally considered his old servant, Frank, who was the immediate jewel of his soul, shining with all the lustre of solid merit. This faithful Indian was the friend, the guide, the Counsellor of his Master! He was his nurse! He dressed and undressed him!—Nor did the great breathing treasury of knowledge ever go out without this steady servant, this trusty support of exalted genius!

> The Doctor had, at one time, some intention of liberally educating Frank; he consulted his genius, his constitution, and inclination; but

he found they would not do. Frank preferred marriage to study; he took to himself a white woman by whom he has had children; and, with the income which his master has left him, he will be enabled to live very comfortably.

The text of Johnson's will was very soon published in full, appearing in the *London Chronicle* and the *St. James's Chronicle* on 23 December, in the *General Advertiser* on 24 December, in the *Morning Chronicle* and the *Morning Herald* on 25 December, and in the *Gentleman's Magazine* for December. As noted above, in his will Johnson left £100 to his housekeeper Mrs. White and £200 to the representatives of William Innys. Under the terms of the codicil Johnson's house in Lichfield was to be sold and the proceeds divided between various distant relatives. He left £100 to the Revd. John Rogers in trust for the care of "Elizabeth Herne, a lunatic," and £200 was settled on Johnson's two godchildren. John Desmoulins received £200 in annuities, Francesco Sastres (a member of Johnson's Essex Head Club) received £5, and eighteen of Johnson's friends received bequests of books.

The cash bequest in the will of £2,000 on trust for Barber was altered by the codicil, which specified that the £750 held by Langton was to be used to purchase the annuity of £70 per annum. The remaining £1,250 was, together with the rest of Johnson's estate after the specific bequests listed above, left to the three executors—Hawkins, Reynolds, and Scott—in trust for Francis Barber. Part of the estate was Johnson's library, which was auctioned in 1785 for £320 9s.[29] Johnson's legacy to Barber was reckoned by Hawkins to be worth about £1,500 in total (apparently in addition to the annuity).

It was a substantial and enormously generous bequest—to earn that sum at the wage he had been paid in the navy, Barber would have had to serve for an improbable 138 years. But the terms are revealing. The money and goods were not left to him outright but on trust, and they were to be applied by the three trustees "in such manner as they shall judge most fit and available to his benefit." In other words, it was the trustees who would be in ultimate control, not Barber. It is clear that Johnson wanted Barber to be well provided for, but he also thought that he needed guidance and, if necessary, limits on the uses to which he could put his inheritance.

When the contents of Johnson's will became public knowledge they caused considerable astonishment in some quarters. The Revd. William Johnson Temple wrote to Boswell, "Think of his making his Will on the

Final page of the will of Samuel Johnson, 9 December 1784. "All the rest residue and remainder of my Estate and Effects I give and bequeath to my said Executors in trust for the said Francis Barber." (The National Archives, PROB 1/19 1784. By permission of The National Archives, London)

very night on which he died, and leaving so large a sum to a Negroe."[30] Johnson's old friend Mrs. Thrale (by now Mrs. Piozzi) was far from happy at the idea that gifts which she had given to Johnson had fallen into the hands of Francis Barber. Twenty-five years after Johnson's death, she tried to get some of them back from Barber's widow. Piozzi recorded in her commonplace book for 1809:

Blackamour

I got my old Pocket book again which I had given the Doctor, and which he had bestowed upon *Blackey;* but my Silver Tea kettle & Lamp, my Portrait, and the Great Chair I had taken so much Pains to work for [Johnson], were all gone irrecoverably.

Four years later, in correspondence with her daughter, she was still complaining that "a Carpet I had worked, and an old Silver Tea-Kettle and Lamp which had been my poor Mother's Virgin Establishment:—They all went to the Blackamoor, with my portrait by some of the Burneys."[31]

But the most hostile reaction of all came from Hawkins, in his *Life of Samuel Johnson,* which was published in March 1787. Hawkins's book is now little read except by scholars, but it had considerable impact at the time. It was effectively the authorised life of Johnson. There had been a number of previous Johnson biographies but they had been little more than booklets of forty or fifty pages, often written by people who had little or no knowledge of their subject. In contrast, Hawkins's *Life* was a volume of over 600 pages, written by a man who had been intimate with Johnson for a period approaching half a century and who was his chief executor. To give it even

Sir John Hawkins (1786), by Robert James. "Francis Barber is an exceedingly worthless fellow." (Faculty of Music Collection, Oxford University/The Bridgeman Art Library)

greater authority, Hawkins's book was first published as Volume I of the eleven-volume *Works of Samuel Johnson* (a collection of which Hawkins was the editor).

For anyone interested in Johnson or those in his circle, Hawkins's work is an essential book, containing much information about Johnson which is not available elsewhere. Hawkins was better placed than anyone to write such an account by reason of his knowledge of Johnson (and his works), the intelligence he brought to the task, and his experience as a biographer. Unfortunately for Hawkins, there were several problems with the book. One is the content: critics were quick to point out that it is in places rambling, tedious, and astonishingly dull. A difficulty of a different kind was that in the wings there was a rival, and much superior, biographer. Boswell launched an assault on Hawkins's volume, conducting an anonymous campaign of denigration in the press. But it was not these activities which sank Hawkins's biography; the simple fact was that Boswell was a great writer, and Hawkins was not. When Boswell's *Life of Samuel Johnson* appeared, four years after Hawkins's, it promptly and permanently eclipsed it. A further problem was that many people did not like Hawkins. As we have seen, Johnson labelled him "unclubbable," and the verdict has stuck: he often seems at best mean-spirited. The portrait he presents of Francis Barber bears this out.

Hawkins sets the tone for his treatment of Barber from the moment he introduces him in his narrative:

> Of this negro-servant much has been said, by those who knew little
> or nothing of him, in justification for that partiality which Johnson
> shewed for him, and his neglect of his own necessitous relations.[32]

The message is clear: those who speak positively of Barber do so out of ignorance, Johnson showed poor judgment in supporting Barber, and there is little which is worth saying about him.

Barber does not feature much in the book, but when he does, the reader is left in no doubt as to Hawkins's views—often expressed at the cost of the topic which Hawkins is actually addressing. The pages dealing with Johnson's last days are in diary form, and they lend an appropriate air of solemnity and inevitability to the account. It is therefore particularly jarring when Hawkins pauses from his narrative to launch an assault on Barber.

In the entry for 9 December 1784, Hawkins reports Johnson's dictation of the codicil, with its provision for Barber. At this point he adds a footnote which takes up half the page in the first edition. Some extracts from this have already been quoted, but it is worth setting it out in full:

> How much soever I approve of the practice of rewarding the fidelity of servants, I cannot but think that, in testamentary dispositions in their favour, some discretion ought to be exercised; and that, in scarce any instance they are to be preferred to those who are allied to the testator either in blood or by affinity. Of the merits of this servant, a judgment may be formed from what I shall hereafter have occasion to say of him. It was hinted to me many years ago, by his master, that he was a loose fellow; and I learned from others, that, after an absence from his service of some years, he married. In his search of a wife, he picked up one of those creatures with whom, in the disposal of themselves, no contrariety of colour is an obstacle. It is said, that soon after his marriage, he became jealous, and, it may be supposed, that he continued so, till, by presenting him first with one, and afterwards with another daughter, of her own colour, his wife put an end to all his doubts on that score. Notwithstanding which, Johnson, in the excess of indiscriminating benevolence, about a year before his death, took the wife and both the children, into his house, and made them a part of his family; and, by the codicil to his will, made a disposition in his favour, to the amount in value of full fifteen hundred pounds.[33]

After digesting this footnote, the reader then returns to the text, which continues, "He [Johnson] was now so weak as to be unable to kneel, and lamented, that he must pray sitting, but, with an effort, he placed himself on his knees, while Mr. Strahan repeated the Lord's Prayer." Hawkins had a good opportunity for second thoughts about the footnote when a revised edition of the book was required four months after the first had been published, but he chose not to take it. He reexamined the note and let it stand almost unchanged. The only amendments he made to it were to show that at the time in question the Barbers had one daughter and not two, and to change the sum Barber inherited from "full fifteen hundred" to "near fifteen hundred." Hawkins's narrative of Johnson's life closes with brief accounts of Johnson's autopsy and funeral, and then the text of Johnson's will and codicil. But that is not the end of the volume. There then follows a Postscript, which takes up seven pages in the first edition and is entirely devoted to attacking Barber.[34]

Hawkins begins by setting out his purpose. The will, he writes, demonstrates Johnson's determination to be *nobilissimus* towards Barber, but "the many lavish encomiums that have been bestowed on this act of bounty, make it necessary to mention some particulars, subsequent to his death, that will serve to shew the short-sightedness of human wisdom, and the effects of ill-directed benevolence." In short, Hawkins sets out to prove that Johnson got it wrong, and that the money should have gone to his relations and not to Barber.

First, Hawkins states how much money Barber received from the estate. He gives this as "little short of £1,500" (at an earlier point in the book he calls it "fully £1,500") and contrasts this with the £235 made from the sale of the Lichfield house, which was shared amongst five relatives. Three of these individuals, says Hawkins, got £58 15s each, and the other two got £29 7s 6d. He then goes on to point out that the executors answered all of Barber's calls for money. Hawkins gives detailed figures, down to the last farthing.

Hawkins then tells the story of Humphrey Heely, a relation of Johnson's who was living in poverty. (Hawkins had visited Heely in the almshouse where he lived with his wife, and he describes the "scene of distress" that met his eyes.) Johnson had previously given Heely money, and Hawkins says that Heely asked Barber for money "a few days after the doctor's decease," whereupon Hawkins told Barber that "seeing he was so great a gainer by his master's will, as to be possessed of almost the whole of his fortune," Barber should supply Heely's needs. According to Hawkins, Barber replied, *"I cannot afford it."* Clearly the reader is being invited to contrast Barber's meanness with Johnson's charity.

The next relation to whom Hawkins turns is Elizabeth Herne, whom he describes as "a first cousin" of Johnson who had been confined in Bedlam and was by then in a madhouse for incurables. Johnson had helped to support her to the tune of £25 a year, and left £100 on trust for her in his will. The named trustee however, the Revd. John Rogers, renounced the legacy, and Hawkins claims that he (Hawkins) must now use the £100 for her maintenance, and when that is exhausted he must arrange for her to be cared for by the parish. Hawkins gives the following account of Barber's response to her predicament:

> Of the craft and selfishness of the doctor's negro-servant, the
> following is a notable instance. At the time of his master's death,

Mrs. Herne's maintenance was about £30 in arrear. I was applied to for the money, and shewed the bill to him [Barber], upon which he immediately went to the mad-house, and insisted with the keeper thereof, that it should be charged on the legacy; but he refused to do it, saying, that the lunatic was placed there by Dr. Johnson, and that it was a debt incurred in his life-time, and, by consequence, payable out of his effects. When this would not do, this artful fellow came to me, and pretended that he could bring a woman to swear that there was nothing due; and, upon my telling him, that I should, notwith-standing, pay the bill, he said, he saw *there was no good intended for him,* and in anger left me.[35]

According to Hawkins, Barber was willing to perpetrate a fraud by persuading a woman to swear that nothing was owed to the madhouse, in order to prevent the bill from being paid out of the estate. Hawkins also points out, by way of contrast, that Bennet Langton, who had been paid £20 by the book-sellers for the manuscript of Johnson's Latin poems, had decided that it would be divided amongst Johnson's poor relations, whereupon Diana Beauclerk had added to that the sum of £30 which was owed by Johnson to her late husband Topham Beauclerk. Hawkins concludes the Postscript and the volume:

> The above facts are so connected with the transactions of Dr. Johnson, in the latter days of his life, that they are part of his history; and the mention of them may serve as a caveat against ostentatious bounty, *favour to negroes,* and testamentary dispositions *in extremis.*[36]

It is by any standard a peculiar way to end a biography. But if we leave aside the appropriateness of giving these charges such prominence in a life of Johnson, that still leaves the questions of what motivated Hawkins and whether his allegations against Barber were true.

The figure of Humphrey Heely loomed large for Hawkins. This is in part because, from the first occasion on which they discussed the matter, Hawkins laid great emphasis on Johnson making financial provision for his relations. This concern for Heely's welfare appears to have become a family trait. Hawkins's daughter, Laetitia-Matilda, devoted five pages of her *Memoirs, Anecdotes, Facts, and Opinions* (1824) to Heely, of whom she memo-rably wrote, "He was the scathed oak of a former century: but a few arid symptoms of foliage testified that he had once been leafy."[37] Following in her father's footsteps, she criticised Johnson's "wild benevolence," and went on:

I know it has been considered an offence of a heinous magnitude, to weigh any claim against the *merits* of Mr. Francis Barber, merits that had no foundation, but in his consultation of his own interest or the perverseness of his admirers; but unless Johnson had, when making his will, entirely lost all recollection of Heely, I know nothing that can excuse his petulant refusal to consider how the residue of his property should be disposed of. My father urged that and every other point of religious and moral obligation, with the gentleness of a divine, and the skill of a lawyer. He had only his own integrity to requite him.[38]

The "gentleness of a divine" is not perhaps a quality readily associated with John Hawkins, but his daughter's account may be influenced by a touch of filial piety. Doubtless many lawyers have only their own integrity to requite them for their services, but whether that was the case with Hawkins is a moot point. It is hard to avoid the suspicion that Hawkins's true concern was not the positive one of providing more for relatives, but the negative one of ensuring that Barber received less. There is no doubt that Johnson did display his customary charity to Heely, in spite of some reservations about whether he and his wife were to be believed about their claims of poverty. "Their representations of their affairs," wrote Johnson, "I have discovered to be such as cannot be trusted." Johnson also described Heely in 1767 as a "near relation." But his claim on Johnson amounted only to the fact that he was at that time married to Johnson's cousin Elizabeth Ford. She died in 1768, and Heely remarried.[39] Heely's claims on Johnson were slight, and on Barber nonexistent. But for Hawkins any relation, no matter how remote, was preferable to a black man—or at least, to this black man.

So far as Elizabeth Herne is concerned, she was not Johnson's "first cousin," but the daughter of a cousin. It seems that the costs of her maintenance were shared between Johnson (who paid about £12 a year) and a family called Prowse, who may have been relations of Herne. Before he died, Johnson agreed with the Revd. John Rogers and Mrs. Mary (Prowse) Rogers to leave £100 to the Revd. Rogers for Herne's benefit, and Rogers undertook to provide for Herne's future by granting an annuity of £23 a year.[40] In short, Rogers, who was a wealthy man, agreed to make full provision for Herne. Whether he renounced the legacy from Johnson, as Hawkins claimed, is not known, nor do we know why he might have done so, but it seems unlikely that Herne would have been left in need given that a wealthy clergyman who clearly felt some sense of obligation towards Herne had agreed to provide for her.

Of course, this does not change the fact that if Hawkins's story about Barber's attempts to prevent him from paying Elizabeth Herne's madhouse bill is true, then it reflects very badly indeed on Barber—after all, what Hawkins says he was suggesting would be outright fraud. It is almost certainly true that the bill was due and was paid from Johnson's estate. Hawkins would hardly have published such a claim if it was false, bearing in mind that his fellow executors were almost certain to read the account. But did Barber suggest concocting a perjury to evade the liability on the estate? If the story is true, it goes a long way towards explaining Hawkins's contempt for Barber; if it is false, it certainly accounts at least partly for the fact that, as we shall see, Barber became bitterly resentful of Hawkins.

There is real difficulty in judging the reliability of the allegations which Hawkins made against Barber. His hostility towards Barber (and its racial undercurrent) is undisguised, but what is impossible to tell at this distance in time is whether Barber is a wholly innocent victim, or whether there was an element of truth in some of the charges Hawkins made against him.

In any event, Barber was not the only one against whom serious allegations were made. Johnson had left the bulk of his wealth on trust for Barber, but when it came to the administration of the estate there was a strong suspicion that John Hawkins had required rather more than just his integrity to requite him. There were two other executors, William Scott and Joshua Reynolds, but in practice they left the day-to-day business of the estate entirely in Hawkins's hands. Scott wrote to Lady Inchiquin in 1794, "During Sir John Hawkins's life, Sir Joshua & myself did not trouble ourselves about the executorship the whole business of which was performed by Sir John."[41] This left Barber in the awkward position of still being beholden to Hawkins. It also put Hawkins in a position of considerable power, and there were credible reports that he abused it.

Reynolds thought Hawkins "not only mean and grovelling in disposition but absolutely dishonest." At least, so Edmund Malone, a close friend of Reynolds, recorded in his journal, and he went on to explain why:

> After the death of Dr. Johnson, [Hawkins] as one of his executors laid hold of his watch and several trinkets, coins, &c., which he said he should take to himself for his trouble—a pretty *liberal* construction

of the rule of law, that an executor may satisfy his own demands in the first instance. Sir Joshua and Sir Wm. Scott, the other executors, remonstrated against this, and with great difficulty *compelled* him to give up the watch, which Dr. Johnson's servant, Francis Barber, now has; but the coins and old pieces of money they could never get.

He likewise seized on a gold-headed cane which some one had by accident left in Dr. Johnson's house previous to his death. They in vain urged that Francis had a right to this till an owner appeared, and should hold it *in usum jus habentes* [for the use of the rightful claimant]. He would not restore it; and his house being soon afterwards consumed by fire, he *said* it was there burnt.[42]

How much weight should be given to this account? Malone is hardly an unbiased witness. He gave substantial assistance to Hawkins's rival, James Boswell, in the preparation of his life of Johnson, and according to Peter Martin, Malone's modern biographer, he had an "almost obsessive dislike towards Hawkins's *Life*," and "briefed Boswell about how to denigrate Hawkins in his biography."[43] But whether true or false, the story of the watch and the cane soon became public knowledge.

The watch was a distinctive and valuable item, and was later described by Hawkins in his biography. It had been made for Johnson in 1768 by the well-known watchmakers Mudge and Dutton at a cost of seventeen guineas. Johnson, who had a horror of not using his time well, had an inscription etched onto the dial plate which read, in Greek, "the night cometh," from the verse in John's Gospel, "I must work the works of him that sent me, while it is day: the night cometh, when no man can work." (He later came to consider the inscription ostentatious and removed the dial plate.)

In another version of the anecdote which was in circulation, Hawkins was said to have obtained a low valuation for the watch with a view to buying it himself, but Barber refused to sell.[44] There is probably some truth in these reports, but there is also reason to believe that Hawkins had an explanation for his actions. In March 1788 Barber wrote to Boswell, "I don't know that Sir John has at present any thing in his Custody of mine except a gold headed Cane which was never accounted for."[45] The following month Boswell attended on Hawkins to obtain any of Johnson's books or papers which were still in his possession. He anticipated a frosty reception, and was taken aback by Hawkins's courtesy:

We sat most serenely opposite to each other in armchairs, and I declare, he talked so well and with such a courteous formality that every five minutes I unloosed a knot of the critical cat-o'-nine-tails which I had prepared for him. How much might human violence and enmity be lessened if men who fight with their pens at a distance would but commune together calmly face to face!

Boswell raised the subject of Barber's complaint about the cane and the watch, and recorded in his journal that "he defended himself, I thought very well, from the charge of the gold-headed cane . . . I told him fairly of Francis's complaint that he did not go first to Mudge, the maker of his master's watch, to get it valued, as his valuation was double that of the others."[46]

Unfortunately Boswell did not record Hawkins's defence to the charge of keeping the stolen cane, nor his response to Barber's complaint about the watch, and we have no way of judging the truth of the stories about them. But what mattered from Barber's perspective was that he certainly did believe that the stories were true, and they were hardly likely to endear Hawkins to Barber.

13. Lichfield

Johnson's legacy left Barber independent and well-off, able to make his own choices and to put them into effect. In fact he was forced to do so, as the home he had enjoyed for so many years with Johnson was now no more, and he had to find somewhere to live. By October of 1785 he had decided to leave London altogether, although he did not do so immediately.[1] After some thirty-four years in the capital, he started a new life in Lichfield.

Barber had good reasons for choosing to settle there. It was familiar territory, as he had accompanied Johnson there on several occasions and had stayed for weeks at a time—easily long enough to come to know such a small city, and to become known there. It was also a place where the Barber family could live much more cheaply than in London. Barber, after all, had never had anything like the sum of money he now possessed, and there were plenty of people in London who would be happy to help him dispose of it. And weighing heavily on Barber were Johnson's exhortations not long before his death that he should move to Lichfield. Barber still felt a strong sense of obligation to comply with his master's wishes.

It was probably not until August 1786 that Francis, Elizabeth, and their two children made the 110-mile journey to Lichfield.[2] Barber was able to make good use of Johnson's local connections, who seem to have welcomed him. He took a house on Stowe Street, where the family stayed for seven years, paying £12 a year in rent.[3] The owner was a Mrs. Jane Gastrell, sister of Molly and Elizabeth Aston. The sisters were almost exact contemporaries of Johnson and had known him all their lives. Barber came to be on good terms with Richard Greene, the owner of the famous Lichfield museum of curiosities and a friend of Johnson's, and also with Anna Seward, a considerable literary figure in Lichfield whose work Johnson admired (though his views were not entirely reciprocated).

Not everybody was quite so welcoming. Lucy Porter, Johnson's stepdaughter from his marriage to Tetty, was still living in Lichfield, and Barber called on her soon after he arrived in Lichfield. Lucy had always had a good relationship with Johnson (unlike her siblings, who would have nothing at all to do with him). Barber presented to Lucy her mother's wedding ring. After Elizabeth Johnson's death in 1752, Johnson had kept it in a small wooden box in which was pasted the inscription "Eheu! Eliz. Johnson, Nupta Jul. 9, 1735. Mortua, eheu! Mart. 17, 1752" (Alas! Elizabeth Johnson, married 9 July 1735. died, alas! 17 March, 1752). It was clearly an item of enormous sentimental value, but Lucy rejected the gift. Her reasons for doing so are unknown; perhaps an item so intimately linked to both her mother's remarriage and her death was simply too disturbing. Barber had the ring enameled and presented it to his wife in memory of Johnson. He had it inscribed "Saml Johnson LLD OB 13 Dec 1784 AE 75."[4]

Lucy Porter had her own memories of Johnson and had no need to learn about him from Barber, but others were fascinated by what he had to tell. Barber became a minor celebrity, sought out by both locals and visitors, eager to hear his tales of Sam Johnson, the son of the local bookseller, who had ended up with a funeral in Westminster Abbey.

Barber soon discovered that connection with a celebrity was not without its disadvantages. In March 1786 Mrs. Piozzi published her *Anecdotes of Samuel Johnson*, with its humiliating account of Barber's embarrassment at the attentions paid to his wife by Mrs. Piozzi's servants, and its sneer at Barber's "delicacy." Hawkins and Boswell were also at work on biographies of Johnson, and this battle of the biographers kept Barber in the public eye. The month after the appearance of Piozzi's volume, "Peter Pindar" (the pseudonym of John Wolcot) published a satirical poem, "Bozzy and Piozzi; or, The British Biographers. A Pair of Town Eclogues," in which Boswell and Piozzi appeal to the judgment of John Hawkins as to who is the more able biographer. As part of her case, Mrs. Piozzi recounts again the anecdote of Hodge the cat:

> To please poor HODGE, the DOCTOR all so kind,
> Went out, and bought him oysters to his mind.

This every day he hid—nor ask'd black FRANK.
Who deem'd himself of much too high a rank,
With vulgar fish-fags, to be forc'd to chat,
And purchase oysters, for a mangy cat.

Barber was trying to build a new life in Lichfield, and this kind of publicity could hardly have been helpful to him and his family, but much worse was to come. In March 1787 John Hawkins published his *Life of Samuel Johnson*, with its onslaught on Barber and its smear on his wife. Extracts from the book soon appeared in numerous papers, and Hawkins's charges became common knowledge, even among those who had not read the volume. For some readers Hawkins's account confirmed their suspicions about the black population as a whole. In June of 1787 a correspondent to the *St. James's Chronicle* wrote, in a letter quoted in a previous chapter, "I am not surprised at the base Ingratitude of Johnson's Black, as mentioned by Sir John Hawkins . . . The Truth is, these People are the worst Race of Men on the habitable Globe."[5] The letter did not go unanswered. A week later one respondent used it as the basis not only of a defence of the black population but also of an attack on slavery. "Philanthropos" wrote from Oxford:

> I was not a little disgusted by some Sentiments which lately appeared in your Paper. Your nameless Correspondent, from the Instance of Francis Barber, takes Occasion to abuse the whole Race of the Negroes. Supposing the Charge to be true (which yet may remain to be proved) that the late petulant and desultory biographer of Dr. Johnson brings against his black Servant, what will this prove?— that the whole Negro Race are deficient in the moral Sense, and that Gratitude and Principle never dwelt in an African Breast! The whole Race of Christians might as well be charged with Hypocrisy and Impurity from the criminal Designs of some few. The Observations of this Correspondent may carry Conviction to those who are engaged in the Slave Trade, and to those alone.[6]

The correspondent went on to launch an impassioned plea for the abolition of the slave trade, "Here Avarice is supported by Cruelty and the Wantonness of Oppression authorized by the Sanction of Law. The Particulars of this most abominable Traffick are too long to be enumerated . . . Surely the Thousands annually sacrificed to Slavery, to Filth, to Wretchedness, and Cruelty, loudly call for some speedy Redress."

Other news items treated Barber less as a basis for serious discussion and more as a figure of fun. The *World and Fashionable Advertiser* wrote:

> *Francis Barber*, Esquire—late the *black servant* of Dr. Samuel Johnson, is applying to the mania of the times, and positively *threatens* a life of his late master! He *further threatens*, in a particular manner, to be regardful of poor Sir John Hawkins. With anecdotes of the watch, &c. &c. &c.
>
> N.B. In *point of writing*, a bett or two have been made, in *Tom Payne*'s shop, that the *Knight* is *beat* by the Negro. This is to be a BLACK LETTER book![7]

The phrase "Black Letter book" was a play on words, alluding to a book printed in Gothic typeface, to Hawkins's profession as an attorney (a black letter book being a law textbook), and, of course, to Barber's colour.

Barber soon heard about Hawkins's account and was deeply offended. In July of 1787 Richard Greene wrote to Boswell, "[Barber], poor man, has been much hurt by Sir J. Hawkins's illiberal treatment."[8] Boswell had been quick to write to Barber to express his sympathy. This was genuine—he liked Barber and had always been on good terms with him. In this case, however, Boswell also had another motive. Barber had been very helpful to Boswell's work on his biography of Johnson, collecting for him some of the proof sheets of the *Lives of the Poets*, sending him original letters, and responding to queries about his life with Johnson. Now Boswell saw an opportunity to gain an advantage over his rival biographer. On 29 June 1787 he wrote to Barber:

> Sir John Hawkins having done gross injustice to the character of the great and good Dr. Johnson, and having written so injuriously of you and Mrs. Barber, as to deserve animadversion, and perhaps to be brought before the spiritual court, I cannot doubt of your inclination to afford me all the helps you can to state the truth fairly, in the Work which I am now preparing for the press.[9]

The spiritual court had jurisdiction over claims for slander. Barber was hardly likely to bring an action against Hawkins, but he was very willing to assist Boswell in any way he could—and if it damaged John Hawkins's interests, so much the better. An opportunity to help Boswell arose in connection with Johnson's diaries.

Johnson had burnt some of these volumes, but he spared at least four-teen notebooks. In his biography Hawkins had boasted of his unique access to the diaries. As an executor of the will he was entitled to temporary posses-sion of them, but he had no right to use them as a source for his book. The person who was entitled to them was Francis Barber, who, as residuary legatee, should have received all of Johnson's personal possessions except those items which had been made the subject of specific bequests. Boswell wanted the diaries, as well as any other materials written by Johnson, to use in his own work. He enclosed with his letter of 29 June a draft of a letter to be signed by Barber and requested him to return three copies of it, one for each of Johnson's executors—Hawkins, Reynolds, and Scott:

> SIR: As residuary legatee of the late Dr. Samuel Johnson I do now request that his Diary and every other book or paper in his hand-writing in the possession of his Executors or any of them be deliv-ered to——on my account as I understand them to be an undoubted part of my property.

The letter was a calculated insult to Hawkins, making it clear that Barber knew that Hawkins had retained materials which were "an undoubted part" of Barber's property—as they certainly were—and had made use of them.

Barber's reply, dated 9 July 1787, to Boswell's request, left him in no doubt of his willingness to assist in any way possible:

> Sir: I had the unspeakable Satisfaction of receiving your Letter on saturday last by the care of Mr. Green, and agreeable to your request with a heart full of Joy and gratitude, I took Pen in hand to enform you that I am happy to find there is still remaining a friend who has the memory of my late good Master at heart that will endeavour to vindicate his cause in opposition to the unfriendly proceedings of his Enimies; as I myself am incapable of to undertake such a task. The aspersions Sir John has thrown out against my Master as having been his own Murderer are intirely groundless, as also his assertion concerning Mr. Heley's applying to me for releif, he never did, neither was he any ways allied to my Master but by having been married to a relation of his who has been long dead

The reference to Hawkins having suggested that Johnson was "his own Murderer" appears to be a garbled account of Hawkins's story of Johnson's last night. Barber must have heard this secondhand, as he had not at this time read Hawkins's book, as he went on to make clear:

> I have not had the mortification to fall in with that impious production of Sir John Hawkins relating to the Life of my Dear Master, but assure yourself Dear Sir it will be to me a subject of the greatest happiness to render abortive the unworthy and false proceedings of the above mention'd Gentleman and from hence you may justly infer that fuller exposition of that basest of Mortals in as much as he has reflected not only on me and my consort, but on the unsullyed Character of the best of beings my affectionate and unparallel Master: if necessity should require it, if God spare my Life (for I am at present very poorly) I would willingly attest what I have related personally.[10]

Barber sent Boswell the authorisation, and a week later Hawkins handed over some (although apparently not all) of the papers.

The incident resulted in Barber's name appearing in the papers once again, the *St. James's Chronicle* for 21–24 July 1787 reporting that Barber had "rescued out of the Hands of Sir John Hawkins all the Diaries and Manuscripts of the Doctor, and deposited them with Mr. Boswell . . . Mr. Barber, we hear, has written a Letter full of honest Indignation at the Aspersions thrown both upon himself and his Master by a Late Biographer."[11]

Given the speed with which this story became public knowledge, and Boswell's love of fighting his battles with Hawkins in the press, it is likely that he was the source of the story. But it seems that Boswell was still not satisfied, and a few months later he wrote to Barber again, requesting a written demand for Hawkins to hand over the diplomas of Johnson's honorary doctorates from Dublin and Oxford, and all other papers or books in his possession which belonged to Johnson. Barber agreed to help, and Boswell again drafted the request:

> I hereby authorise you to demand from Sir John Hawkins all books or papers of any sort which belonged to the late Dr. Samuel Johnson, that may be in his possession.[12]

The terms were again likely to irritate Hawkins—a formal demand (which Barber was perfectly entitled to make) in peremptory language, implying that Hawkins had not complied with his obligations as executor.

Forty years later, Hawkins's daughter, Laetitia-Matilda, read this letter from Boswell to Barber and described it as an "act of violence."[13] Barber sent Boswell the demand (changing the words "the late" to "my late Master"), and Boswell notified Hawkins. This resulted in the 19 April 1788 meeting between Boswell and Hawkins where, as we have seen, Boswell raised the matters of the gold-headed cane and the watch and was taken by surprise at the courteous reception he received from Hawkins. He was given the few items which Hawkins still had in his possession, which amounted only to three pamphlets, the diplomas of Johnson's Dublin and Oxford degrees, and a few other papers.[14]

Hawkins's *Life of Samuel Johnson* prompted a mocking review in the August 1787 issue of the *Gentleman's Magazine*. It was the work of Richard Porson, a noted classical scholar who had a sideline in making witty pseudonymous contributions to the newspapers. Porson included in the review a parody of a "missing" page from the *Life* in which Hawkins tells the story of the watch:

> And here, touching this watch already by me mentioned, I insert a notable instance of the craft and selfishness of the Doctor's Negro servant. A few days after that whereon Dr. Johnson died, this artful fellow came to me, and surrendered the watch, saying at the same time, that his master had delivered it to him a day or two before his demise, with such demeanour and gestures, that he did verily believe that it was his intention that he, namely Frank, should keep the same. Myself knowing that no sort of credit was due to a black domestic and favourite servant, and withal considering that the wearing thereof would be more proper for myself, and that I had got nothing by my trust of executor save sundry old books, and coach-hire for journies during the discharge of the said office . . . I took the watch from him, intending to have it appraised by my own jeweller, a very honest and expert artificer, and, in so doing, to have bought it as cheap as I could for myself, let it cost what it would. Upon my signifying this my intention to Frank, the impudent Negro said, "he plainly saw there was no good intended for him;" and in anger left me.[15]

Hawkins was the target of Porson's parody, but its publication meant that once again Barber's name appeared in print. The attack on Barber by Hawkins in his *Life of Samuel Johnson* and the surrounding publicity were sufficient to make 1787 a very unpleasant year for the Barbers, and it was not over yet. In November, the newspapers announced a new publication:

> This Day are Published, Price Two Shillings
>
> MORE LAST WORDS OF DR. JOHNSON, Consisting of important and valuable ANECDOTES . . . with some original and interesting stories of a private nature, relative to that great man.
>
> To which are added, several singular and unaccountable facts relative to his Biographical Executor, formerly Chairman of the Quarter Sessions.
>
> By FRANCIS BARBER[16]

Anyone who rushed out to purchase a copy of this work in the hope of reading an account of Samuel Johnson written by his former servant would have been disappointed. As the title page of the volume stated, the work was by "Francis, Barber," the crucial comma having been unaccountably omitted from the newspaper advertisements. The preface made it clear that the author was anxious to avoid any possible confusion:

> I am not the late Dr. Johnson's black, but his white, servant. My name is Francis, and I had the honour of dressing his wig . . . Were I apprehensive that my name's being suffered to stand in the title page of the present production could, in any degree, injure the sale of the invaluable work which is soon expected from that learned gentleman, Francis Barber, the words should have been omitted. I am conscious that I have forestalled many anecdotes which he otherwise would have made known: so many, indeed, that, from the moment of this pamphlet's publication, he will be so incensed as to look black in the face ever afterwards. . . . Our names are not so similar as to delude the public into the idea that Mr. Francis, the barber, is Mr. Francis Barber.[17]

The booklet consisted of fifty pages of scatological humour, together with some rather feeble imitations of Johnson's style:

> Mrs. Macaulay, the historian . . . was once crowned with laurel on her birth-day . . . and she returned the compliment by begging to kiss the Doctor's hand. "Madam," said the Doctor, "you are at

liberty to kiss my *hand,* as a *woman;* but as a *whig,* you ought to think it an honour to be permitted to kiss my——"[18]

Some careless readers supposed the work to be Barber's, and it sold well enough to justify a second edition. The *European Magazine* reported that "by those who only read the title-page to this horrid mass of fraud as well as nonsense, it was, at first credulously supposed, that poor Frank Barber, the Doctor's black servant . . . had commenced author."[19]

Barber was mortified at the appearance of the publication, and at the obvious association with his name, and he wrote to the newspapers denying that he was connected with it. But his attempts merely served to increase the publicity. The *Morning Chronicle and London Advertiser* for 26 November announced that "Francis Barber, who states himself to be the black servant

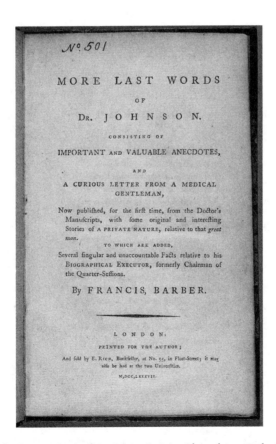

The title page of *More Last Words of Dr. Johnson* (1787), with its play on Barber's name. (Reproduced courtesy Hyde Collection, Houghton Library, Harvard University, 2003J-SJ1106)

of Doctor Johnson, must make his personal appearance before the Printer, accompanied by some known friend of the Deceased Doctor, ere the Letter signed Francis Barber can be admitted. Nothing but ocular demonstration can persuade the Printer to pronounce black to be white."

A supposed disclaimer appeared shortly afterwards:

> I, FRANCIS BARBER, DOCTOR JOHNSON's Black, think it honestly my duty to tell everybody that the pamphlet just now printed, called "More last Words of Dr. Johnson," is not my penmanship . . . I have had some disputes with one of my Master's Executors, yet that's all made up; and be it how it will, I would not have told, if I had been so minded, half so much of him as they have said in that Pamphlet; or of Mrs. Thrale or any of my Master's friends, no, not for all what he left me.[20]

It was a notice which was calculated to increase interest in the pamphlet, and the next in the series carried on the running joke at Barber's expense:

> WHEREAS an Advertisement has appeared in this Paper, impudently signed with the name of FRANCIS BARBER, and falsely stating that the new Pamphlet, called More Last Words of Dr. Johnson, is not written by him, I do hereby contradict the assertion, and publicly protest that the Production alluded to is written by me,
>
> FRANCIS BARBER[21]

In spite of all this unwelcome attention there is some evidence that Barber was still regarded as a respectable neighbour by those who knew him in Lichfield. In July 1788 local householders in his ward elected him a dozener, a sort of petty constable responsible for bringing before the Portmote Court complaints concerning minor offences such as assaults, gossiping, or failure to attend the watch.[22] The dozeners also had a ceremonial role, taking part in such occasions as the "chairing" of a newly elected Member of Parliament and the Lichfield Greenhill Bower. There was no parliamentary election while Barber was a dozener, but the Bower took place on Whit Monday 1789, during Barber's period of service.

The Bower was a daylong festival which had its origins in the Court of Array or View of Men and Arms, an annual review of the local defence forces. It featured music, dance, processions, gunfire, and (according to one 1730s account) "as much ale as [the participants] can possibly drink."[23] It was understandably a very popular event. The proceedings commenced early in the morning when the sheriff, the town clerk, and the bailiffs were escorted from the Guildhall in the centre of Lichfield to Greenhill, where a bower had been erected. The dignitaries were accompanied by the two manorial constables, ten armed men, eight morris dancers, a fool, and a band of musicians playing drums and fifes.

After the Court of Array or View of Men and Arms had been proclaimed, the city officials remained in the bower whilst the rest of the procession marched off to the first ward and summoned its dozeners such as Barber. The party was then led by the dozeners, each carrying a halberd (the symbol of his office) and a "posy," a decoration of flowers and greenery or a puppet with garlands. They marched through the ward while a volley was fired over each house, and then back to the bower, the procession now including all the householders of that ward (on pain of a 1d fine). The constables' party then repeated the procedure for the next ward, and so on until all the twenty-one wards had been summoned. Each return to the bower was marked by more food and drink. Writing in 1801, the Staffordshire historian Stebbing Shaw noted, "It is generally late in the evening before they have finished their painful task." The last procession of the day involved all the marchers, including the dozeners with their halberds and posies. They marched back from Greenhill along Bore Street and Sadler Street (now called Market Street), passing on the way the house where Johnson had been born and brought up. He had watched the procession in the 1720s, and saw it again in 1779.[24] In the marketplace the town clerk gave a speech, the dozeners placed their posies in St. Mary's Church, "God Save the King" was sung, and everyone went home.

Barber lasted only a year as a dozener. His term of office was not renewed in July 1789, and he was never reelected. He was now about forty-seven, and for some years his troubles had been increasingly compounded by ill health. Medical bills increased the demands on his financial resources, which had been further stretched by the birth of his fourth child, Ann, in November 1786.[25] In his July 1787 letter to Boswell (discussed above), Barber reported that he was "at present very poorly," and in March 1788 he wrote that he had been prevented from writing sooner, "not having been very well."[26] On 2 April 1788 he wrote to Boswell again, apologising that he had not been able to write sooner, "having had return of my old complaint." He went on:

Whit Monday (late eighteenth century), by C. E. Stringer. This painting of the Lichfield Whit Monday procession includes the city dozeners such as Barber. The corner house in the centre is Johnson's birthplace. (From an extra-illustrated copy of Thomas Harwood, *The History and Antiquities of the Church and City of Lichfield* [Cadell and Davies, 1806], courtesy of The Bodleian Libraries, The University of Oxford, Vet. A6 d. 1024 pp. 177–390, pullout before 353)

My disorder together with that of three of my Children lately having had the Small pox, has been very expensive to me, so that I am at present rather distressed, and find some difficulty to discharge my Rent for this year; for which reason I shall ever acknowledge as a particular favour if you would advance me Ten pound (which I will repay as I can turn myself about) to release me from my present uneasy situation.[27]

Barber's reference to "three of my children" is puzzling. The phrase seems to suggest that he had at least four surviving children, but the only Barber children known to have been living in April 1788 were Elizabeth, Samuel, and Ann. The Barbers' first son, also named Samuel, had died in 1775. No record of any other child has been found, and in 1799 Barber stated on oath that he had three children. It seems most likely that it is simply a misleading choice of wording in this letter. Barber's letters often contain mistakes of grammar or spelling and misuse of words, and on at least one occasion he had a draft letter corrected by a friend.

The sum of money which Barber wanted to borrow was substantial (almost exactly what he had earned in a year in the navy), but Boswell promptly replied, "As I am very sensible of your obliging disposition towards me, I am glad that I can accommodate you with the sum which you want, for which I enclose you a Bank Post Bill." Boswell had also given some thought to ways in which Barber could improve his financial position: "Some of your old Master's friends have thought that your opening a little shop for a few books and stationary wares in Lichfield might be a good thing for you. You may consult, and consider of it."[28]

Barber never took up the idea of opening a shop. By December of 1788, he was writing to Bishop Percy, again about the subjects of health and money:

> The infirmatives I have incessantly laboured under, together with those, attendant on age; not to mention the severe Illness, from which my Wife has with great difficulty recovered and the indisposition of my eldest Daughter is continually subject to, have universally Concurred, and in some measure compelled me to sollicit your Lordship to remit me (if convenient) the sum of Fifty pounds from the Bond together with the small Interest due thereon the the [*sic*] 10th of November last.
>
> I should not have troubled your Lordship, but as Christmas is drawing near and it is customary for Apothecaries and other Tradespeople to bring in their accounts some of which I have already received, and much larger than I ever expected—I have it not in my power, *without the assistance of your Lordship,* to discharge the same with my Quarterly annuity, except I leave myself destitute of money.[29]

The letter is signed by Barber but has been written by someone else, suggesting that ill health prevented him from writing personally. (He later mentioned a problem with his eyesight.) The bond to which Barber referred was the £150 lent by Johnson to Percy and referred to in Johnson's will. The Bishop had last sent money to Barber in March of that year, when he remitted £45. This sum was six years' interest, which for some reason had not been paid. On this occasion Percy promptly complied with Barber's request, sending him £57 10s on 26 December 1788, as repayment of £50 of the capital of the loan, together with interest.[30]

The constant references to money raise the question of what had happened to Johnson's legacy. The significance for the Barbers of the £1,500 inheritance and the £70 annuity becomes clear when it is compared to the wages they were receiving from Johnson—7s a week for Frank and 5s a week for Elizabeth, in total £31 4s a year. (In addition, they were provided with board and lodging, and Johnson probably bought their clothes.) In the 1780s a footman in a household with a number of servants might earn 13 or 14 guineas a year, and a maid of all work might make 9 or 10 guineas as well as tips, clothing, board, and lodging. Even among the most highly skilled craftsmen there were very few who could hope to make anything like £70 a year.[31]

In his *Life of Samuel Johnson* Hawkins gives some details about the payments to Barber under Johnson's will:

> From the time of the doctor's decease, myself, and my colleagues the other executors, answered all the calls of Francis for money. On the 6th day of September 1785, we had advanced him £106. By the 13th of December following, he had received of Mr. Langton for his annuity, and of Mess. Barclay and Perkins for interest, as much as made that sum £183 and on the 15th of the same month, a year and two days after his master's death, he came to me, saying, that he wanted more money, for that a few halfpence was all that he had left. Upon my settling with him in August 1786, it appeared that, exclusive of his annuity, he had received £337 and, after delivering to him the bond for £150 mentioned in the will, I paid him a balance of £196 15s 4d 3/4.[32]

According to this account, by 15 December 1785 Barber had spent almost £289—a very substantial sum of money. Assuming that the £106 paid on 6 September 1785 is not part of the figure of £337, then by August 1786 Barber had received at least £639 15s 4 3/4d, as well as the annuity. (The bond for £150 delivered to Barber is the document evidencing the loan to Percy, not the actual money.) At that point the account was settled so far as Hawkins was concerned. In November 1786 he wrote to Bishop Percy, "Francis Barber is an exceedingly worthless fellow. He is gone to reside at Lichfield, and I have settled my account with him."[33] It is not clear how these sums relate to the total value of the bequest. As we have seen, Hawkins recorded this as being "near fifteen hundred pounds" and "a sum little short of £1500."[34]

The suggestion that Barber went through the money quickly is supported by Laetitia-Matilda Hawkins, who wrote:

> When my father had to carry the will into effect, he was obstructed in every way by Francis. As fast as he drew money, so fast he

spent it, and came for more. I remember seeing him, with all the vulgar insolence of a hackney-coachman, chuck up a few half-pence, which, he said, without rendering any reason, were all he had remaining of a large sum which he had received very shortly before, and urging Sir J. H. most indecorously to precipitation for which he might have been called to account; and this, when, had it not been that my father laboured the point incessantly, Francis, after all his master's vain boasting, and unfeeling disregard of nearer connections, would have been left to the labour of his hands for a subsistence. My father then lost all consideration for the fellow, who, as if he had had only the justification of the acting executor in view, as quickly as possible reduced himself to the refuge of a workhouse.[35]

That John Hawkins "lost all consideration for the fellow" is not perhaps saying a great deal. But even if we make allowances for some exaggeration—so far as is known Barber was never in a workhouse—it does seem that Barber ran through his legacy at some speed, and was unable to live on the £70 a year. He was not good at handling money, no doubt in part because he was unused to dealing with such sums. (There is evidence that he did not, at first, understand how the payment of the annuity would work; in October 1786 Bennet Langton wrote to him, explaining that a sum was payable every quarter by George Stubbs, "to repeat, what I have said before very distinctly.")[36] An account of the life of Barber's son Samuel recorded that "his parents were improvident, strove to make a figure in the world, lived above their means, and dissipated their property."[37] This may not be very reliable, as it was written from secondhand information and was not published until 1829, but contemporary witnesses tell the same story. Late in 1790 Anna Seward wrote to Boswell:

> I am afraid Poor Frank Barber has been very imprudent and that Doctor Johnson's kindness has but little answered its purpose. I have given him three guineas for a carpet so worn, & thread bare, that it is not worth *one*. I was pleased with the idea of treading upon a surface so classical, & did not wish to have a good bargain.[38]

On 29 September 1790 Barber was writing to Boswell in despair about his situation. He once again used a third party to pen the letter, as "my Eyes are not so good as they were some time back."

I wish I never had come to reside at this Place, but being persuaded by my late poor dear worthy Master, to whom I was, and ought, in duty bound, to oblige, was the occasion. Some time ago, I was extreamly ill for a considerable time, which of course incurred a long Doctor's Bill, which when I came to pay astonished me greatly at the Total thereof, however I paid it: viz. 23.5.6, and some few months prior thereto, I observe, I paid him, and another of the Faculty, upon Account of myself, my Wife and Family—14 £. odd.

I have also been at a great Expence in the care and Education of my Children, as it is my wish, upon my Master's Account, to see them Scholars.

In the picture painted by Barber, he had at first been welcomed by local tradesmen who, doubtless knowing of the legacy, had been eager to extend him credit. But that had all come to an end:

When I first came here, people never minded, *but rather urged to entrust me* with Articles into the House, but now they see me rather reduced, (but can assure you has not been through my Extravagancy in the least, but trusting in mankind to be honest and just, put too much Confidence in them, who have now rewarded me for my pains,) and through some spiteful Enemy, or busy person, several with whom I dealt, hasteily have sent in their Bills, pressing immediate payment, as if in a manner they would eat me at once, and as my Quarterly payment (as it becomes due) will not be sufficient to discharge the same and to leave me a farthing in Pocket to subsist upon, and having no friend here to assist me, or confide in; beg you will assist me in my distressed situation.[39]

Barber asked Boswell for another loan, this time of £20, and also hoped for assistance in finding employment. He wrote that on the day of Johnson's funeral Edmund Burke had offered to assist if he ever wanted to go into service, and added, "I could wish [Burke], you, or some of my Worthy Master's ffriends would get me a Place in the Stamp Office—India-house, etc. I will leave this dead place as I cannot get any Employ therein." Boswell had helped Barber by lending him money on a previous occasion, but he now had substantial debts of his own (as well as five growing children to provide for) and was trying to obtain a loan in order to buy some land.[40] He replied to Barber, declining to lend him money but pointing out that the repayment terms Barber was offering Boswell would in fact be sufficient to satisfy Barber's creditors. There was a note of reproach too in his response. The original letter has not survived but Boswell summarised its contents in his register of letters:

> Reminding him that his worthy Master was attacked for the extraordinary liberality of the provision which he left to him. It would be a sad thing if the World should know that even that does not maintain him decently; advising him against leaving Lichfield which his Master recommended as his residence—there he can live much cheaper, and with fewer temptations than in London.[41]

There is no further surviving correspondence between Barber and Boswell, but the following year John Holt wrote to Boswell, seeking information about Barber. Holt was a schoolmaster and antiquarian and the regular contributor of a "Meteorological Diary" to the *Gentleman's Magazine*. In June 1793 he visited Lichfield and sought out Barber. He wrote about his visit in his column in the *Magazine:*

> Francis is about 48, low of stature, marked with the small-pox; has lost his teeth; appears aged and infirm, clean and neat, but his cloaths the worse for wear; a green coat, his late Master's cloaths, all worn out. He spends his time in fishing, cultivating a few potatoes, and a little reading.
>
> He laments that he has lost the countenance and table of Miss S——, Mr.——and many other respectable good friends, through his own imprudence and low connexions.[42]

The "Miss S" referred to was probably Anna Seward. Clearly, Barber was no longer acceptable company to her.

It was probably in the same year that the Barbers left the house in Stowe Street, which had been their home since coming to Lichfield. It may have been that the rent of £12 a year was now beyond them. They subsequently moved several times but never again paid a rent as high as £10.[43] As the money ran out, Barber turned to one of the few resources which was left to him. His master and friend Samuel Johnson remained a subject of enormous interest, and collectors were willing to pay for items associated with him. Barber started to sell off some of the objects he had inherited—Johnson's bible, ink stand, and even the infamous watch, the very one which had been at the heart of the controversy with John Hawkins. In the spring of 1794 Canon Hugh Bailye of Lichfield Cathedral wrote to a friend:

> O how . . . will Boswell envy me! No less than Dr. Johnson's watch is now in my possession! . . . I purchased it of Francis Barber, his black servant, who is now settled at Lichfield, and I am afraid in great want, though his master left him almost all his property. But he has a wife, poor fellow, that brings him both black and white children (alternately); this strange chemical mixture has produced that bitter portion poverty. This is not the Philosopher's stone.[44]

The Barbers' son Samuel was of a darker skin colour than his sister Elizabeth. (In 1863 Mary Webb [Hickman] Emery recalled that her father, Gregory Hickman, a Staffordshire surgeon, had employed "a mulatto servant, Samuel Barber" in about 1797.)[45] As Bailye's comments demonstrate, it was a circumstance which provoked local gossip about his mother.

There are many accounts of other items which were sold by Barber at this time, but some memorabilia were handed down to his son Samuel. One is particularly intriguing. Mary Webb Emery recalled that Samuel Barber had possessed several valuable articles which were said to have belonged to Johnson and which had been given to Hickman by Francis Barber (or possibly by Samuel Barber). These included "a gold headed cane." Perhaps the famous cane which Hawkins was supposed to have kept eventually found its way to Barber.

The sale of the watch was not sufficient to keep the family going for long. Nothing had come of Barber's request to Boswell to help him find employment, and any hopes Barber may have had of further assistance from that quarter ended with Boswell's death in May 1795. Barber badly needed more income, and fortunately he saw an opportunity. When Dr. Charles Burney sought out Barber in Lichfield in 1797, he discovered that he had left the city for good. He had moved to Burntwood, a small village just a few miles away, and there he set up a school. Samuel Johnson's determination to make a scholar of Barber seems to have paid off at last, and he may have been the first black schoolmaster in Britain.[46] Fittingly, the school was just a mile away from Edial, where Johnson had established a school more than sixty years earlier, though his experience was not a happy one—Johnson's venture had ended in failure after less than two years.

Barber must have judged that Burntwood was a suitable location for a school, perhaps because the village already had a charity school, which had been established in 1770. Nothing is known about Barber's school, but it seems unlikely that he intended to compete with the well-established charity institution. It is probable that his school was an elementary school, aimed at young children who might then go on to the charity school.

Barber could also claim that Burntwood was a healthy spot for children. David Moss, master of the charity school from 1782 until 1808, advertised "the well known salubrity of Burntwood, as bordering on that healthful spot, Cannock Chase," and proudly boasted of a cold bath, erected at considerable expense within twenty yards of the school, "for the use and convenience of such young gentlemen whose parents may be desirous of such an accommodation."[47]

Setting up a school was an act of considerable boldness, possibly touched by desperation, on Barber's part—especially if he knew that Johnson's attempt had been unsuccessful. There was no telling how the populace would react to their children being taught by a black man—and a former slave, at that—however well educated. A similar situation arose a few years later when an applicant for a teaching job in Bisley in Gloucestershire was required to produce a testimonial from a referee. The reference was generally positive but added, "Unfortunately he is a Mulatto, a native of the West Indies, which circumstances, added to a family of nine children, has kept him down in the world—Where so dark a complexion is not objected to, he would make a very valuable Schoolmaster."[48]

Whether because of attitudes to Barber's colour or for some other reason, the school was not a success. National economic problems caused by the war with France may have been a factor: prices rose very steeply in 1799 and leapt by 36 percent in 1800.[49] Barber's financial difficulties continued, and in October 1799 he was obliged, as noted earlier, to appear before a magistrate to be examined under the Poor Law, an appearance which carried with it the hope of receiving some assistance, but also an underlying threat.

The Poor Law was a complicated system under which every parish was obliged to collect money from those who could afford it and to make payments to those in need. In order for Barber to qualify for such relief, he had to have a "settlement" in the parish; the purpose of the examination was to determine whether in fact he did. The issue was particularly acute because the examination would determine not only whether he might obtain some very modest financial support from the parish, but also whether he and his family could remain there. A pauper who became a charge on a parish but who did not have a settlement there could be forcibly returned to the parish—perhaps hundreds of miles away—where he or she did have a settlement.[50] It was not uncommon for paupers to be passed from one parish to another. Only three months before Barber's examination his son Samuel had been paid 6d by the overseers of the poor to attend a woman who was being sent from Burntwood to her former parish.[51]

In his statement, which was taken on oath, Barber said that he was about fifty-two, and that he had been born "in Jamaica in the West Indies of which Island his parents were Natives."[52] (As we have seen, his belief about his age was probably incorrect.) He went on to state:

> That he hath lived in various services but the last place in which he was hired and served a Year was with Dr. Samuel Johnson in Bolt Court Fleet Street in the Parish of Saint Dunstans in the West in the City of London with whom he resided about Thirty-Four Years and until the Doctors death. That soon after Dr. Johnson died this Examinant went to live in the Parish of Saint Chad in the City and County of Lichfield where he resided in a House then belonging to Mrs. Gastrell for about seven Years for which he paid the yearly Rent of Twelve Pounds. That he hath since rented at different times several other Houses but never at any time Rented Ten Pounds a Year. That he hath now resident with him in Burntwood aforesaid his Wife named Elizabeth and three children Elizabeth aged about fifteen years Samuel aged about thirteen years and Ann aged about ten years.

Barber was wrong about the ages of his children, who were not fifteen, thirteen, and ten, but seventeen, fifteen, and twelve, respectively. But the key matters which decided the issue of his settlement were that he had served Johnson for over a year in the parish of St. Dunstan in the West, that he had lived in St. Chad's parish for several years, paying over £10 a year in rent, and that he had not paid over £10 a year since then. Serving a master for over a year or renting at more than £10 a year could establish a settlement, so Barber probably had a settlement in both St. Dunstan's and St. Chad's, but not in Burntwood. The result of the examination was that if he or his family became a burden on the parish, they could be returned to Lichfield or London.

Francis and Elizabeth Barber remained in Burntwood, however, so it seems that they were never quite so desperate as to need parish assistance. (The records of the parish overseer of the poor show no payments to them.) They were to spend the last months of their life together in Burntwood.

There is one surprising feature of Barber's Poor Law examination. He is described as "of the township of Burntwood ... yeoman." The term "yeoman" could be used in different senses. Johnson provided four meanings in his *Dictionary of the English Language* (1755):

1. A man of a small estate in land; a farmer; a gentleman farmer.
2. It seems to have been anciently a kind of ceremonious title given to soldiers: whence we have still yeomen of the guard.
3. It was probably a freeholder not advanced to the rank of a gentleman.
4. It seems to have had likewise the notion of a gentleman servant.

Of these meanings the fourth seems to be the one intended. (It recalls Steele's reference to the esquire's loyal and long-standing servant, the description which Boswell applied to Barber.) Whatever its precise meaning, it seems to suggest that Barber was still regarded as having a certain social status in the community.

Barber had always suffered from ill health of some unspecified kind—"a sickly lad ... a malady in his throat," "extreamly ill," "my old complaint," "a troublesome disorder"—and his health deteriorated during 1800.[53] He was attended by Dr. Richard Wright, grandson of the Richard Greene whom Barber had known in Lichfield in the 1780s, and in gratitude he gave to Dr. Wright a copy of *The Satires of Juvenal* which had belonged to Johnson. (He probably had no other means of paying him.) Barber did not respond to the treatment, and it was decided that an operation was required. In December he was taken into the Staffordshire General Infirmary. Surviving records show that the eleven patients admitted during the week ending Friday 12 December 1800 included Francis Barber.[54]

The fact that Barber was admitted to the Infirmary confirms his impoverished condition. The hospital (whose "physician extraordinary" was Erasmus Darwin, grandfather of Charles) had been established in 1766 as a charity and admitted only poor patients, the rules laying down that "no patients be admitted who are able to subsist themselves, and pay for medicines." It also indicates that he still had at least one local supporter, as anyone who was to be admitted to the Infirmary (except for an accident victim) had to have a letter of recommendation from a benefactor of the hospital. It is not known who sponsored Barber, but one of those with the right to nominate patients was Canon Hugh Bailye of Lichfield Cathedral, who had bought Johnson's watch from Barber five years earlier. Perhaps the infamous watch had this last part to play in Barber's story.

The nature of Barber's illness remains unknown. It could not have been regarded as incurable because of a strict rule that only patients believed to be curable would be admitted. The rules stated:

> That . . . no persons disordered in their senses, suspected to have the smallpox or other infectious distempers; having epileptic or convulsive fits; scrofulous complaints of long standing; habitual ulcers; cancers not admitting of an operation; consumptions or dropsies in their last stages; in a dying condition, or judged incurable, be admitted as in-patients; or if inadvertently admitted, be suffered to continue.

The prospect of an operation would have been daunting in pre-anaesthetic days when a little laudanum (a mixture of opium and sherry) or just alcohol would have been the best pain relief available. Whether the recovery rate was helped by the diet is not clear: on Friday, 12 December, the meals provided for patients such as Barber were a pint of milk porridge and four ounces of bread for breakfast, bread or suety pudding washed down with a pint of beer at dinner, and a pint of gruel for supper.

The operation was performed not long after Barber's admission to the Infirmary. It was described in his obituary in the *Gentleman's Magazine* as "painful" and was not a success. He lingered for a month, but on 13 January 1801 he died, aged about fifty-seven or fifty-eight. He was buried in the churchyard of St. Mary's Church, Stafford, on 28 January. The record of burials for that date includes "Francis Barber from the Infirmary." Underneath the entry an unknown hand has written "Dr Johnson's negro servant."[55]

14. Afterlives

When Francis Barber died in 1801, the annuity of £70 a year came to an end. Indeed, his lack of money suggests that he was no longer receiving the payments, perhaps having sold the right for a lump sum. His widow Elizabeth was left with little source of income, and with two daughters at home to support. Their son Samuel had left home: the Barbers had been anxious to give him a good education, and he had been sent to a boarding school in Lichfield. He left the school around 1799 and, as noted earlier, was employed for several years as a servant by Gregory Hickman, a surgeon in Burslem, some thirty-five miles from Lichfield.[1] The Johnson connection had served Samuel Barber well; Hickman was a distant relation of Johnson, and his grandfather had known Johnson.

The Barbers' elder daughter, Elizabeth, did not survive her father long. She died in Burntwood in March 1802, at the age of twenty.[2] Barber's widow and their surviving daughter, Ann, moved back to Lichfield, where they once again lived on Stowe Street and kept a day school for children. Johnson's old friend Mrs. Thrale (now Mrs. Piozzi), who visited Lichfield in April 1809, was sceptical about Ann's paternity:

> I saw a Girl at Lichfield lately—who *called herself*—and was *called* by others, the Daughter of Dr. Johnson's Negro Francis. She was rather a remarkably *fair* Girl, & approaching to pretty.[3]

The school did not make much money, and Elizabeth Barber was reduced to selling mementos of Dr. Johnson, as Francis had done before her. The Revd. Thomas Whalley, the clergyman who visited Mrs. Barber in 1810, wrote in a letter to the *European Magazine* that she "had in her possession many articles formerly the property of the Doctor, which 'her necessities and not her will' have obliged her to part with."[4] One of the last items she parted with was the miniature painting of Johnson which he had given to her many years earlier.

Whalley's letter included an unfavourable account of Mrs. Piozzi's actions on her visit the previous year. As we have seen, even though Johnson by that time had been dead for twenty-five years, Piozzi still resented the fact that Francis Barber had inherited items which had been her gifts to Johnson. She wanted them back, and at last an opportunity arose. Travelling from London to her estate at Brynbella in Wales, she stopped over at the George Inn in Lichfield and summoned Elizabeth Barber. The call to attend on a wealthy lady may have aroused some hopes in the impoverished widow, but if so they were soon dashed as it became clear that Mrs. Piozzi's principal concern was with the gifts she had given to Johnson. Whalley recounted what occurred:

> I also heard of a *pocket-book* purchased in France by a *literary lady*, one of his warm admirers, and presented to him (the Doctor) by her. This lady, in passing through Lichfield, on her road into Wales, a short time since, sent, from the George-inn, to Mrs. Barber, expressing a wish *to speak with* and *to serve her*—but, at the interview, the *pocket-book* was principally inquired after, and it was reluctantly given back to the ORIGINAL DONOR, who hailed it, in a poetical rhapsody, as "a long lost friend restored"—yet the remuneration given to the poor woman for it was scarcely its value as "*Leather and Prunella*"!!!

Whalley's readers would have understood that the book's value as "leather and prunella" was its scrap value. This account was not entirely fair to Mrs. Piozzi; she may have been more interested in the pocket-book than in Elizabeth Barber, but she was aware of the family's poverty, recording that they were "in sad want," and gave her a guinea for the book. The money may not have been much to Mrs. Piozzi, but it was more than a week's wages for many people, almost certainly including Elizabeth Barber.[5]

Elizabeth Barber died in Lichfield in 1816, at the age of sixty, and Ann went to live with her brother Samuel. He had left the service of Gregory Hickman some years earlier and entered the employment of the famous

Burslem potter Enoch Wood, who had been an apprentice of Josiah Wedgwood. During the nineteenth century the pottery industry of Staffordshire expanded enormously, so that by 1900 there were 300 factories making china and earthenware in the towns which made up the area known as "the potteries" (of which Burslem was one). The manufacturers included such famous names as Wedgwood, Spode, and Minton. Samuel Barber became a potter's printer, preparing the designs which would be transferred onto the pottery, and the first of several generations of Barbers to work in that trade.

The best source of information about Samuel Barber is an appreciation of his life which was published in *The Primitive Methodist Magazine* in 1829, although some allowance has to be made for the fact that it clearly reflects the perspective of the magazine's readership.[6] According to this account, as a young man Samuel Barber seems to have been something of a dandy, enjoying music and dancing and spending much time dressing his hair. He was, as he afterwards expressed it, "as proud a fop as ever lived."

In 1806, however, Barber's life changed dramatically under the influence of the flourishing Methodist movement. Methodism was a considerable force in Staffordshire, and its heart was in Burslem, the site of the first Methodist Society in the county. John Wesley preached there and at other places nearby on many occasions. "At Burslem I was obliged to preach abroad," wrote Wesley in his journal in March 1790, "such were the multitudes of the people." At the age of twenty-three Samuel Barber experienced a profound Christian conversion, becoming very active among the Methodists and serving as a local preacher in 1809.

Just a few years later, Burslem was the centre of a group which broke away from the Wesleyan Methodists. A practice which developed locally (adopted from American revivalist movements) was the holding of "camp meetings," open-air gatherings at which exuberant preaching, singing, and prayer would go on deep into the night. One such meeting took place in 1807 on Mow Cop, a hill near Stoke-on-Trent, lasting from six in the morning until eight in the evening, and it attracted the disapproval of the more conservative Wesleyan authorities, who ordered that there should be no more camp meetings. Some local Methodists refused to comply, and the conflict resulted in the expulsion of two figures who had been a considerable influence on Barber, Hugh Bourne and William Clowes. Bourne was expelled from the Methodist Society in 1808 and Clowes in 1810. The two men became the leading figures in a movement known as the Primitive Methodist Connexion, and Barber joined them. The Primitive Methodists were much more emotional than the Wesleyan Methodists, their worship being marked by loud cries and exorcisms.

In 1811 Samuel Barber's commitment to the Primitive Methodists was further deepened when he married Frances Sherwin, who was also active in the movement. The couple had six children, of whom two died young and one did not marry. As to the remaining offspring, Martha Barber married one John Sneyd, and the couple immigrated to the United States in 1848. Two years later, Enoch Barber followed in their footsteps; it may well be that there are Barber descendants living in the United States today. The oldest child of Samuel and Frances Barber was Isaac, who was born in 1813.[7]

Samuel became a well-known preacher and leader within the Primitive Methodists, despite working fourteen- to sixteen-hour days at the potteries. He journeyed hundreds of miles, sometimes travelling up to twenty miles on a Sunday to preach and then returning the same day. He was not thought of as a great preacher—it was said of him that "as a preacher, his talents were not of the first order." Nonetheless he was highly regarded, perhaps because "he was an advocate for short meetings, and usually spoke to the people in a brief, concise way."

Samuel Barber died on 6 July 1828. By that time the Primitive Methodists numbered over 31,000, and Samuel was the eleventh preacher of fifty-five in terms of seniority on the Tunstall preaching circuit. But his status as a preacher was not of interest to the newspapers which reported his death, and they did not mention it. What made him newsworthy was that he was "son of the late Mr. Francis Barber, the faithful (black) servant, and residuary legatee of the great Dr. Samuel Johnson."[8]

Like his father, Isaac Barber worked in the potteries, becoming a mould maker in Burslem at Pinder, Bourne and Hope's, earthenware manufacturers who were later to become Doultons, the china makers. One of Isaac's colleagues there was John Lockwood Kipling (father of Rudyard), who was articled as a designer and modeller from about 1851 to 1858. (In 1865 he immigrated to India to take up a post as professor of architectural sculpture, and he spent most of the rest of his life there.) Writing in 1908, Kipling recalled that Isaac Barber had "a certain hoarse quality in his voice, which I have since heard in many lands . . . woolly hair and mulatto features." He also remarked that Barber was "not a particularly good workman, nor was he popular with his fellows, being a dull and not very intelligent man . . . not in the least an interesting person. I do not recall a single suggestive fact or recollection being drawn from him, and yet I frequently talked with him."

It is impossible to say whether Isaac Barber was actually so completely devoid of interest, or whether this simply reflects the memories of a man in his seventies recalling an acquaintance after a gap of fifty years. It may be too that Kipling's views were tainted by a degree of scepticism about whether Isaac was who he claimed to be: Kipling described him as "a man of colour . . . claiming to be a descendant of Frank Barber, Dr. Johnson's servant."[9]

Isaac Barber married Martha Brian in 1848, and they had four children, one of whom is believed to have died young. The others were Enoch (born 1849), Edward (born 1854), and Sarah (born 1857). All three of these great-grandchildren of Francis Barber worked in the pottery industries, Enoch as a mould maker, Edward as a hollow ware presser (responsible for pressing clay into moulds for the manufacture of jugs and pots), and Sarah as a gilder of pottery. They all married and had between them eleven children, the great-great-grandchildren of Francis Barber. The total number of the subsequent descendants of Francis Barber is not known, but it is possible to follow the history of at least one line right down to the present day.[10]

Isaac's son Enoch married Louisa Parker in 1878. They had four children: Frances, William Edward ("Ted"), Frederick, and Hilda. Ted was a mould maker, like his father and grandfather before him (though he also served in the army for a time), and he was baptised and brought up in the Primitive Methodists. He married Sarah Rowley, and they had eight children, seven of whom married and had, between them, twenty children.

Ted and Sarah's third son, Norman Barber, was born in 1920 and died in 1986. He was the first for several generations not to go into the pottery industries, working as a jeweller throughout his life, with the exception of the years 1939–45, when he served in the Royal Artillery, reaching the rank of Battery Sergeant Major. He married Audrey Keighley in 1946, and the couple settled in Burslem and had three children: Cedric, Stephen, and Sandra.

Cedric Barber served as a police officer and later worked in insurance sales. He married Lesley Brace, and they had two children, Christopher (born in 1974) and Caroline (born in 1978). Christopher and Caroline are in the seventh generation to be descended directly from Francis Barber. This is only one line of descent; in all probability there are hundreds of other members of that generation.

The question is sometimes asked: if thousands of black people lived in Britain in the eighteenth century, what became of them? Francis Barber and his descendants provide at least part of the answer. Like so many others in Staffordshire, they worked in the pottery factories and worshipped with the Methodists. In wartime they served in the armed forces. They married and had children and grandchildren. In short, they formed part of the everyday life of the country. To this day Francis Barber's descendants continue to live in Staffordshire.

How do these modern-day Barbers regard their ancestor Francis? There are signs that attitudes have changed over the years. Dennis Barber (a sixth-generation descendant born in 1930) was fascinated by the story which was passed down to him and wanted to find out more, an attitude that was shared by his contemporaries: "Most people think it's wonderful," he recalled. "People that I worked with thought it was a fascinating story." But when he was a child the matter was regarded as not quite respectable:

> It was not a subject spoken about outside the family . . . My mother didn't like to hear any talk about Francis Barber. My father always raised it and called him Mr Barber. My mother always used to turn around and say, "Look, don't talk about that Black man in front of the children." . . . I think it's because she was the older generation.[11]

For Dennis's cousin Cedric Barber (born in 1948 and also a sixth-generation descendant) the discovery that he was descended from a black slave was a positive experience. "My 'black roots' have risen to the forefront of my consciousness in recent years, and I have to say that this awareness of my family has revolutionised my life," he wrote. "Finding my family was African, and all that that meant (slavery, ill-treatment) was also very emotional."[12]

Several years have passed since I attended the lecture in Dr. Johnson's House, and I am back there once again, viewing the same picture of the young black man. On the previous occasion there were many other visitors, but this time the building is closed to the public because a small team is making a BBC television documentary entitled *The Black Eighteenth Century*.[13]

The programme takes as its starting point several portraits of black men and women of the period. Ignatius Sancho is one of those featured. He was born on a slave ship around 1729, and became a domestic servant and later a grocer in Westminster. His published letters have made him perhaps the best-known black Briton of his time. His portrait by Gainsborough now hangs in the National Gallery of Canada. Dido Elizabeth Belle also features in the programme. As discussed earlier, she was the mixed-race great-niece of Lord Mansfield and was brought up in his household alongside Lady Elizabeth Murray, another great-niece. The two girls were painted together in their teens, looking affectionate and happy in each other's company.

Another picture which appears in *The Black Eighteenth Century* is the portrait of the black man which hangs in Dr. Johnson's House. Cedric Barber is filmed in front of it, expressing his pride in his ancestor. We know the history of Francis Barber, but what about the history of this painting? And is the face in the picture really that of Francis Barber?[14]

The archives of Dr. Johnson's House show that the portrait which hangs there was at one time the property of Sir James Knight-Bruce (1791–1866), a judge of the High Court, and it was passed down through the family to his great-grandson David Minlore. In 1933 Minlore agreed to exhibiting the picture for a few months in Dr. Johnson's House.

The House had recently been bought by Cecil Harmsworth, a Liberal Member of Parliament. It had gone through many uses since Johnson's day and had recently been a cheap boardinghouse. When Harmsworth bought it, the building was in a state of considerable disrepair and seemed to be fit for nothing but demolition, but he was determined to save it for the public. He restored it and handed it over to a charitable trust in 1929. When the picture was displayed in the House in 1933 Harmsworth took a great interest in it, and in the connection to Johnson. The following year Minlore indicated that he planned to sell the portrait in the United States, but Harmsworth was determined that it should stay in the House. In July 1934 he bought it from Minlore for £40 and gave it to the House.[15]

The correspondence surrounding the acquisition of the portrait shows that Harmsworth was anxious to establish the identities of both the sitter and the artist. He wrote to Arundel Esdaile, Secretary of the British Museum, "The question is, is it Francis Barber, and is it by Sir Joshua?" Esdaile consulted Edward Croft-Murray, then Assistant Keeper in the Department of Prints and Drawings and later to become a well-known art historian. Croft-Murray concluded that the portrait was not an original by Joshua Reynolds, but a copy. He added, "It *is* however a portrait of Francis Barber," but he gave no reasons for this confident identification.[16]

The history of the picture is much better known today, and it is now established that the painting which hangs in Dr. Johnson's House is a copy of a portrait by Joshua Reynolds. The date of the original is uncertain. Nicholas Penny, who curated the Joshua Reynolds exhibition at the Royal Academy of Arts in 1986, wrote that it is "exceedingly hard to date this study on stylistic grounds, but c.1770 seems likely." Similarly David Mannings and Martin Postle, in their magisterial *Sir Joshua Reynolds: A Complete Catalogue of His Paintings* (2000), describe it as "Painted c.1770(?)."[17] The history of the original portrait can be traced forward to the present day. Following Reynolds's death the picture was sold at auction by Greenwood's in 1796. The purchaser was Sir George Beaumont, a close friend of Reynolds's. It remained in the Beaumont family until 1902, when it was sold to the well-known art gallery Colnaghi. Over the next eighty years it passed through various hands until 1983, when it was sold by the Comtessa Alexandre de Castéja to the Menil Foundation collection in Texas, where it remains.

The identity of the artist who painted the copy which hangs in Dr. Johnson's House is unknown. David Minlore told Cecil Harmsworth that he was certain that it was by James Northcote (who certainly painted copies of numerous works by Reynolds), and his assessment is probably the origin of the statement "Attributed to James Northcote," which now appears on the picture frame. Modern expert opinion, however, rejects that attribution.[18] It is likely that a number of artists had access to the original painting, as it is well known that Reynolds encouraged his pupils to copy his work. There was also opportunity for copies to be made at a later date, as pictures which were exhibited at the British Institute for Promoting the Fine Arts (as the Reynolds original was in 1813 and 1823) were commonly left there for some weeks, in order to allow young painters to copy them. This explains the fact that at least five other copies of this particular portrait exist: the British Museum and the Victoria and Albert Museum both have copies, Tate Britain has two, and there is a miniature copy in the Hyde Collection at Harvard.

It seems likely that the painter of the picture which hangs in Johnson's House will remain unidentified, but what of the identity of the sitter? When the portrait was put up for sale in Paris by the Comtessa de Castéja in 1983, it was described in the sale catalogue as "Portrait de Frank Barber, serviteur du Docteur Samuel Johnson."[19] The Menil Foundation catalogue describes it more circumspectly as "A Young Black." Many writers have reproduced this picture, stating that the face is that of Francis Barber. John Wain, Walter

A Young Black (c. 1770), by Joshua Reynolds. A copy of this portrait hangs in Dr. Johnson's House, London. (Reproduced courtesy Menil Collection, Houston, Texas. Photograph by Hickey-Robertson, Houston)

Jackson Bate, and Jeffrey Meyers all do so in their biographies of Samuel Johnson, and Folarin Shyllon and Gretchen Gerzina do likewise in their studies of British black history.[20] Any Internet search for references to Francis Barber is likely to bring up this picture. Not everyone, however, has been convinced that the portrait is of Francis Barber. A note of caution was sounded one hundred years ago by Aleyn Lyell Reade, who wrote that the identification was "yet to be proved."[21]

The identification of the sitter as Francis Barber rests on two pieces of evidence. The first is an entry which appears in Joshua Reynolds's pocket book for 23 April 1767. It did not become public knowledge until 1865, when Charles Leslie and Tom Taylor published their *Life and Times of Sir Joshua Reynolds*, which reproduced many extracts from Reynolds's pocket books. In their printed list of sitters for April 1767 appears the name "Frank." Leslie and Taylor added after this entry a cautious suggestion: "(?Barber, Johnson's black servant)." But in 1899, when Algernon Graves and William Vine Cronin published their work, *A History of the Works of Sir Joshua Reynolds*, the tentative nature of the identification had vanished and they categorically described the portrait as being of "Francis Barber, Dr. Johnson's black servant."[22]

In fact the evidence of the pocket book is far from clear, for several reasons. The first is that Leslie and Taylor misread the entry, which reads not "Frank" but "Franks," as Nicholas Penny pointed out in 1986.[23] Penny suggested that it is a reference to the members of the Franks family, whom Reynolds was painting around that time, but it seems unlikely that any member of the Franks family would have been referred to simply as "Franks." Throughout, the pocket book entries meticulously use the correct title of the sitter: Mr., Mrs., Miss, Master, Captain, Sir, and so on. There were sixteen sittings for the Franks family paintings, and on each occasion the entry is for "Mr Franks," "Mrs Franks," or "Miss Franks." In any event, the paintings of members of the Franks family were completed and paid for in 1766, well before 23 April 1767.[24]

A reference to "Frank" seems more likely than the rather discourteous "Franks." It is possible that the entry is simply a slip of the pen and that "Frank" was intended. If this is the case, then it refers to someone in Reynolds's acquaintance who was referred to simply as "Frank," and Francis Barber remains a possible candidate. If it is a reference to Barber, it probably does indicate a sitting for a portrait. (The pocket books include social and business engagements as well as sittings, but it is unlikely that Reynolds would have had such an appointment with the servant of his old friend.)

The second clue regarding the identity of the subject comes from the description of the picture as it appeared in various exhibition catalogues. As noted above, the portrait was first owned by Sir George Beaumont, the

seventh baronet, who bought it in 1796, at the Greenwood's auction. (It was
described in the sale catalogue as "Study of a black man's head.")[25] Beaumont
was a wealthy collector and patron whose gift of paintings to the nation was
to form the basis of the National Gallery.[26] He was also a talented amateur
artist and a friend of Reynolds, who had painted his portrait. When the
British Institution for Promoting the Fine Arts was founded in 1805 he was
closely involved, serving as one of the Committee of Subscribers and one of
the first Directors, and in 1813 he helped to arrange a retrospective exhibition
of Reynolds's work at the Institution. Beaumont lent the portrait for display
in that exhibition, and it appears in the exhibition catalogue as "Portrait of a
Black Servant of Sir Joshua Reynolds."[27]

In this light it is very difficult to see how the portrait can be of Francis
Barber. Beaumont had known Reynolds well and was in a position to say
whether the picture was of his servant. As an organiser of the exhibition it is
unlikely that he would have permitted the catalogue entry to appear if he did
not believe it to be correct. Additional evidence supports this identification:
as noted earlier, James Northcote wrote that Reynolds portrayed his black
footman "in several pictures."[28] It seems most likely that the picture is indeed
of Reynolds's servant.

So what is the origin of the claim that the figure in the portrait is Francis
Barber? Its source can be traced to the catalogue of another exhibition, the
*Catalogue of the Art Treasures of the United Kingdom collected at Manchester
in 1857*. Here the painting was described as "A Negro. ? Frank Barber, Dr.
Johnson's Black Servant."[29] Even that identification (qualified as it was by a
question mark) was given with some reservations. George Scharf, the curator
of the exhibition, noted that "the pictures are all described under the names
given by the present owners." The owner at that time was another Sir George
Beaumont (the ninth baronet, born in 1828), nephew of the original owner,
who had died in 1827. In other words, the identification of the portrait as
being of Francis Barber was first made over fifty years after Barber's death by
an owner of the picture who had been born over twenty-five years after that
death. There is no reason to believe that his claim was true.

How much does it matter that the face in the picture is probably not
that of Francis Barber? Of course an authenticated portrait would be of
enormous interest, but the Reynolds picture and the story of Francis Barber
are both significant in their own right, irrespective of any link between them.
Of one thing we can be certain: the portrait is of a young black man who

lived in London in the mid eighteenth century. In spite of the best efforts of historians, the details of many such lives are likely to remain unknown. The Reynolds portrait, together with its numerous copies, provide a permanent reminder that a black community did exist and formed part of the social fabric of eighteenth-century Britain. It is particularly appropriate that a copy should hang in Dr. Johnson's House, which was home to one such young black man, the former slave Francis Barber.

There are no memorials to Barber, although perhaps the occasional passerby in Streatham wonders at the name of "Francis Barber Close." His legacy lies in his numerous descendants, but also in the story of one man's journey from Jamaican slavery to freedom in England. At its heart is the bond between Barber and Samuel Johnson. It was in many ways a father-son relationship, with all that encompasses in terms of intimacy, possessiveness, exasperation, and love. Johnson had an authoritarian side to his character, yet for the most part he treated Barber with respect and affection, providing him with a home, an education, and the means to live once he was gone. Barber regarded Johnson with honour, giving him support and companionship in the darkest of his often very dark days. Much of what each contributed to the other's life is unknowable to us, but in their actions we have the clearest possible indication of how each regarded the other. Samuel Johnson named Francis Barber his heir; Francis Barber named both his sons "Samuel."

Acknowledgments

This book has been a long time in the writing. My interest in the subject of slavery in Britain in the eighteenth century was first sparked by a talk given to the Johnson Society of London by Peter Street in 1999. I have learned a great deal about eighteenth-century life and literature in the congenial company of this Society. At a later stage my proposal for this book was awarded the Biographers' Club prize (now renamed the Tony Lothian prize). I am grateful to the Club and to its founder, Andrew Lownie, for the encouragement this provided.

Over the years I have spent many enjoyable hours in Dr. Johnson's House, where Francis Barber lived, and which is always a pleasure to visit. Natasha McEnroe, Stephanie Pickford, and Morwenna Rae (successive Curators of the House) and Celine McDaid (Deputy Curator) have assisted in many ways. It is a privilege to serve as a director of Dr. Johnson's House Trust, and I am grateful to my fellow directors and governors for allowing me to benefit from their expertise, and for permission to quote from the archives of the Trust. In Lichfield, Joanne Wilson, Museums and Heritage Officer at the Samuel Johnson Birthplace Museum, gave invaluable help, especially concerning Barber's later years.

I am grateful for the assistance of knowledgeable archivists and librarians at the following institutions: the Beinecke Rare Book and Manuscript Library, Yale University; the Bodleian Library, Oxford; the British Library; the Guildhall Library, London; the Heinz Archive and Library of the National Portrait Gallery; Hertfordshire Archives and Local Studies; Kent History and Library Centre; the Library of Congress; Lincoln's Inn Library; the London Library; London Metropolitan Archives; the National Archives, Kew; the National Maritime Museum, Greenwich; the New-York Historical Society; the library of Pembroke College, Oxford; the Royal Academy of

Arts; Senate House Library, University of London; the Society of Antiquaries of London; and the Society of Apothecaries.

I am indebted to all the writers listed in the bibliography, but Aleyn Lyell Reade demands particular mention. His *Johnsonian Gleanings*, published in eleven volumes between 1909 and 1952, are a remarkable achievement, and have been my constant source of reference. I have also made particular use of Marshall Waingrow's edition of *The Correspondence and Other Papers of James Boswell Relating to the Making of the 'Life of Johnson.'*

Some of the material in this book has been developed in presentations to well-informed audiences at the Friends of the Georgian Society of Jamaica; the Johnson Society of London; the Black Georgians study day at the Hunterian Museum; at Dr. Johnson's House; and at the annual meeting of The Johnsonians in New York. I thank the editors of the *Johnsonian News Letter*, the *New Rambler*, and *Editing Lives: Essays in Contemporary Textual and Biographical Studies in Honor of O M Brack, Jr.*, for allowing me to use in revised form material which first appeared in articles in those publications.

Many individuals have responded generously to queries or helped in other ways. I wish to thank Cedric Barber, James G. Basker, John Bathurst, Thomas F. Bonnell, the late O M Brack Jr., Trevor Burnard, John Davies, Catherine Dille, Charles R. Foy, William Jacob, Lyle Larsen, Sheila O'Connell, John Overholt, Julian Pooley, Nicholas Rogers, and Peter Sabor. Particular thanks go to James J. Caudle: chapter 6 is heavily dependent upon work on Edward Ferrand, on which we collaborated. I am especially grateful to my good friends Trevor Cooper and Gordon Turnbull, who both read the manuscript in full and made numerous helpful suggestions. At Yale University Press Eric Brandt, Chris Rogers, Erica Hanson, and Jeff Schier have been all that an author could hope for, combining enthusiasm with expertise. I wish to thank also the anonymous readers for the Press for their helpful comments.

The Fortunes of Francis Barber has not been written in the soft obscurities of retirement, or under the shelter of academick bowers. My day job is in maritime law, and I wish to express my appreciation to my colleagues at Stephenson Harwood, who have displayed interest in Francis Barber and Samuel Johnson in a manner which was both courteous and almost wholly convincing. For many years we were based in St. Paul's Churchyard, and my daily journey to work took me along Fleet Street, past the church of St.

Dunstan in the West, and up Ludgate Hill towards the Cathedral. For anyone interested in Francis Barber's London it is hard to imagine a greater piece of good fortune.

Family and friends have encouraged, supported, and endured nobly throughout. My late brother David took a keen interest in the early stages of the work; I like to think that he would have enjoyed the outcome. Perhaps one day Sarah and Rebecca will be equally interested. We have it on good authority that life has no pleasure higher or nobler than that of friendship: I should like to express my gratitude for many years of friendship to Monica Cooper, John Curtin, Nancy Johnson, Mike Murphy, Pip Murphy, Andy Roberts, Neil Roberts, Tracey Roberts, and Jennifer Ullman, who have all uncomplainingly heard a good deal about Francis Barber and Samuel Johnson. But my greatest debt is to Kate, without whom this book would not have been started, let alone finished.

Notes

Full details of all works cited in the notes by short title are given in the bibliography. Unless otherwise indicated, references to *Boswell's Life of Johnson* are to *Boswell's Life of Johnson*, ed. George Birkbeck Hill, revised by L. F. Powell, 6 vols. (Oxford: Clarendon Press, 1934–1964), and references to Hawkins, *Life of Johnson*, are to John Hawkins, *The Life of Samuel Johnson, LL.D.*, ed. O M Brack, Jr. (Athens and London: University of Georgia Press, 2009). References to Waingrow, *Correspondence*, are to *The Correspondence and Other Papers of James Boswell Relating to the Making of the Life of Johnson*, ed. Marshall Waingrow, 2d ed., corrected and enlarged (Edinburgh and New Haven: Edinburgh University Press and Yale University Press, 2001).

CHAPTER I. THE HOUSE IN GOUGH SQUARE

1. Sheila O'Connell, "Hitting the Headlines in Johnson's London," unpublished lecture delivered at Dr. Johnson's House, 18 February 2004. In *London 1753* O'Connell provides a vivid portrait of London as Francis Barber knew it. For Taylor, see 150, for Maclaine see 259–61, 263, and for Snell see 111–12.
2. Winder, *Bloody Foreigners*, 105.
3. *Evening Standard*, 9 February 2004, 15. Olaudah Equiano (c.1745–1797) was the author of *The Interesting Narrative of the Life of Olaudah Equiano, or Gustavus Vassa, the African* (London, 1789). Ignatius Sancho (c.1729–1780) was the author of the posthumously published *Letters of the Late Ignatius Sancho, an African* (London, 1782).
4. Hochschild, *Bury the Chains*, 143.
5. Wain, *Frank* (broadcast 1982, published 1984); Maureen Lawrence, *Resurrection* (unpublished play first performed 1996, winner of the LWT Plays on Stage Award for 1997); Martin, *Incomparable World* (1996); Phillips, *Foreigners* (2007).

CHAPTER 2. "THE DUNGHILL OF THE UNIVERSE"

My account of the Bathurst family and Barber's early years in Jamaica is derived from Reade, *Johnsonian Gleanings*, Pt II, and Larsen, *Dr. Johnson's Household*. For the background history of Jamaica and of slavery, I have made particular use of Dunn, *Sugar and Slaves*, Craton and Walvin, *A Jamaican Plantation*, Higman, *Jamaica Surveyed*, and Walvin, *Black Ivory*.

1. *Boswell's Life of Johnson*, I, 34.
2. Parish register of St. Mary's, Lichfield, for 7 September 1709, cited by Reade, *The Reades of Blackwood Hall*, 200.
3. Boswell's letter of 15 July 1786, with Barber's replies, is printed in Waingrow, *Correspondence*, 127–31, with detailed annotation. For the suggestion that the interview was conducted by Boswell in person see 128, n. 1.
4. Waingrow, *Correspondence*, 127.
5. Poor Law examination of Francis Barber, 4 October 1799, Samuel Johnson Birthplace Museum, Lichfield.
6. Waingrow, *Correspondence*, 127.
7. On slave families, see Walvin, *Black Ivory*, 171–84.
8. Deeds of sale August 1749 and 30 September 1749, Deed 137, the Jamaica Archives, cited by Larsen, *Dr. Johnson's Household*, 25, 135. I am grateful to Lyle Larsen for providing information about these deeds and copies of the texts.
9. Will of Richard Bathurst, 14 August 1756, The National Archives, PROB 11/824. The distinction between "negro" and "mulatto" in the West Indies is discussed by Winthrop Jordan in "American Chiaroscuro: The Status and Definition of Mulattoes in the British Colonies," 194–200.
10. Craton, *Searching for the Invisible Man*, 55.
11. Burnard, "Slave Naming Patterns."
12. Craton, *Searching for the Invisible Man*.
13. Reade, *The Reades of Blackwood Hall*.
14. Deed of sale, 23 September 1747, Deed 131, the Jamaica Archives, cited by Larsen, *Dr. Johnson's Household*, 25, 135.
15. Patterson, *The Sociology of Slavery*, 174–81.
16. My account of the early history of Jamaica is based on Dunn, *Sugar and Slaves*, esp. 147–65.
17. Burnard, "European Migration to Jamaica 1655–1780," 781.
18. *A Proclamation for the Encouraging of Planters in His Majesties Island of Jamaica in the West-Indies* (1661).
19. Walvin, *Black Ivory*, 5.

20. Larsen, *Dr. Johnson's Household*, 24; Reade, *Johnsonian Gleanings*, Pt II, 4.

21. *Calendar of State Papers, Colonial Series, America and West Indies*, Vol. 10, 1677–1680, 286, 406, and *Calendar of State Papers, Colonial Series, America and West Indies*, Vol. 13 (1689–1692), 471; Roby, *Members of the Assembly of Jamaica*, 41–42, 83–84.

22. Long, *History of Jamaica*, II, 485–92.

23. The figure of 1,020,000 is for disembarkations, 91 percent of which are documented, and 9 percent are estimates; see Eltis and Richardson, *Atlas of the Transatlantic Slave Trade*, Map 154, "Jamaica: African coastal origins of slaves and home ports of vessels carrying them, 1607–1857." The figure of 15.1 percent average mortality is taken from Map 120, "Slave mortality and voyage length for slaves arriving in Caribbean regions from Africa, 1701–1770."

24. Burnard, "European Migration to Jamaica 1655–1780," 772; Long, *History of Jamaica*, II, 79.

25. For the Jamaican slave laws see Dunn, *Sugar and Slaves*, 238–46; Smith, "The legal status of Jamaican slaves before the anti-slavery movement," and Gaspar, "Rigid and Inclement."

26. Anonymous [Edward Ward], *A Trip to Jamaica*, 14, 16.

27. Long, *History of Jamaica*, II, 74–79, 435.

28. See the extract from a plan of the Orange River estate reproduced by Higman in *Jamaica Surveyed*, 245.

29. Thistlewood, *In Miserable Slavery*, 287.

30. Larsen, *Dr. Johnson's Household*, 25.

31. My account of the experience of child slaves is based on Roughley, *The Jamaica Planter's Guide*, 103–27, Walvin, *Black Ivory*, and Teelucksingh, "The 'Invisible Child' in British West Indian Slavery."

32. Roughley, *The Jamaica Planter's Guide*, 16.

33. Chenoweth, "The Eighteenth-Century Climate of Jamaica," 54, Table 14.

34. The diaries have been edited by Douglas Hall and published as Thistlewood, *In Miserable Slavery*. My account of Thistlewood is based on Burnard, *Mastery, Tyranny and Desire*.

35. Thistlewood, *In Miserable Slavery*, 236–37.

36. Burnard, *Mastery, Tyranny and Desire*, 93, 106–15.

37. Diary entry for 31 October 1768, Thistlewood, *In Miserable Slavery*, 168.

38. Ibid., 250–51.

39. Ibid., 73.

40. Ibid., 73, 72.

41. Ibid., 79–80.

42. Ibid., 87.

43. Burnard, *Mastery, Tyranny and Desire*, 156.

44. Thistlewood, *In Miserable Slavery*, 72.

45. Long, *The History of Jamaica*, II, 487.

46. Burnard, *Mastery, Tyranny and Desire*, 29–34.

47. Johnson, *An Introduction to the Political State of Great Britain*, in Johnson, *Political Writings*, 137.

48. Baptism of Richard Bathurst, 20 June 1722, Register of baptisms, marriages and burials, St. Andrew, Jamaica, 1664 to 1807, I, 54 (scanned copy of the register viewed online at familysearch.org); Richard Bathurst to Samuel Johnson, 18 March 1757, printed in Harwood, *The History and Antiquities of the Church and City of Lichfield*, 451–52.

49. *Boswell's Life of Johnson*, IV, 28.

50. Waldstreicher, *Runaway America*, 144; Wise, *Though the Heavens May Fall*, 5–6; Cairns, "Knight v. Wedderburn," 244–46. For an account of visitors to Britain from the America colonies, many of whom brought slaves with them, see Flavell, *When London Was Capital of America*.

51. Anonymous, *A Trip Through Town*, 6.

52. Craton and Walvin, *A Jamaican Plantation*, 153, n. 62; Higman, *Jamaica Surveyed*, 122.

53. Dunn, *Sugar and Slaves*, 253.

54. Quoted by Walvin, *Black Ivory*, 190.

55. Craton and Walvin, *A Jamaican Plantation*, 139, 142 (favoured positions, financial provision); Dunn, *Sugar and Slaves*, 254 (baptism).

56. Marriage of Richard Bathurst and Katharine [Catharine] Phillips, 22 June 1721, and burial of Catharine Phillips, 31 October 1726, Register of baptisms, marriages and burials, St. Andrew, Jamaica, 1664 to 1807, I, 198, 281. The other children of Richard and Catharine Bathurst were Robert (baptised 10 September 1724, buried 29 June 1726) and Elizabeth (baptised 3 March 1726, buried 3 May 1731); see 54, 55, 281, 283. Scanned copies of the registers viewed online at familysearch.org.

57. Will of Richard Bathurst, 24 April 1754, The National Archives, PROB/11/824/149.

58. The possibility of Bathurst being Barber's father was first suggested by two dramatists. John Wain raised the idea in a BBC radio play broadcast in 1982 and published in 1984 (*Frank*, 30), as did Maureen Lawrence in her unpublished play *Resurrection* (first performed 1996). Jeffrey Meyers claims that

Barber "could conceivably have been the son of Bathurst" (*Samuel Johnson: The Struggle*, 8, 288) and James G. Basker argues that Barber was "most probably" Bathurst's son ("Johnson and Slavery," 39).

CHAPTER 3. A NEW NAME

1. Hawkins, *Life of Johnson*, 134–35; Wilson, *The History of the Middlesex Hospital*, xiv, 189, 191.
2. For the smells and sounds of London at this time, see Schwartz, *Daily Life in Johnson's London*, 3–30. The speech by Lord Tyrconnel is quoted by Schwartz at 21.
3. Burnard, "European Migration to Jamaica 1655–1780," Table I; Finlay and Shearer, "Population growth and suburban expansion," Table 1.
4. Quoted in Fryer, *Staying Power*, 10. For the black population in England in the sixteenth and seventeenth centuries, see 4–13.
5. *Daily Journal*, 5 April 1723, quoted in Equiano, *The Interesting Narrative*, ed. Sollors, 230.
6. Equiano, *The Interesting Narrative*, ed. Carretta, 85. (Unless otherwise indicated, all references to *The Interesting Narrative* are to the Carretta edition.)
7. *London Chronicle*, 19–22 October 1765.
8. Barker, *The African Link*, 34.
9. Walvin, *Black and White*, 46.
10. Chater, *Untold Histories*, 26. An earlier study had suggested a figure of at least 5,000 in London at any one time in the late eighteenth century; see Myers, *Reconstructing the Black Past*, 27.
11. Chater, *Untold Histories*, 27.
12. Norton, "The Fate of Some Black Loyalists of the American Revolution," 406, n. 11, citing lists in The National Archives, T 1/638 and T 1/643.
13. Chater, *Untold Histories*, 35; Gregory and Stevenson, *Britain in the Eighteenth Century*, 289; Finlay and Shearer, "Population growth and suburban expansion," Table 1.
14. Hawkins, *Life of Johnson*, 197.
15. Travis Glasson discusses the tensions within Anglicanism concerning the issue of baptism and the attitude to slavery in *Mastering Christianity*.
16. *Butts v. Penny* (1677) 2 Lev 201; 83 ER 518.
17. These entries from city of London parish registers now in London Metropolitan Archives are cited from "Guildhall Library Manuscripts Section, Black and Asian people discovered in records held by the

Manuscripts Section," online at http://www.history.ac.uk/gh/baentries. htm.

18. Quoted by Drescher, "Manumission in a Society without Slave Law," 95.

19. Equiano, *The Interesting Narrative*, 93–94.

20. Opinion of the Attorney-General and the Solicitor-General, 1729, printed in Walvin, *The Black Presence*, 94–95.

21. Baker, *The Law's Two Bodies*, 88.

22. *Pearne v. Lisle* (1749) Ambler 75; 27 ER 47.

23. Cooke, *The Life of Samuel Johnson, LL.D.*, 133.

24. Brack and Kelley, *Samuel Johnson's Early Biographers*, 91–108.

25. Chater, *Untold Histories*, 181–82. I am grateful to the Ven. Dr. William Jacob for guidance on baptismal practice in the eighteenth century.

26. Larsen, *Dr. Johnson's Household*, 25.

27. Reade, *Johnsonian Gleanings*, Pt II, 9–10.

28. Thomas Percy to James Boswell, 29 February 1788, Waingrow, *Correspondence*, 209.

29. Slater, *Charles Dickens*, 113, 116.

30. Waingrow, *Correspondence*, 127.

31. For Dr. Bathurst, see Ingledew, "Samuel Johnson's Jamaican Connections," 1–3, and Wiltshire, *Samuel Johnson in the Medical World*, 94–96.

32. Hawkins, *Life of Johnson*, 142–43.

33. Wilson, *The History of the Middlesex Hospital*, 190–91.

34. Wiltshire, *Samuel Johnson in the Medical World*, 112.

35. *Thraliana*, 184.

36. Piozzi, *Anecdotes*, 66. In 1762 Bathurst became an army doctor and sailed on the British expedition to attack the port of Havana in Cuba, the heart of Spanish power in the region. He died there in August of that year.

37. Samuel Johnson to George Hay, 9 November 1759, *The Letters of Samuel Johnson*, I, 187–88.

CHAPTER 4. JOHNSON

There are numerous biographies of Samuel Johnson. For the basic narrative of his life I have relied, in particular, on *Boswell's Life of Johnson;* Clifford, *Young Samuel Johnson* and *Dictionary Johnson;* DeMaria, Jr., *The Life of Samuel Johnson;* and Nokes, *Samuel Johnson: A Life.*

1. Anonymous [William Johnson Temple], *The Character of Doctor Johnson* (1792), quoted in *Dr Johnson: Interviews and Recollections*, 23–24.

2. Entry for 18 October 1773, in *The Journal of a Tour to the Hebrides, Boswell's Life of Johnson*, V, 329.

3. For the diagnosis of Tourette's syndrome, see T. J. Murray, "Dr. Samuel Johnson's Movement Disorder." Wiltshire reviews a number of suggested causes of Johnson's movement disorder in *Samuel Johnson in the Medical World*, 29–34.

4. Hawkins, *Memoirs*, I, 86.

5. *Boswell's Life of Johnson*, IV, 425. Johnson's manner of walking with his left arm under his chin is described by Hawkins in her *Memoirs*, I, 86.

6. Burney, *The Early Journals and Letters of Fanny Burney, Vol. II 1774–1777*, 225.

7. *Boswell's Life of Johnson*, I, 146–47; Ozias Humphry to William Humphry, 19 September 1764, quoted in *Johnsonian Miscellanies*, II, 400.

8. *Boswell's Life of Johnson*, I, 94; Boswell, *London Journal*, 220; Burney, *The Early Journals and Letters of Fanny Burney, Vol. III 1778–1779*, 73; Reynolds, "Recollections of Dr. Johnson," 281.

9. *Boswell's Life of Johnson*, I, 531.

10. Ibid.

11. Allen Reddick explains the nature of Johnson's false start in *The Making of Johnson's Dictionary*, 25–54.

12. Samuel Johnson to William Strahan, 1 November 1751, *The Letters of Samuel Johnson*, I, 50.

13. *Boswell's Life of Johnson*, V, 215.

14. Shaw, *Memoirs of the Life and Writings of the Late Dr. Samuel Johnson*, 34.

15. Samuel Johnson to Thomas Warton, 21 December 1754, *The Letters of Samuel Johnson*, I, 190.

16. Piozzi, *Anecdotes*, 114; Waingrow, *Correspondence*, 128. Barber elsewhere wrote that "at my coming to Live with [Johnson] I found that Mrs. Johnson was Dead and was Buried about a fortnight" (Francis Barber to James Boswell, 20 December 1789, Waingrow, *Correspondence*, 228). The burial took place on 26 March 1752 (Clifford, *Dictionary Johnson*, 98).

17. Piozzi, *Anecdotes*, 89.

18. Hawkins, *Life of Johnson*, 197.

19. *European Magazine*, 1798, 376, quoted in *Johnsonian Miscellanies*, II, 396.

20. Burney, *The Early Journals and Letters of Fanny Burney, Vol. III The Streatham Years: Part I, 1778–1779*, 255–56.

21. Samuel Johnson to Hester Maria Thrale, 29 July 1771, *The Letters of Samuel Johnson*, I, 378.

22. Piozzi, *Anecdotes*, 67.

23. The descriptions of Johnson are quoted from various sources by Rogers, *Johnson and Boswell: The Transit of Caledonia*, 99–100.

24. Waingrow, *Correspondence*, 128.

25. My account of the house and the garret is based on two papers by Natasha McEnroe, former curator of Dr. Johnson's House, "17, Gough Square," and "The Dictionary Garret: Anatomy of a Room."

26. *Boswell's Life of Johnson*, I, 188.

27. Steevens, "Anecdotes by George Steevens," 317.

28. Waingrow, *Correspondence*, 127–28.

29. Ibid., 128.

30. Samuel Johnson to Bennet Langton, 21 May 1775, *The Letters of Samuel Johnson*, II, 208.

31. Reddick, *The Making of Johnson's Dictionary*. On Barber, see especially 66–67 and 212.

32. Stephens, "Literacy in England, Scotland and Wales, 1500–1900," 555.

33. Johnson, review of Soame Jenyns, *A Free Inquiry into the Nature and Origin of Evil, Literary Magazine*, XIII, 15 April–15 May 1757, in Johnson, *A Commentary on Mr. Pope's Principles of Morality*, 397–432 at 410.

34. *Boswell's Life of Johnson*, I, 45.

35. Indenture between Peter Joye and William Savage, parson of St. Ann, Blackfriars, 22 February 1716, London Metropolitan Archives, MS 9192/1, 20, 513–16; Gillian Joye, "Peter Joye's Charity School, St. Ann, Blackfriars in the Eighteenth Century" (unpublished thesis, 1990, Guildhall Library) 53; *The Gazeteer and New Daily Advertiser*, 18 March 1766, 2.

36. Waingrow, *Correspondence*, 127.

37. Baptisms of Mary Coxeter (12 March 1739), Anne Coxeter (20 June 1741), and Thomas Coxeter (31 May 1744), Register of baptisms, marriages and burials, St. Anne, Blackfriars, 1710–1812, scanned copy online at ancestry. co.uk; *Boswell's Life of Johnson*, III, 158, n. 1; Waingrow, *Correspondence*, 129, n. 8; *The London Evening Post*, 25–28 April 1747, records the death of Thomas Coxeter at his home in Bridewell Precinct.

38. Glynn and Glynn, *The Life and Death of Smallpox*, 1; Davenport, Schwarz and Boulton, "The decline of adult smallpox," 1290.

39. I am grateful to Gordon Turnbull for a sight of his forthcoming article, "Samuel Johnson, Francis Barber," which establishes conclusively the whereabouts of the school run by Desmoulins. It had previously been

wrongly thought that Desmoulins taught at the Birmingham Free Grammar School, and that Barber attended that school; see Joseph Hill and Robert K. Dent, *Memorials of the Old Square* (Birmingham: Achilles Taylor, 1897), 38–39, quoted by Reade, *The Reades of Blackwood Hill*, 230.

CHAPTER 5. SERVANT OR SLAVE?

1. Meldrum, *Domestic Service and Gender 1660–1750*, 14.
2. White, *London in the Eighteenth Century*, 228.
3. Meldrum, *Domestic Service and Gender 1660–1750*, 15.
4. Hawkins, *Life of Johnson*, 197.
5. Meteorological Journalist [John Holt], "An Excursion from Walton to London," *Gentleman's Magazine* 1793, 619–20.
6. Waingrow, *Correspondence*, 128. For Deyman, see Caudle and Bundock, "A newly identified apothecary," Appendix. In the replies to his questionnaire Boswell took down the name as "Diamond."
7. Davis, *Thomas Percy: A Scholar–Cleric in the Age of Johnson*, 39.
8. On Levett and Williams, see Larsen, *Dr. Johnson's Household*, passim.
9. *Gentleman's Magazine*, 55 (1785), Pt 1, 101.
10. Ibid.
11. Francis Burney to Susanna Elizabeth Burney, post 16–21 September 1778, Burney, *The Early Journals and Letters of Fanny Burney, Vol. III The Streatham Years: Part I, 1778–1779*, 48.
12. Hawkins, *Life of Johnson*, 195.
13. Baretti, MS note on *Piozzi Letters*, quoted in *Boswell's Life of Johnson*, II, 99, n. 2. To similar effect is Boswell, journal entry for 18 April 1778, *Boswell in Extremes*, 301.
14. Hawkins, *Life of Johnson*, 195–96.
15. Ibid., 245–46.
16. Paley, Malcolmson, and Hunter, "Parliament and Slavery, 1660–c.1710." In 1764 one unknown member of the House of Lords proposed a clause regulating "in what Manner . . . Slaves . . . may be used in England," but the proposed measure was never considered as Parliament was prorogued shortly afterwards; see Paley et al., 258.
17. Baker, *An Introduction to English Legal History*, 468–72.
18. John Rushworth, *Historical Collections* (London, 1680), quoted by Fryer, *Staying Power*, 113.

19. *Smith v. Browne and Cooper*, 2 Salk. 666, 90 ER 1172 at 1173.

20. *Pearne v. Lisle* (1749), Ambler 75, 27 ER 47 at 48.

21. *Shanley v. Harvey* (1762), 2 Eden 125, 28 ER 844.

22. *The London Gazette* 1694, quoted in Shyllon, *Black People in Britain*, 11.

23. Shyllon, *Black People in Britain*, 14. For other instances of the use of slave collars, see Fryer, *Staying Power*, 22. A clear illustration of such a collar from about 1700 appears in the portrait of James Drummond, second titular Duke of Perth, by Sir John Baptiste de Medina (National Galleries of Scotland).

24. Shyllon, *Black People in Britain*, 13.

25. The figure of forty is derived from the lists in Myers, *Reconstructing the Black Past*, 58 and 146, and Chater, *Untold Histories*, 86 and 98, taking into account the overlap between the two. For the records of slave sales in Scotland see Whyte, *Scotland and the Abolition of Black Slavery, 1756–1838*, 14.

26. *The Slave, Grace*, 2 Hagg. 94 at 105; ER 179 at 182–83.

27. Walvin, *Black and White*, 50.

28. See the entries for those dates in Johnson's diaries in Johnson, *Diaries, Prayers, and Annals*.

29. Will of Richard Bathurst, 24 April 1754, The National Archives, PROB/11/824/149.

30. For discussion of master–servant relations and the role of the head of the household, see Hecht, *The Domestic Servant Class in Eighteenth-Century England*, 71–101, and Meldrum, *Domestic Service and Gender 1660–1750*, 34–67.

31. J. Dod and R. Cleaver, *A Godly Forme of Household Government* (London, 1612), quoted by Meldrum, *Domestic Service and Gender 1660–1750*, 37; William Darrell, *The Gentleman Instructed, in the Conduct of a Virtuous and Happy Life* (1727), quoted in Hecht, *The Domestic Servant Class in Eighteenth-Century England*, 75.

32. Tadmor, *Family and Friends in Eighteenth-Century England*.

33. Entry for 13 July 1755 in Johnson, *Diaries, Prayers, and Annals*, 57.

34. Patrick Delaney, *Twenty Sermons upon Social Duties* (1750), quoted in Hecht, *The Domestic Servant Class in Eighteenth-Century England*, 72.

35. *Rambler* No. 68, Johnson, *The Rambler*, III, 360–61.

36. Hoole, *Journal Narrative Relative to Johnson's Last Illness*, n.p., entry for 5 December 1784. A lucid introduction to Johnson's Christian beliefs is Suarez, "Johnson's Christian Thought."

37. Johnson, *Diaries, Prayers, and Annals*, 294–95.

CHAPTER 6. AN APOTHECARY IN CHEAPSIDE

My discussion of Edward Ferrand in this chapter is heavily indebted to collaborative work with James J. Caudle, who identified Ferrand as the apothecary whose name Boswell wrote as Farren. This collaboration resulted in two publications, Caudle and Bundock, *The Runaway and the Apothecary*, and Caudle and Bundock, "A Newly Identified Apothecary in Boswell's *Life of Johnson*." I gratefully acknowledge my debt to James Caudle's research skills and knowledge of eighteenth-century history.

1. Samuel Johnson to Lewis Paul, Autumn 1756, *The Letters of Samuel Johnson*, I, 115, 145. Barber told Boswell that he left "about 1757;" see Waingrow, *Correspondence*, 127.

2. Waingrow, *Correspondence*, 127; Samuel Johnson to George Hay, 9 November 1759, *The Letters of Samuel Johnson*, I, 188.

3. The date of his death is unknown. The parish register for St. Mary Magdalene Church, Lincoln, now in Lincolnshire Record Office, shows that Bathurst was buried there on 21 April 1755. I am grateful to Lynda Hotchkiss of the Lincolnshire County Council Genealogical Research Service for locating this record.

4. Will of Richard Bathurst, 24 April 1754, The National Archives, PROB/11/824/149.

5. Reade, *Johnsonian Gleanings*, Pt II, 3, note.

6. Waingrow, *Correspondence*, 127.

7. Several runaway advertisements are reproduced in File and Power, *Black Settlers in Britain 1555–1958*, Figs 10.1–10.6.

8. *Public Advertiser*, 13 November 1761.

9. *Daily Advertiser*, 14 and 15 February 1757. The advertisements were discovered by Betty Rizzo; see "The Elopement of Francis Barber."

10. Waingrow, *Correspondence*, 127.

11. For a full account of Ferrand, see Caudle and Bundock, "A Newly Identified Apothecary in Boswell's *Life of Johnson*."

12. Mortimer, *The Universal Director*, 57.

13. For Hingeston, see Society of Apothecaries Court Minute Book, 1745–1767, 68, 187v. For Spalding, see ibid., 116v. All Court Minute books referred to in this chapter are held at the Worshipful Society of Apothecaries of London.

14. Will of Edward Ferrand, 28 April 1767, The National Archives, PROB 11/946/294.

15. For his appointment to the committee which managed the Physic Garden, see Court Minute Book, 1745–1767, 134, 147v, 158v, 177v, 197v, and 205.

16. Ibid., 1745–1767, 127.

17. Ibid., 196–97; Court Minute Book, 1767–1778, 1, 28.

18. Bannerman, *Registers of St. Mary Le Bow, Cheapside,* 62–63.

19. Ferrand's charitable activities are discussed in Caudle and Bundock, "A Newly Identified Apothecary in Boswell's *Life of Johnson.*"

20. Wall, Cameron, and Underwood, *A History of the Worshipful Society of Apothecaries of London Vol. I, 1617–1815,* 187; Court Minute Book, 1745–1767, 19v.

21. Court Minute Book, 1745–1767, 136.

22. Ibid., 139v–41.

23. Society of Apothecaries Rough Court Minute Book, 1776–1783 [n.p.], Special Court of Assistants, 14 January 1783.

24. On the different kinds and conditions of apprenticeship, see George, *London Life in the Eighteenth Century,* 221–61.

25. Quoted in Corfield, "From Poison Peddlers to Civic Worthies," 5.

26. Bate, *Samuel Johnson,* 326.

27. Court Minute Book, 1745–1767, 116v.

28. Wall, Cameron, and Underwood, *A History of the Worshipful Society of Apothecaries of London,* 78.

29. For Satia see Sherwood, "Blacks in the Gordon Riots," Aldous, *My Ancestors Were Freemen of the City of London,* 30–31, and Chater, *Untold Histories,* 231–32.

30. The proclamation is set out in Walvin, *The Black Presence,* 65.

31. Waingrow, *Correspondence,* 127.

CHAPTER 7. THE *STAG*

For the background to Barber's naval service I have relied on two books by N. A. M. Rodger: *The Wooden World* and *The Command of the Ocean.* On the operations of the press gangs, I have referred to Nicholas Rogers, *The Press Gang.*

1. *Boswell's Life of Johnson,* II, 438.

2. *Boswell's Life of Johnson,* III, 266 ("abhorrence"); *Boswell's Life of Johnson,* II, 438 ("gaol").

3. *Boswell: The Ominous Years,* 271–72.

4. Wain, *Samuel Johnson,* 267; Jones, "Barber, Francis." For similar comments, see Bate, *Samuel Johnson,* 326, and Clifford, *Dictionary Johnson,* 201.

5. Tobias Smollett to John Wilkes, 16 March 1759, *The Letters of Tobias Smollett*, 75.

6. Hoare, *Memoirs of Granville Sharp, Esq*, 168.

7. For a detailed modern treatment of the press gang see Rogers, *The Press Gang*.

8. Rodger, *The Wooden World*, 167.

9. Gradish, *The Manning of the British Navy During the Seven Years' War*, 212. On the difficulty of interpreting the recruitment figures, see Rodger, *The Wooden World*, 145–49.

10. Muster book of the *Princess Royal*, The National Archives, ADM 36/6541, 127.

11. Waingrow, *Correspondence*, 127.

12. Myers, *Reconstructing the Black Past*, 74.

13. Morgan, "Black Experiences in Britain's Maritime World," 131, n. 25.

14. Foy, "Uncovering Hidden Lives: Developing a Database of Mariners in the Black Atlantic"; Foy, "Ports of Slavery, Ports of Freedom." I am grateful to Charles Foy for the provision of additional information.

15. Lewis, *A Social History of the Navy 1793–1815*, 129.

16. Carretta, *Equiano the African*, 74–75.

17. Rodger, *The Wooden World*, 159.

18. Carretta, *Equiano the African*, 86–88; Rodger, *The Wooden World*, 161.

19. Rodger, *The Wooden World*, 159.

20. Gradish, *The Manning of the British Navy During the Seven Years' War*, 73; The National Archives, ADM 36/6755, 1. The figure is the same throughout Barber's naval career.

21. White, *London in the Eighteenth Century*, 234.

22. Chater, *Untold Histories*, 85, 98.

23. My account of Equiano's naval career is derived from Equiano, *The Interesting Narrative*, and Carretta, *Equiano the African*.

24. Equiano, *The Interesting Narrative*, 139.

25. For the incidents in Savannah see Equiano, *The Interesting Narrative*, 139–41, 158, 159.

26. Ibid., 164.

27. Muster book of the *Golden Fleece*, The National Archives, ADM 36/7153, 27; Muster book of the *Princess Royal*, The National Archives, ADM 36/6540, 178.

28. Rodger, *The Command of the Ocean*, 220–23.

29. Lyon, *The Sailing Navy List*, 33.

30. The National Archives, ADM 36/6541, 127, ADM 36/6542, 32 (date of discharge). The log of Captain Tindal, Captain of the *Stag*, records that men were received on board from the *Princess Royal* on both 18 and 21 December; see The National Archives, ADM 51/894, Part 2.

31. Lyon, *The Sailing Navy List*, 83.

32. Muster book of the *Stag*, 14 February 1759, The National Archives, ADM 36/6755, 14.

33. He was described as "a sickly lad of delicate frame" (Tobias Smollett to John Wilkes, 16 March 1759, *The Letters of Tobias Smollett*, 75) and, at a much later date, as "low of stature" (Meteorological Journalist [John Holt], "An Excursion from Walton to London," 619–20).

34. Quoted in Gradish, *The Manning of the British Navy During the Seven Years' War*, 74.

35. Rodger, *The Wooden World*, 80.

36. Ibid., 212.

37. Log of Captain Tindal, The National Archives, ADM 51/894, Part 2.

38. Lloyd, *The British Seaman 1200–1860*, 219.

39. The National Archives, ADM 36/6755, 49, 70, 85, 101, 115. I have not been able to account for Barber's whereabouts from 3 to 14 March 1759, but he then reappears in the muster books of the *Princess Royal*, with a date of entry and appearance as 14 March 1759 from "Nore Stag," and is discharged for victualling (meaning that the *Princess Royal* was no longer responsible for providing his food and drink) on 28 March, "Lent Raven" (muster books of HMS *Princess Royal*, The National Archives, ADM 36/6541, 315 and ADM 36/6542, 170).

40. Lyon, *The Sailing Navy List;* Admiralty order to Captain Long of the *Raven*, 20 March 1759, The National Archives, ADM 2/82, 338; captain's log for the period April–June 1759, The National Archives, ADM 51/772, Part 6.

41. Captain's log of Captain Henry Angel, 31 May 1759, The National Archives, ADM 51/894, Part 2. The prize money was shared out on 2 April 1760; see Captain Angel's log for that date.

42. Tobias Smollett to John Wilkes, 16 March 1759, *The Letters of Tobias Smollett*, 75; Samuel Johnson to George Hay, 9 November 1759, *The Letters of Samuel Johnson*, I, 188.

43. For example, Admiralty Pay Book, HMS *Stagg*, 1 September 1759–29 February 1760, The National Archives, ADM 32/169, shows that when Barber was paid gross wages of £6 3s 6d on 14 February 1761, 9s 6d was deducted for tobacco.

44. The muster book of the *Raven* shows him as discharged into the *Stag* on 14 July (The National Archives, ADM 36/6435, 186). But Commander Long's log for 15 July records, "We anchored in the Downes . . . & found lying there . . . the Stagg" (The National Archives, ADM 51/772, Part 6).

45. Middleton, *The Bells of Victory*, 107–8; Corbett, *England in the Seven Years' War*, II, 17–70.

46. Clowes, *The Royal Navy*, III, 223; Log of Captain Angel, The National Archives, ADM 51/894. For William Boys, see Rodger, *The Wooden World*, 53.

47. Log of Captain Angel, 17 and 18 October 1759, The National Archives, ADM 51/894, Part 2.

48. Log of Captain Angel, 18 October 1759, The National Archives, ADM 51/894, Part 2.

49. Middleton, *The Bells of Victory*, 136; Corbett, *England in the Seven Years' War*, 47.

50. Middleton, *The Bells of Victory*, 142–45.

51. Muster books of the *Stag*, The National Archives, ADM 36/6756, 93, 111.

52. Letter from Captain Angel to John Clevland, 8 August 1760, Captain's letters 1758 to 1761, The National Archives, ADM 1/1442, Part 8. Barber told Boswell that his naval service continued until three days before George II died (which occurred on 25 October 1760); see Waingrow, *Correspondence*, 127, 129, n. 13. However, the naval records are clear and are to be preferred to Barber's memory on this point.

53. Tobias Smollett to John Wilkes, 16 March 1759, *The Letters of Tobias Smollett*, 75.

54. For Johnson's relationship with Wilkes, see Liebert, *The Bear and the Phoenix*.

55. Tobias Smollett to John Wilkes, 24 March 1759, *The Letters of Tobias Smollett*, 76.

56. Tobias Smollett to John Wilkes, 1 April 1759, *The Letters of Tobias Smollett*, 77.

57. Samuel Johnson to George Hay, 9 November 1759, *The Letters of Samuel Johnson*, I, 187–88.

58. Waingrow, *Correspondence*, 127.

59. *Boswell's Life of Johnson*, I, 348.

60. Wain, *Samuel Johnson*, 267; Jones, "Barber, Francis."

61. Middleton, *The Bells of Victory*, 109–10. Johnson was well aware of the large numbers who died from disease; see *Thoughts on the Late Transactions respecting Falkland's Islands* (1771), in Johnson, *Political Writings*, 346–86 at 370–71.

62. Samuel Johnson to Lucy Porter, 9 August 1759, *The Letters of Samuel Johnson*, I, 187.

CHAPTER 8. "A RACE NATURALLY INFERIOR"

1. *Johsonian Miscellanies*, II, 416, 418.
2. Boswell, *London Journal 1762–1763*, 229.
3. *James Boswell's Life of Johnson: An Edition of the Original Manuscript*, Vol. I, 273.
4. *New Monthly Magazine*, Vol. X (July–December 1818), 386.
5. Quoted by Hecht, *Domestic Servant Class*, 127–28.
6. *London Chronicle*, 16–18 February 1764, 166.
7. Quoted in Gerzina, *Black London*, 35.
8. Ibid., 24.
9. John Fielding, *Penal Laws* (1768), quoted in Walvin, *The Black Presence*, 66.
10. *Thraliana*, I, 475.
11. Lambert, *Edmund Burke of Beaconsfield*, 69.
12. Northcote, *Life of Sir Joshua Reynolds*, I, 185–86, 204.
13. The picture was presumably painted in the early 1840s, as it was first exhibited in 1845; see Mitchell, *Picturing the Past*, 184. The painting is not from life: James E. Doyle (1822–1892) was born after all those in the painting had died, but portraits of all the subjects (except the black servant) had circulated widely. For the occasion when Barber served at Joshua Reynolds's house, see Frances Reynolds, "Recollections of Dr. Johnson" [1831], in *Johnsonian Miscellanies*, II, 276.
14. The account that follows is from Northcote, *Life of Sir Joshua Reynolds*, I, 204–6.
15. *Idler* 82, 10 November 1759; Johnson, The *Idler and the Adventurer*, 254–58 at 256–57.
16. Frances Reynolds, *An Enquiry Concerning the Principles of Taste*, 25–27. For Johnson's views on *An Enquiry*, see ii–iv.
17. My account of the development of theories of race is based on Hudson, "From 'Nation' to 'Race' "; Eze, *Race and the Enlightenment;* and Kitson, " 'Candid Reflections.' "
18. Goldsmith, *A History of The Earth and Animated Nature* (1774) in *Works of Oliver Goldsmith* VI, 86–87, II, 94. Goldsmith's views are discussed by Wheeler in *The Complexion of Race*, 180–81.
19. *St. James's Chronicle*, 8 June 1787.

20. Barker, *The African Link*, 24.

21. Quoted by Pittock, *James Boswell*, 28.

22. *Boswell for the Defence 1769–1774*, xvi. On Boswell's support for the oppressed see Pittock, *James Boswell*, 27–29.

23. Clarkson, *History of the Rise, Progress, and Accomplishment of the Abolition of the African Slave-Trade*, I, 252–53. According to Clarkson, the "strong expressions" were: "Mr. Boswell, after saying the planters would urge that the Africans were made happier by being carried from their own country to the West Indies, observed, 'Be it so. But we have no right to make people happy against their will' " (253).

24. Boswell, *No Abolition of Slavery*, lines 243–48.

25. For some instances from the 1790s, see Brady, *James Boswell: The Later Years*, 464–65.

26. See, for example, 21 March 1772, "Frank and I were pleased to renew our old acquaintance" (*Boswell for the Defence*, 40); 29 May 1783, "I then gave Frank a crown and bid him drink his master's health, or take good care of him" (*Boswell, The Applause of the Jury*, 154). See also the correspondence between Boswell and Barber quoted in chapter 13 below.

27. Francis Barber to James Boswell, 7 January 1786, Waingrow, *Correspondence*, 107; Boswell, *The Correspondence of James Boswell with David Garrick, Edmund Burke, and Edmond Malone*, 282, n. 5.

28. Francis Barber to James Boswell, 2 April 1788, and James Boswell to Francis Barber, 11 April 1788, Waingrow, *Correspondence*, 215–16.

29. *Boswell's Life of Johnson*, IV, 404; I, 237; III, 222.

30. Ibid., I, 239, n. 1.

31. Ibid., IV, 401 (December 1784). Boswell also published in his *Life of Johnson* several of Johnson's affectionate letters to Barber; see *Boswell's Life of Johnson*, II, 62–63, 115–16.

32. Ibid., III, 200–201.

33. Johnson, "The Life of Admiral Drake," *Gentleman's Magazine* 1740, in *Early Biographical Writings*, 37–66, at 38.

34. I owe this point to James G. Basker, "Johnson and Slavery," 37. My discussion of Johnson and slavery is indebted to a series of articles on the subject by Basker: "Samuel Johnson and the African-American Reader," " 'The Next Insurrection': Johnson, Race and Rebellion," "Intimations of Abolitionism in 1759: Johnson, Hawkesworth and *Oroonoko*," "Multicultural Perspectives: Johnson, Race and Gender," "Johnson, Boswell, and the Abolition of Slavery," and "Johnson and Slavery."

35. Johnson, *An Introduction to the Political State of Great Britain* (1756), in Johnson, *Political Writings*, 137.

36. For the Associates of Dr. Bray, see Pennington, "Thomas Bray's associates," and Glasson, *Mastering Christianity*.

37. Samuel Johnson to William Drummond, 13 August 1766, *The Letters of Samuel Johnson*, I, 268–71.

38. Maurice J. Quinlan, "Dr. Franklin Meets Dr. Johnson"; letter from Benjamin Franklin to Deborah Franklin, 27 June 1760, *The Papers of Benjamin Franklin*, Vol. 9, 173–75. For a full discussion of Franklin's complex attitudes towards slavery see Waldstreicher, *Runaway America*.

39. Johnson, *The Idler and Adventurer*, 252–54 at 253.

40. Johnson, Introduction to *The World Displayed* [1759], in *Samuel Johnson's Prefaces and Dedications*, 216–37 at 227.

41. Johnson, *The Idler and Adventurer*, 269–72 at 270.

42. *Critical Review*, 7 (December 1759), 480–86; Basker, "Intimations of Abolitionism in 1759: Johnson, Hawkesworth and *Oroonoko*."

43. For details of the slave revolts and their reporting, see Basker, " 'The Next Insurrection': Johnson, Race and Rebellion;" for the *Somerset* case, see chapter 10 below; and on the *Zong* see Walvin, *The Zong*.

44. Samuel Johnson to William Drummond, 13 August 1766, *The Letters of Samuel Johnson*, I, 269.

45. *Boswell's Life of Johnson*, V, 20.

46. Johnson, *A Journey to the Western Islands of Scotland*, 44. For Johnson's attitudes towards other cultures see Curley, *Samuel Johnson and the Age of Travel*, especially 17, 84–85, 105, 231.

47. Leslie and Taylor, *Life and Times of Sir Joshua Reynolds*, II, 460.

48. Introduction to *The World Displayed*, in *Samuel Johnson's Prefaces and Dedications*, 227; Johnson, *A Voyage to Abyssinia*, 3–4. For discussion of Johnson's attitude to imperialism, see Hudson, *Samuel Johnson and the Making of Modern England*, 170–220, and Greene, *Evaluating Empire and Confronting Colonialism in Eighteenth-Century Britain*, 16–17, 93–95.

49. Piozzi, *Anecdotes*, 131, 111–12, 130.

50. *Rambler* 14, 5 May 1750, Johnson, *The Rambler*, III, 75.

CHAPTER 9. "THIS IS YOUR SCHOLAR!"

1. *Boswell's Life of Johnson*, II, 4–5.

2. "Vicinus," "Bishop-Stortford School destroyed; its Library preserved." My account of the school is based on this article, on *A History of Hertfordshire*

(Victoria County History), II, 81–82, and III, 294, and on Minute book of the Trustees of the Stortford Charity—extracts relating to the school, Hertfordshire Archives and Local Studies, D/P 21 29/33 (cited below as "Minute book").

3. *St. James's Chronicle*, 14–17 November 1767.

4. Letter from L. Pigott to Trustees of the Stortford Charity, November 1767 (date illegible, but after 25 November), Hertfordshire Archives, D/P 21 25/1.

5. *St. James's Chronicle*, 1–3 December 1767 and 8–10 December 1767.

6. Samuel Johnson to Joseph Smith, 1 March 1770, and to Francis Barber, 25 September 1770 and 7 December 1770, *The Letters of Samuel Johnson*, I, 334, 350, 353.

7. Thomas Percy to James Boswell, 29 February 1788, Waingrow, *Correspondence*, 209; *James Boswell's Life of Johnson: An Edition of the Original Manuscript*, Vol. 1, 293. In the manuscript, Boswell noted that Johnson's "smile of approbation" at his servant's Latin occurred after Barber "had been at a school in the country." Boswell at first placed the incident in 1763, but later deleted the passage, possibly recognising that it must have occurred after Barber's time in Bishop's Stortford.

8. Samuel Johnson to Francis Barber, 28 May 1768, *The Letters of Samuel Johnson*, I, 315.

9. Undated letter from Trustees, Hertfordshire Archives, D/P 21 25/1, calling a meeting for 29 July 1769; Minute book, 29 July, 4 September, and 26 December 1769.

10. *St. James's Chronicle*, 26–28 December 1769.

11. Tompson, *Classics or Charity?*, 31.

12. Samuel Johnson to Francis Barber, 25 September 1770, *The Letters of Samuel Johnson*, I, 350.

13. *Boswell's Life of Johnson*, III, 385.

14. Samuel Johnson to Hester Thrale, 14 November 1778, *The Letters of Samuel Johnson*, III, 140.

15. Samuel Johnson to Francis Barber, 7 December 1770, *The Letters of Samuel Johnson*, I, 353.

16. Pye, "John Phillips—An Eighteenth-Century Hatter."

17. Hecht, *The Domestic Servant Class in Eighteenth-Century England*, 99.

18. Quinlan, "Dr. Franklin Meets Dr. Johnson"; Bundock, "The Making of Johnson's *Prayers and Meditations*," 86–87.

19. Johnson, *Diaries, Prayers and Annals*, 17.

20. Tompson, *Classics or Charity?*, 31–32.

21. Cooke, *The Life of Samuel Johnson, LL.D.* [1785], in *The Early Biographies of Samuel Johnson*, 91–135 at 133.

22. For Quaque see Glasson, *Mastering Christianity*, 171–95. James G. Basker first suggested that Johnson might have had the example of Quaque in mind; see Basker, "Johnson and Slavery," 46.

23. *London Chronicle*, 18–20 July 1765.

24. For a full account of such missionary activities, see Andrews, *Native Apostles*.

25. *St. James's Chronicle*, 22–25 July 1769.

26. Chapman, "The Formal Parts of Johnson's Letters," 151.

27. For a full account of Hawkins's life see Davis, *A Proof of Eminence*.

28. Burney, *The Early Journals and Letters of Fanny Burney, Vol. III The Streatham Years: Part I, 1778–1779*, 76.

29. Hawkins, *Life of Johnson*, 197–98.

30. Ibid., 198, note.

31. Minute book, entry for [?]1 January 1770.

32. Samuel Johnson to Joseph Smith, 1 March 1770, *The Letters of Samuel Johnson*, I, 334.

33. Samuel Johnson to Hester Thrale, 20 June 1771, *The Letters of Samuel Johnson*, I, 364.

34. *Boswell for the Defence 1769–1774*, 40.

CHAPTER 10. SLAVERY ON TRIAL

1. McGuffie, *Samuel Johnson in the British Press*.

2. *Town and Country Magazine*, April 1771, 184.

3. Samuel Johnson to George Hay, 9 November 1759, *The Letters of Samuel Johnson*, I, 187–88.

4. *The London Packet, or New Evening Post*, 3–5 July 1771.

5. Samuel Johnson to Hester Thrale, 20 June 1771, *The Letters of Samuel Johnson*, I, 364.

6. *Aris's Birmingham Gazette*, 11 November 1771.

7. *Morning Chronicle and London Advertiser*, 28 May 1773.

8. My account of Strong's case is based on Hoare, *Memoirs of Granville Sharp*, and Granville Sharp, "An Account of the Occasion which compelled Granville Sharp to study Law and undertake the Defence of Negro Slaves in England," Gloucestershire Record Office, D 3549.

9. Hoare, *Memoirs of Granville Sharp*, 36.

10. Sharp, "An Account," f. 4.

11. Sharp, *A Representation of the Injustice and Dangerous Tendency of Tolerating Slavery, or of Admitting the Least Claim to Private Property in the Persons of Men, in England* (London, 1769).

12. The account I give here of the *Somerset* case is based on the more detailed consideration in my article "Slavery on Trial." Steven M. Wise has published a full discussion of the case in *Though the Heavens May Fall*.

13. Adams, "Dido Elizabeth Belle"; Minney, "The Search for Dido"; Wise, *Though the Heavens May Fall*, 78–79.

14. This quotation is taken from a transcript of part of the trial, "Case involving James Sommersett, a negro, in Court of King's Bench, 1772," n.p., f. 11, in the Granville Sharp collection of the New-York Historical Society, which appears to be a verbatim report. Unless otherwise indicated, other quotations from counsels' arguments are taken from Lofft, *Reports of Cases Adjudged in the Court of King's Bench*. Lofft's note of the arguments is clearly not verbatim but seems to have been regarded as reliable by Francis Hargrave, one of Somerset's counsel; see Hargrave, *A Complete Collection of State-Trials*, 339.

15. "Case involving James Sommersett, a negro, in Court of King's Bench, 1772," f. 38.

16. Lofft, *Reports of Cases Adjudged in the Court of King's Bench*, 19.

17. Wise, *Though the Heavens May Fall*, 209.

18. *Middlesex Journal*, 23 June 1772, quoted by Shyllon, *Black Slaves in Britain*, 110; *London Packet*, 26–29 June 1772, quoted by Hecht, *Continental and Colonial Servants*, 49.

19. Schama, *Rough Crossings*, 63.

20. Burke, *A Letter to the Sheriffs of Bristol* (1777), quoted by Vincent Carretta, introduction to Cugoano, *Thoughts and Sentiments on the Evil of Slavery*, xi–xii.

21. Quoted by Wiecek, "*Somerset:* Lord Mansfield and the Legitimacy of Slavery," 115–16, n. 105. For newspaper coverage in the colonies of the *Somerset* case, see Blumrosen and Blumrosen, *Slave Nation*, 277.

22. *Morison's Dictionary of Decisions 1540–1808*, XXXIII, 4545; Hailes, *Decisions of the Lords of Council and Session from 1766 to 1791*, 776–80. See Cairns, "Knight v. Wedderburn," and Cairns, "The Definition of Slavery in Eighteenth-Century Thinking."

23. Quoted by Cairns, "The Definition of Slavery," 80.

24. Samuel Johnson to James Boswell, 2 July 1776, *The Letters of Samuel Johnson*, II, 349.
25. John Maclaurin, *Additional Information for Joseph Knight, a Negro of Africa, Pursuer; against John Wedderburn of Ballandean, Esq; Defender* (20 April 1776), 41–44.
26. Samuel Johnson to James Boswell 6 July 1776, *The Letters of Samuel Johnson*, II, 349–50.
27. Samuel Johnson to James Boswell, 22 July 1777. *The Letters of Samuel Johnson*, III, 42.
28. *Boswell in Extremes*, 182–83.
29. Boswell, *The Life of Samuel Johnson* (1791), I, 589, n. 4.
30. Pottle, *The Literary Career of James Boswell*, 168, 212; Brady, *James Boswell: The Later Years 1769–1795*, 478; *James Boswell's Life of Johnson: An Edition of the Original Manuscript*, Vol. 3, xvi, 145–47; Boswell, *The Life of Samuel Johnson* (2d ed., 1793), "Additions to Dr. Johnson's Life . . . after the second edition was printed," *ix (*recte* *xiv)–*xviii; Boswell, *The Principal Corrections and Additions* (1793), 21.
31. *Boswell's Life of Johnson*, III, 203.
32. Hailes, *Decisions of the Lords of Council and Session*, 777.
33. Long, *Candid Reflections*, quoted in Walvin, *The Black Presence*, 68.

CHAPTER 11. "NOBODY BUT FRANK"

1. *Thraliana*, I, 175.
2. Piozzi, *Anecdotes*, 131; letter from the Revd. Thomas Sedgwick Whalley to the *European Magazine*, 21 September 1810, quoted by Reade, *Johnsonian Gleanings*, Pt II, 81; *Boswell's Life of Johnson*, II, 76.
3. Register of Marriages at St. Dunstan in the West, 1762–1779, London Metropolitan Archives.
4. Register of Baptisms, St. Andrew, Holborn, London Metropolitan Archives. This suggestion was made by Ingledew, "Some new light on Francis Barber." See also Berrett, "Francis Barber's marriage and children: a correction."
5. Chater, *Untold Histories*, 30.
6. Carretta, *Equiano the African*, 217.
7. Quoted in Equiano, *The Interesting Narrative*, 371.
8. *Cobbett's Weekly Political Register*, 16 June 1804, cols. 935–36, quoted by Peter Fryer, *Staying Power*, 234–35.

9. Hawkins, *Life of Johnson,* 357, note.

10. Piozzi, *Anecdotes,* 145.

11. Boswell, *The Life of Samuel Johnson with Marginal Comments by Hester Lynch Thrale Piozzi,* III, 280, marginal note b.

12. *Boswell's Life of Johnson,* IV, 197

13. *Thraliana,* I, 184 ("a Blackamoor and his Wife") and 532 ("Black Francis & his White Wife's Bastard"); Piozzi, *Anecdotes,* 131 ("Francis and his white wife . . . his Desdemona").

14. Register of Baptisms in the Parish of St. Bridget als St. Bride, 1736–1812; Register of Burials in the Parish of St. Bridget als St. Bride, 1736–1812 (Samuel Barber buried 20 April 1775); Register of Christenings in the Parish of St. Andrew, Holborn, 1781–1792, all in London Metropolitan Archives.

15. Samuel Johnson to Mrs. Thrale, 24 November 1781, *The Letters of Samuel Johnson,* III, 375.

16. Samuel Johnson to Edmund Allen, 26 November 1781, *The Letters of Samuel Johnson,* III, 376.

17. *Thraliana,* 531–32, entry written 18 April 1782; Reade, *Johnsonian Gleanings,* Pt IX, 208; Mrs. Piozzi's Commonplace Book, quoted in *Johnsonian Gleanings,* Pt IX, 208.

18. Hawkins, *Life of Johnson,* 357, note.

19. *Thraliana,* I, 184; Cooke, *The Life of Samuel Johnson* (1785), in *The Early Biographies of Samuel Johnson,* 133.

20. *Thraliana,* I, 184, 531–32.

21. Boswell, *The Applause of the Jury,* 112; Gordon Turnbull, "Not a woman in sight."

22. Samuel Johnson to Lucy Porter, 19 October 1779, *The Letters of Samuel Johnson,* III, 190.

23. Burney, *The Early Journals and Letters of Fanny Burney, Vol. III The Streatham Years: Part I, 1778–1779,* 148–49.

24. Samuel Johnson to Mrs. Thrale, 14 November 1778, *The Letters of Samuel Johnson,* III, 140.

25. *James Boswell's Life of Johnson: An Edition of the Original Manuscript,* Vol. 3, 1776–1780, 217. The passage was mislaid and never used in the *Life of Johnson;* see Bonnell's discussion at xvi and 217, n. 4.

26. Samuel Johnson to Edmund Allen, 7 June 1784, *The Letters of Samuel Johnson,* IV, 332; Johnson, *Diaries, Prayers and Annals,* 285.

27. Burney, *The Early Journals and Letters of Fanny Burney, Vol. III The Streatham Years: Part I, 1778–1779,* 147.

28. *Gentleman's Magazine* 1793, 619–20.

29. Samuel Johnson to Robert Levet, 22 October 1775, *The Letters of Samuel Johnson*, II, 273.

30. Samuel Johnson to Robert Levet, 23 September 1776 and 21 October 1776, *The Letters of Samuel Johnson*, II, 357, 358.

31. Edward Williamson, Bishop of Swansea and Brecon, "Dr Johnson and the Prayer Book."

32. The volume is now in the Samuel Johnson Birthplace Museum, Lichfield.

33. Reade, *Johnsonian Gleanings*, Pt II, 85. An illustration of the miniature appears in Overholt and Horrocks, *A Monument More Durable Than Brass*, 50.

34. Martin, *Samuel Johnson: A Biography* 372; Nokes, *Samuel Johnson: A Life*, 260; Meyers, *Samuel Johnson: The Struggle*, 290–91; *Oxford Dictionary of National Biography*, art. "Francis Barber."

35. Piozzi, *Anecdotes*, 131.

36. *Boswell's Life of Johnson*, II, 215.

37. Johnson, *Diaries, Prayers, and Annals*, 225, 297, 313.

38. Samuel Johnson to Mrs. Thrale, 13 September 1777, *The Letters of Samuel Johnson*, III, 66.

39. "On the Death of Dr. Robert Levet," Johnson, *Poems*, 313–15.

40. Samuel Johnson to William Hunter, 2 June 1778, *The Letters of Samuel Johnson*, III, 117.

41. Samuel Johnson to Lucy Porter, 2 March 1782, *The Letters of Samuel Johnson*, IV, 15.

42. Samuel Johnson to Hester Thrale, 5 June 1783, *The Letters of Samuel Johnson*, IV, 145.

43. Samuel Johnson to Hester Thrale, 19 June 1783, *The Letters of Samuel Johnson*, IV, 151–52.

44. Samuel Johnson to Hester Thrale, 28 June 1783, *The Letters of Samuel Johnson*, IV, 160.

45. Samuel Johnson to Joshua Reynolds, 6 September 1783, *The Letters of Samuel Johnson*, IV, 195.

46. Samuel Johnson to Francis Barber, 16 September 1783, *The Letters of Samuel Johnson*, IV, 199.

47. Murphy, *An Essay on the Life and Genius of Samuel Johnson, LL.D.*, 440.

48. Samuel Johnson to Hester Thrale, 27 December 1783, *The Letters of Samuel Johnson*, IV, 265.

49. He was baptised at St. Dunstan's in the West on 18 January 1784; see Register of Baptisms in the Parish of St. Dunstan in the West, 1771–1794, London

Metropolitan Archives. The register gives the Barbers' address as "Bolt Court."

50. *Boswell's Life of Johnson*, IV, 284.

51. Samuel Johnson to Mrs. White, 2 November 1784, *The Letters of Samuel Johnson*, IV, 433.

52. Samuel Johnson to Hester Thrale, 15 January 1777, *The Letters of Samuel Johnson*, III, 4.

53. Samuel Johnson to Dr. Richard Brocklesby, 30 August 1784, *The Letters of Samuel Johnson*, IV, 386; diary entry, 19 October 1784, Johnson, *Diaries, Prayers, and Annals*, 403. Johnson's medical problems are discussed by John Wiltshire in *Samuel Johnson in the Medical World*.

54. Quoted in *The Letters of Samuel Johnson*, IV, 204, n. 1.

55. Samuel Johnson to Joshua Reynolds, 18 September 1784, *The Letters of Samuel Johnson*, IV, 407. For Johnson's subscription to a balloon, see his letter to Hester Maria Thrale, 31 January 1784, ibid., 279, and for his letter of 22 September 1783 to Mrs. Thrale about balloons, see ibid., 203–5.

56. *London Chronicle*, 17 November 1784.

57. Ibid.

58. Samuel Johnson to Edmund Hector, 17 November 1784, *The Letters of Samuel Johnson*, IV, 437–38.

59. Hoole, *Journal Narrative Relative to Dr Johnson's Last Illness*, n.p., entry for Saturday, 20 November 1784.

60. *Gentleman's Magazine* 1793, 619–20.

CHAPTER 12. HAWKINS V. BARBER

1. Samuel Johnson to John Hawkins, 7 November 1784, *The Letters of Samuel Johnson*, IV, 436.

2. Hawkins, *Life of Samuel Johnson*, 353.

3. Hawkins narrates the history of the making of Johnson's will in his *Life of Samuel Johnson*, 340, 349, 351–53, and 356. The text of the will and its codicil are set out at 360–62.

4. Hoole, *Journal Narrative Relative to Doctor Johnson's Last Illness*, n.p., entry for 30 November 1784.

5. T. D. Boswell to James Boswell, 31 December 1784, Beinecke Rare Book and Manuscript Library, Yale University, GEN MSS 89, C 506.

6. Boswell, *Boswell: The Applause of the Jury, 1782–1785*, 291.

7. *Boswell's Life of Johnson*, IV, 395–96. For a full account of the matter see Pottle, "The Dark Hints of Hawkins and Boswell."

8. Boswell, *London Journal 1762–1763*, 273.

9. Richard Brocklesby to James Boswell, 13 December 1784, Waingrow, *Correspondence*, 21; *Boswell: The English Experiment 1785–1789*, 19.

10. Johnson, *An Account of the Life of Dr. Samuel Johnson*. For Barber's role in preserving the account, see v.

11. I have discussed in more detail the events of this day and the controversy concerning the diaries in "Did John Hawkins Steal Johnson's Diary?"

12. Hyde, "Not in Chapman," 319.

13. Windham, *Diary*, 28–29.

14. Reade, *Johnsonian Gleanings*, Pt II, 58–60. The memorial of the annuity is enrolled on the Close Rolls, The National Archives, C 54/6717.

15. Diary entry, 11 December 1784. I am grateful to Peter Sabor and Stewart Cooke for providing a transcription from the manuscript of Frances Burney's diary. The manuscript differs in minor respects from the text published in D'Arblay, *Diary and Letters of Madame D'Arblay*, II, 280.

16. T. D. Boswell to James Boswell, 31 December 1784, noted above.

17. Ibid.

18. *Boswell's Life of Johnson*, IV, 417.

19. James Boswell printed extracts from T. D. Boswell's letter in *Life of Johnson*, IV, 417–18.

20. *Boswell's Life of Johnson*, IV, 418; Gordon Turnbull, "Not a Woman in Sight."

21. T. D. Boswell to James Boswell, 31 December 1784, noted above.

22. Hawkins, *Life of Johnson*, 357–59; Windham, *The Diary of the Right Hon William Windham 1784 to 1810*, 31–32.

23. John Hoole to William Bowles, 14 December 1784, in Hoole, *Five Letters and a Dream of Johnson*, 16–17.

24. Hawkins, *Life of Johnson*, 358.

25. *Public Advertiser*, 21 December 1784; "Anecdotes of George Steevens," in *Johnsoniana*, 199–201.

26. Hawkins, *Life of Johnson*, 359.

27. Charles Burney to Thomas Twining, 25 December 1784, Burney, *The Letters of Dr. Charles Burney, Vol. I, 1751–1784*, 459–60.

28. Laetitia-Matilda Hawkins, *Memoirs*, I, 224, 153–54.

29. Fleeman, "Revenue of a writer," 223, 230, n. 80.

30. William Johnson Temple to James Boswell, 6 January 1785, Waingrow, *Correspondence*, 35.

31. Commonplace book entry, 1809, quoted in Reade, *Johnsonian Gleanings*, Pt IX, 208–9; Hester Piozzi to Lady Keith, 15 May 1813, Piozzi, *The Piozzi Letters*, Vol. 5, *1811–1816*, 197.

32. Hawkins, *Life of Johnson*, 197–98.

33. Hawkins, *The Life of Dr. Samuel Johnson* (1787), 586, footnote; Hawkins, *Life of Johnson*, 356–57, footnote.

34. Hawkins, *The Life of Dr. Samuel Johnson* (1787), 596–602; Hawkins, *Life of Johnson*, 362–66.

35. Hawkins, *Life of Johnson*, 365–66, footnote.

36. Ibid., 366.

37. Hawkins, *Memoirs*, I, 223.

38. Ibid., 222.

39. For Johnson's comments on Heely, see letters to William Drummond, 24 October 1767, and to Lucy Porter, 7 June 1768, *The Letters of Samuel Johnson*, I, 289–90, 315–16. For Heely, see Reade, *The Reades of Blackwood Hill*, 57–58, and Reade, *Johnsonian Gleanings*, Pt X, 175.

40. Reade, *The Reades of Blackwood Hill*, 179–82; Reade, *Johnsonian Gleanings*, Pt X, 179.

41. Lord Stowell (William Scott) to Lady Inchiquin, 1794, James Marshall and Marie-Louise Osborn Collection, Beinecke Rare Book and Manuscript Library, Yale University, Osborn MSS File 14562.

42. Malone's journal was published by James Prior as "Maloniana"; see Prior, *Life of Edmond Malone*, 426.

43. Martin, *Edmond Malone*, 148.

44. Hawkins, *Life of Johnson*, 277; Reade, *Johnsonian Gleanings*, Pt II, 55, 77.

45. Francis Barber to James Boswell, 12 March 1788, Waingrow, *Correspondence*, 213.

46. Journal entry for 19 April 1788, *Boswell: The English Experiment 1785–1789*, 212–13.

CHAPTER 13. LICHFIELD

1. "Never did I hear till yesterday that [Barber] was in Lichfield . . . he is becoming an inhabitant," Anna Seward to James Boswell, 12 October 1785, Beinecke Rare Book and Manuscript Library, Yale University, GEN MSS 89 C2472–2474.

2. Reade, *Johnsonian Gleanings*, Pt II, 65.

3. Francis Barber to James Boswell, 16 October 1790 (addressed from Stowe Street), and Poor Law examination of Francis Barber, 4 October 1799

(rented for seven years at £12), Samuel Johnson Birthplace Museum, Lichfield.

4. *Boswell's Life of Johnson*, I, 237, n. 1; *James Boswell's Life of Johnson: An Edition of the Original Manuscript*, Vol. 1, 171, n. 5; Reade, *Johnsonian Gleanings*, Pt I, 57. The ring is now in the Samuel Johnson Birthplace Museum, Lichfield.

5. *St. James's Chronicle*, 7–9 June 1787.

6. *St. James's Chronicle*, 14–16 June 1787.

7. *World and Fashionable Advertiser*, 31 March 1787.

8. Richard Greene to James Boswell, 8 July 1787, Waingrow, *Correspondence*, 175–76.

9. James Boswell to Francis Barber, 29 June 1787, Waingrow, *Correspondence*, 173.

10. Francis Barber to James Boswell, 9 July 1787, Waingrow, *Correspondence*, 176–77.

11. *St. James's Chronicle*, 21–24 July 1787.

12. James Boswell to Francis Barber, 20 March 1788, Waingrow, *Correspondence*, 214–16.

13. Travel diary of Laetitia-Matilda Hawkins for July 1827, quoted by de Castro, "Laetitia Hawkins and Boswell," 373–74.

14. *Boswell: The English Experiment 1785–1789*, 212–13.

15. *Gentleman's Magazine*, August 1787, 752–53.

16. *World and Fashionable Advertiser*, 8, 15, and 19 November 1787.

17. "Francis, Barber," *More Last Words of Dr. Johnson*, v–viii.

18. Ibid., 20.

19. *European Magazine and London Review*, December 1787, 466–67.

20. *The World*, 27 November 1787.

21. *The World*, 28 November 1787.

22. John Davies drew my attention to the references to Barber in the Lichfield Portmote Court Book 1778–1818, D77/6/5, Lichfield Record Office. I am grateful to Joanne Wilson for inspecting the entries and providing copies.

23. My account of the Bower is based primarily on Roy Judge's very full description in "The Morris in Lichfield." I have also made use of Harwood, *History and Antiquities of the Church and City of Lichfield*, 354; Hopkins, *Dr. Johnson's Lichfield*, 204–5; and *A History of Staffordshire, Vol. 14: Lichfield (Victoria County Histories)*, 159–60. The Greenhill Bower is still celebrated in Lichfield today.

24. Samuel Johnson to Hester Thrale, 29 May 1779, *The Letters of Samuel Johnson*, III, 166.

25. Ann was baptised at St. Chad's, Lichfield, on 7 November 1786.

26. Francis Barber to James Boswell, 9 July 1787 and 12 March 1788, Waingrow, *Correspondence*, 176–77 and 213–14.

27. Francis Barber to James Boswell, 2 April 1788, Waingrow, *Correspondence*, 215–16.

28. James Boswell to Francis Barber, 11 April 1788, Waingrow, *Correspondence*, 216.

29. Francis Barber to Bishop Percy, 16 December 1788, Samuel Johnson Birthplace Museum, Lichfield.

30. "A state of the Account between the Bishop of Dromore and the Executors of the late Dr. Samuel Johnson" and Thomas Percy to Francis Barber, 26 December 1788, both in the Samuel Johnson Birthplace Museum, Lichfield.

31. Hecht, *Domestic Servant Class*, 144, 148; Burnett, *History of the Cost of Living*, 180–81.

32. Hawkins, *Life of Samuel Johnson*, 363.

33. John Hawkins to Thomas Percy, 7 November 1786, quoted in Reade, *Johnsonian Gleanings*, Pt II, 65.

34. Hawkins, *Life of Samuel Johnson*, 357, note, 362.

35. Hawkins, *Memoirs*, I, 153–54.

36. Bennet Langton to Francis Barber, 6 October 1786, quoted in Reade, *Johnsonian Gleanings*, Pt II, 65.

37. John Smith, "Memoir of Samuel Barber, a Local Preacher," 82.

38. Anna Seward to James Boswell, 16 October 1790, Beinecke Rare Book and Manuscript Library, Yale University, C 2474.

39. Francis Barber to James Boswell, 29 September 1790, Waingrow, *Correspondence*, 261–62.

40. Waingrow, *Correspondence*, 264; *Boswell: The Great Biographer 1789–1795*, 108–9.

41. James Boswell to Francis Barber, 11 October 1790, summarised in Boswell's register of letters, Waingrow, *Correspondence*, 264.

42. *Gentleman's Magazine* 1793, 619–20. Holt was identified as author of the anonymous column by James M. Kuist, *The Nichols File of The Gentleman's Magazine: Attributions of Authorship and Other Documentation in Editorial Papers at the Folger Library* (1982), cited by Emily Lorraine de Montluzin on her website "Attributions of Authorship in the Gentleman's Magazine,

1731–1868: An Electronic Union List," at http://etext.virginia.edu/bsuva/gm2/index.html.

43. Poor Law examination of Francis Barber, 4 October 1799, Samuel Johnson Birthplace Museum, Lichfield.

44. Hugh Bailye to Richard Polwhele, 1794, quoted in Reade, *Johnsonian Gleanings*, Pt II, 77.

45. Reade, *Johnsonian Gleanings*, Pt II, 88.

46. For a survey, see Marika Sherwood, "Black school teachers in Britain in the eighteenth and nineteenth centuries."

47. *A History of Staffordshire, Vol. 14: Lichfield (Victoria County Histories)*, 224, 227; "School and cold bath at Burntwood near Lichfield," *Lloyd's Evening Post*, 9–11 January 1793.

48. Walvin, *Black and White*, 60–61, 76, quoting letter of Richard Raikes, 5 July 1815, Gloucestershire County Record Office.

49. Twigger, *Inflation*, Table 1; Burnett, *History of the Cost of Living*, 198.

50. Holdsworth, *A History of English Law*, X, 256–57.

51. Accounts of the overseer of the poor of Burntwood, Edgell, and Woodhouses for the year ending at Easter 1800, entry for 16 July 1799 (consulted on microfilm, London Family History Centre at The National Archives).

52. Poor Law examination of Francis Barber, 4 October 1799, Samuel Johnson Birthplace Museum, Lichfield.

53. Tobias Smollett to John Wilkes, 16 March 1759, *The Letters of Tobias Smollett*, 75 ("sickly . . . malady"); Francis Barber to James Boswell, 2 April 1788 ("old complaint") and 29 September 1790 ("extreamly ill"), Waingrow, *Correspondence*, 215–16 and 261–62; "Meteorological Journalist," "An Excursion from Walton to London" ("troublesome disorder").

54. Johnson, "The Last Days of Frank Barber."

55. *Gentleman's Magazine* LXXI (1801), Pt 1, 190; Register of baptisms and burials, Stafford St. Mary, Staffordshire Record Office, F 1399/4. The entry is reproduced on the Staffordshire County Council website under "Sources for black and Asian history."

CHAPTER 14. AFTERLIVES

1. Reade, *Johnsonian Gleanings*, Pt II, 88, footnote.

2. Ibid., 81.

3. Mrs. Piozzi's Commonplace Book, quoted in *Johnsonian Gleanings*, Pt IX, 208.

4. Letter from the Revd. Thomas Whalley to the *European Magazine*, 21 September 1810, quoted in Reade, *Johnsonian Gleanings*, Pt II, 81.

5. Mrs. Piozzi's commonplace book, quoted in *Johnsonian Gleanings*, Pt II, 82, Pt IX, 208–9. In 1810 a semi-skilled labourer would have earned about 16s a week, which was reckoned to be barely sufficient for subsistence, and an agricultural labourer about 12s a week (Burnett, *History of the Cost of Living*, 251).

6. John Smith, "Memoir of Samuel Barber, a Local Preacher." My account of Samuel Barber is based on this memoir, together with Kendall, *The Origin and History of the Primitive Methodist Church*, and Bebbington, *Evangelicalism in Modern Britain*.

7. Isaac's date of birth is given as "about 1817" in Reade, *Johnsonian Gleanings*, Pt II, 98. Parish records of St. John, Burslem, Staffordshire, 1713–1888, transcribed at ancestry.co.uk, give his date of birth as 28 November 1813.

8. *The Derby Mercury*, 16 July 1828.

9. John Lockwood Kipling to Aleyn Lyell Reade, 11 February 1908, quoted in Reade, *Johnsonian Gleanings*, Pt II, 99–100.

10. Unless otherwise indicated, my account of the Barber family history is based on Reade, *Johnsonian Gleanings*, Pt II, 86–102; Barber, *Slaves Sinners and Saints;* and the Barber family tree which appears in Grosvenor and Chapman, *West Africa, West Indies, West Midlands*, fig. 11.6. In 1839 Isaac Barber married Maria Walden (died 1847?) and they had a daughter Martha, a potter (born 1844, died 1860). The daughter of Isaac and Martha Barber who died young was Rosehannah (born 1850, died 1851).

11. Martin, *Britain's Slave Trade*, 142–43. See also Syal, "Dr. Johnson's Black Servant Proved to Be My Ancestor."

12. Barber, *Slaves Sinners and Saints*, 219–20.

13. *The Black Eighteenth Century* (BBC TV, 2007), directed by Helen Scholes and produced by David Okuefuna.

14. I discuss the painting in more detail in my article "Searching for the Invisible Man: The Images of Francis Barber."

15. David Minlore to Cecil Harmsworth, 29 June 1934 and Cecil Harmsworth to David Minlore, 26 July 1934, archives of Dr. Johnson's House.

16. Cecil Harmsworth to Arundel Esdaile, 28 June 1934; memo from Edward Croft-Murray to Arundel Esdaile, 30 June 1934, archives of Dr. Johnson's House.

17. Penny, *Reynolds*, 246; Mannings and Postle, *Sir Joshua Reynolds: A Complete Catalogue of His Paintings*, Text Volume, 498. The portrait appears in the Plates Volume, fig. 1011.

18. Waterhouse, "Study of a Black Man by Joshua Reynolds," 112.

19. *Tableaux anciens et du xix siècle argenterie meubles et objets d'art du xviii siècle tapis appertenant à la comtesse A. de Casteja,* 12.

20. Wain, *Samuel Johnson,* fig. 24; Bate, *Samuel Johnson,* illustration 20; Meyers, *Samuel Johnson: The Struggle,* illustration 12, between 272 and 273. Nokes, *Samuel Johnson: A Life,* captions the image "Francis Barber" (illustration 11, between 200 and 201), but in his list of illustrations describes it more cautiously as "A Young Black (?Francis Barber)" (399). F. O. Shyllon, *Black Slaves in Britain,* facing 117; Gerzina, *Black London: Life before Emancipation,* illustration 7, between 116 and 117.

21. Reade, *Johnsonian Gleanings,* Pt II, 104.

22. Leslie and Taylor, *Life and Times of Sir Joshua Reynolds,* I, 282; Graves and Cronin, *A History of the Works of Sir Joshua Reynolds,* I, 49; II, 525.

23. Penny, *Reynolds,* 245.

24. See the entries in the pocket books for 27, 30 March and 3, 6, 14 April 1761 and 17 January 1765, 10 April 1766 (Mr Franks); 17, 24, 28 March, 2 April 1766 (Mrs Franks); and 20, 24, 27 March, 2, 10 April (Miss Franks). The pocket books are now in the Research Library and Archive of the Royal Academy of Arts. For the payments, see Mannings and Postle, *Sir Joshua Reynolds: A Complete Catalogue of His Paintings,* Text Volume, 205–6.

25. Typed copy in the National Portrait Gallery archive of *Catalogue of Portraits . . . by the late Sir Joshua Reynolds . . . which will be sold at auction by Mr Greenwood, 14th April 1796,* No. 53 for 15 April 1796. It was sold to Sir George Beaumont for £18 18s.

26. For information on George Beaumont I have relied on Fullerton, "Patronage and Pedagogy," and Owens and Blayney Brown, *Collector of Genius: A Life of Sir George Beaumont.*

27. British Institution, *Catalogue of Pictures by the late Sir Joshua Reynolds,* first catalogue, 21, No 140. (The exhibition closed on 12 June and reopened on 14 June, to allow some of the paintings to be removed and others to replace them; see West, *Recollections of the British Institution for Promoting the Fine Arts in the United Kingdom,* 148. The present portrait does not appear in the second catalogue of that exhibition.)

28. Northcote, *The Life of Sir Joshua Reynolds,* I, 185–86.

29. *Catalogue of the Art Treasures of the United Kingdom collected at Manchester in 1857,* Nos. 58, 80.

Bibliography

Adams, Gene. "Dido Elizabeth Belle: A Black Girl at Kenwood." *Camden History Review* 12 (1984), 10–14.

Aldous, Vivienne E. *My Ancestors Were Freemen of the City of London*. London: Society of Genealogists, 1999.

Andrews, Edward E. *Native Apostles: Black and Indian Missionaries in the British Atlantic World*. Cambridge, MA, and London: Harvard University Press, 2013.

Anonymous. *A Trip Through Town*. London, 1735.

Anonymous [Edward Ward]. *A Trip to Jamaica: With a True Character of the People and Island*. 3d ed. London, 1698.

Baker, J. H. *An Introduction to English Legal History*. 4th ed. London: Butterworths, 2002.

————. *The Law's Two Bodies: Some Evidential Problems in English Legal History*. Oxford: Oxford University Press, 2001.

Bannerman, W. Bruce, ed. *The Registers of St. Mary Le Bow, Cheapside; All Hallows, Honey Lane; and St. Pancras, Soper Lane, London—Part I: Baptisms and Burials*. London: Harleian Society, 1914.

Barber, Cedric. *Slaves Sinners and Saints: A True Story of the Barber Family over Three Centuries*. Stoke-on-Trent: Tentmaker, 2008.

Barker, Anthony J. *The African Link: British Attitudes to the Negro in the Era of the Atlantic Slave Trade, 1550–1807*. London: Frank Cass, 1978.

Basker, James G. "Intimations of Abolitionism in 1759: Johnson, Hawkesworth and *Oroonoko*." In *The Age of Johnson*, vol. 12, ed. Paul J. Korshin and Jack Lynch, 47–66. New York: AMS, 2001.

————. "Johnson and Slavery." In *Johnson After Three Centuries: New Light on Texts and Contexts*, ed. Thomas A. Horrocks and Howard D. Weinbrot, 29–50. Cambridge, MA: Houghton Library, 2011.

———. "Johnson, Boswell, and the Abolition of Slavery." *New Rambler* (2002), 36–48.

———. "Multicultural Perspectives: Johnson, Race and Gender." In *Johnson Re-Visioned: Looking Before and After*, ed. Philip Smallwood, 64–79. Lewisburg: Bucknell University Press, 2001.

———. " 'The Next Insurrection': Johnson, Race and Rebellion." In *The Age of Johnson*, vol. 11, ed. Paul J. Korshin and Jack Lynch, 37–49. New York: AMS, 2000.

———. "Samuel Johnson and the African-American Reader." *New Rambler* (1994–1995), 47–57.

Bate, Walter Jackson. *Samuel Johnson*. London: Chatto & Windus, 1978.

Bebbington, David. *Evangelicalism in Modern Britain: A History from the 1730s to the 1980s*. London: Unwin Hyman, 1989.

Berrett, A. M. "Francis Barber's Marriage and Children: a Correction." *Notes and Queries* 35 (1998), 193.

Blumrosen, Alfred W., and Ruth G. Blumrosen. *Slave Nation: How Slavery United the Colonies and Sparked the American Revolution*. Naperville, IL: Sourcebooks, 2005.

Boswell, James. *Boswell for the Defence 1769–1774*, ed. William K. Wimsatt, Jr., and Frederick A. Pottle. London: Heinemann, 1960.

———. *Boswell in Extremes 1776–1778*, ed. Charles McC. Weis and Frederick A. Pottle. London: Heinemann, 1971.

———. *Boswell's Life of Johnson*, ed. George Birkbeck Hill, revised by L. F. Powell, 6 vols. Oxford: Clarendon Press, 1934–64.

———. *Boswell: The Applause of the Jury 1782–1785*, ed. Irma S. Lustig and Frederick A. Pottle. London: Heinemann, 1981.

———. *Boswell: The English Experiment 1785–1789*, ed. Irma S. Lustig and Frederick A. Pottle. New York: McGraw-Hill, 1986.

———. *Boswell: The Great Biographer 1789–1795*, ed. Marlies K. Danziger and Frank Brady. London: Heinemann, 1989.

———. *Boswell: The Ominous Years 1774–1776*, ed. Charles Ryskamp and Frederick A. Pottle. London: Heinemann, 1963.

———. *The Correspondence and Other Papers of James Boswell Relating to the Making of the Life of Johnson*, ed. Marshall Waingrow. 2d ed., corrected and enlarged. Edinburgh: Edinburgh University Press; and New Haven: Yale University Press, 2001.

———. *The Correspondence of James Boswell with David Garrick, Edmund Burke, and Edmond Malone*, ed. Peter S. Baker, Thomas W. Copeland,

George M. Kahrl, Rachel McClellan, and James M. Osborn. Heinemann: London, 1986.

———. *James Boswell's Life of Johnson: An Edition of the Original Manuscript in Four Volumes, Vol. 1, 1709–1765*, ed. Marshall Waingrow. Edinburgh: Edinburgh University Press; New Haven and London: Yale University Press, 1994.

———. *James Boswell's Life of Johnson: An Edition of the Original Manuscript in Four Volumes, Vol. 3, 1776–1780*, ed. Thomas F. Bonnell. Edinburgh: Edinburgh University Press; New Haven and London: Yale University Press, 2012.

———. *The Life of Samuel Johnson*. London, 1791.

———. *The Life of Samuel Johnson*. 2d ed. London, 1793.

———. *The Life of Samuel Johnson with Marginal Comments by Hester Lynch Thrale Piozzi*. New York: Heritage, 1963.

———. *London Journal 1762–1763*, ed. Gordon Turnbull. London: Penguin, 2010.

———. *No Abolition of Slavery; or The Universal Empire of Love: A Poem*. London, 1791.

———. *The Principal Corrections and Additions to the First Edition of Mr. Boswell's Life of Dr. Johnson*. London, 1793.

Brack, O M, Jr., and Robert E. Kelley. *Samuel Johnson's Early Biographers*. Iowa City: University of Iowa Press, 1971.

Brady, Frank. *James Boswell: The Later Years 1769–1795*. New York: McGraw-Hill, 1984.

British Institution. *Catalogue of Pictures by the late Sir Joshua Reynolds, first catalogue*. London: W. Bulmer, 1813.

Bundock, Michael. "Did John Hawkins Steal Johnson's Diary?" In *The Age of Johnson*, vol. 21, ed. Jack Lynch, 77–92. New York: AMS, 2011.

———. "The Making of Johnson's *Prayers and Meditations*." In *The Age of Johnson*, vol. 14, ed. Jack Lynch, 77–97. New York: AMS, 2003.

———. "Searching for the Invisible Man: The Images of Francis Barber." In *Editing Lives: Essays in Contemporary Textual and Biographical Studies in Honor of O M Brack, Jr.*, ed. Jesse Swan, 107–22. Lewisburg: Bucknell University Press, 2013.

———. "Slavery on Trial: The *Somerset* Case, 1772." *New Rambler* (2006–7), 54–68.

Burnard, Trevor. "European Migration to Jamaica 1655–1780." *The William and Mary Quarterly*, vol. 53, no. 4 (October 1996), 769–96.

———. *Mastery, Tyranny and Desire: Thomas Thistlewood and His Slaves in the Anglo-Jamaican World*. Chapel Hill and London: University of North Carolina Press, 2004.

———. "Slave Naming Patterns: Onomastics and the Taxonomy of Race in Eighteenth-Century Jamaica." *Journal of Interdisciplinary History*, vol. 31, no. 3 (Winter 2001), 325–46.

Burnett, John. *A History of the Cost of Living*. Harmondsworth: Penguin, 1969.

Burney, Charles. *The Letters of Dr Charles Burney, Vol. I, 1751–1784*, ed. Alvaro Ribeiro, SJ. Oxford: Clarendon Press, 1991.

Burney, Fanny. *The Early Journals and Letters of Fanny Burney, Vol. II 1774–1777*, ed. Lars E. Troide. Oxford: Clarendon Press, 1990.

———. *The Early Journals and Letters of Fanny Burney, Vol. III The Streatham Years: Part I, 1778–1779*, ed. Lars E. Troide and Stewart J. Cooke. Oxford: Clarendon Press, 1994.

Cairns, J. W. "After Somerset: The Scottish Experience." *Journal of Legal History*, vol. 33, no. 3 (2012), 291–312.

———. "The Definition of Slavery in Eighteenth-Century Thinking." In *The Legal Understanding of Slavery: From the Historical to the Contemporary*, ed. Jean Allain, 61–84. Oxford: Oxford University Press, 2012.

———. "Knight v. Wedderburn." In *The Oxford Companion to Black British History*, ed. David Dabydeen, John Gilmore, and Cecily Jones, 244–46. Oxford: Oxford University Press, 2007.

Calendar of State Papers, Colonial Series, America and West Indies, Vol. 10, 1677–1680, ed. Noel Sainsbury and J. W. Fortescue. London, HMSO, 1896.

Calendar of State Papers, Colonial Series, America and West Indies, Vol. 13, 1689–1692, ed. J. W. Fortescue. London: HMSO, 1901.

Carretta, Vincent. *Equiano the African: Biography of a Self-Made Man*. Athens: University of Georgia Press, 2005.

Catalogue of Portraits . . . by the late Sir Joshua Reynolds . . . which will be sold at auction by Mr. Greenwood, 14th April 1796. Typed copy, Heinz Archive and Library, National Portrait Gallery.

Catalogue of the Art Treasures of the United Kingdom collected at Manchester in 1857, catalogue by G. Scharf jun and others. London: Bradbury and Evans, n.d. [1857].

Caudle, James J., and Michael Bundock. "A Newly Identified Apothecary in Boswell's *Life of Johnson*: Edward Ferrand (1691–1769)." *Journal of Medical Biography*, vol. 22, no. 2 (2014), 71–80.

————. *The Runaway and the Apothecary: Francis Barber, Edward Ferrand and the "Life of Johnson."* Privately printed for The Johnsonians, 2011.

Chapman, R. W. "The Formal Parts of Johnson's Letters." In *Essays on the Eighteenth Century,* ed. James Sutherland and F. P. Wilson, 147–54. Oxford: Clarendon Press, 1945.

Chater, Kathleen. *Untold Histories: Black People in England and Wales During the Period of the British Slave Trade, c. 1660–1807.* Manchester: Manchester University Press, 2009.

Chenoweth, Michael. "The Eighteenth-Century Climate of Jamaica, Derived from the Journals of Thomas Thistlewood, 1750–1786." *Transactions of the American Philosophical Society,* New Series, vol. 93, no. 2 (2003), 1–153.

Clarkson, Thomas. *The History of the Rise, Progress, and Accomplishment of the Abolition of the African Slave-Trade by the British Parliament.* London: Longman, 1808.

Clifford, James, *Dictionary Johnson.* London: Heinemann, 1979.

————. *Young Samuel Johnson.* London: Heinemann, 1955.

Clowes, William Laird. *The Royal Navy: A History from the Earliest Times to the Present.* 1898, repr., New York: AMS, 1966.

Cooke, John. *The Macaroni Jester, and Pantheon of Wit, etc.* London, 1773.

Corbett, Julian S. *England in the Seven Years' War: A Study in Combined Strategy.* London: Longmans, Green, 1907.

Corfield, Penelope J. "From Poison Peddlers to Civic Worthies: The Reputation of the Apothecaries in Georgian England." *Social History of Medicine,* vol. 22 (2009), 1–22.

Craton, Michael. *Searching for the Invisible Man: Slaves and Plantation Life in Jamaica.* Cambridge, MA, and London: Harvard University Press, 1978.

Craton, Michael, and James Walvin. *A Jamaican Plantation: The History of Worthy Park, 1670–1970.* London: W. H. Allen, 1970.

Cugoano, Quobna Ottobah. *Thoughts and Sentiments on the Evil of Slavery,* ed. Vincent Carretta. Harmondsworth: Penguin, 1999.

Curley, Thomas M. *Samuel Johnson and the Age of Travel.* Athens: University of Georgia Press, 1976.

Cussans, John Edwin. *History of Hertfordshire.* London, 1870–81.

D'Arblay, Madame. *Diary and Letters of Madame D'Arblay,* ed. Charlotte Barrett, notes by Austin Dobson. London: Macmillan, 1904.

Davenport, Romola, Leonard Schwarz, and Jeremy Boulton. "The Decline of Adult Smallpox in Eighteenth-Century London." *Economic History Review,* vol. 64, no. 4 (November 2011), 1289–1314.

Davis, Bertram H. *A Proof of Eminence: The Life of Sir John Hawkins.* Bloomington: Indiana University Press, 1973.

———. *Thomas Percy: A Scholar-Cleric in the Age of Johnson.* Philadelphia: University of Pennsylvania Press, 1989.

De Castro, J. Paul. "Laetitia Hawkins and Boswell." *Notes and Queries,* vol. 185, no. 13 (1943), 373–74.

DeMaria, Robert, Jr. *The Life of Samuel Johnson: A Critical Biography.* Oxford: Blackwell, 1993.

de Montluzin, Emily Lorraine. "Attributions of Authorship in the Gentleman's Magazine, 1731–1868." http://etext.virginia.edu/bsuva/gm2/index.html.

Drescher, Seymour. "Manumission in a Society Without Slave Law: Eighteenth Century England." *Slavery and Abolition,* vol. 10, no. 3 (December 1989), 84–101.

Dr. Johnson: Interviews and Recollections, ed. Norman Page. Totowa, NJ: Barnes and Noble, 1987.

Dunn, Richard S. *Sugar and Slaves: The Rise of the Planter Class in the English West Indies 1664–1713.* London: Jonathan Cape, 1973.

The Early Biographies of Samuel Johnson, ed. O M Brack, Jr., and Robert E. Kelley. Iowa City: University of Iowa Press, 1974.

Eltis, David, and David Richardson. *Atlas of the Transatlantic Slave Trade.* New Haven and London: Yale University Press, 2010.

Equiano, Olaudah. *The Interesting Narrative and Other Writings,* ed. Vincent Carretta. London: Penguin, 2003.

———. *The Interesting Narrative of the Life of Olaudah Equiano,* ed. Werner Sollors. New York: W. W. Norton, 2001.

Eze, Emmanuel Chukwudi. *Race and the Enlightenment: A Reader.* Oxford: Blackwell, 1997.

File, Nigel, and Chris Power. *Black Settlers in Britain 1555–1958.* London: Heinemann, 1981.

Finlay, Roger, and Beatrice Sheare. "Population Growth and Suburban Expansion." In *The Making of the Metropolis: London 1500–1750,* ed. A. L. Beier and Roger Finlay, 37–59. London: Longman, 1986.

Flavell, Julie. *When London Was Capital of America.* New Haven and London: Yale University Press, 2010.

Fleeman, J. D. "The Revenue of a Writer: Samuel Johnson's Literary Earnings." In *Studies in the Book Trade in Honour of Graham Pollard,* 211–30. Oxford: Oxford Bibliographical Society, 1975.

Foy, Charles R. "Ports of Slavery, Ports of Freedom." Unpublished PhD dissertation, online at http://rucore.libraries.rutgers.edu/etd/.

———. "Uncovering Hidden Lives: Developing a Database of Mariners in the Black Atlantic." *Common-Place*, vol. 9, no. 2 (January 2009).

"Francis, Barber" (pseudonym). *More Last Words of Dr. Johnson, Consisting of Important and Valuable Anecdotes and a Curious Letter from a Medical Gentleman*. London, 1787.

Franklin, Benjamin. *The Papers of Benjamin Franklin*, vol. 9, ed. Leonard W. Labaree. New Haven: Yale University Press, 1966.

Fryer, Peter. *Staying Power: The History of Black People in Britain*. London: Pluto, 1984.

Fullerton, Peter. "Patronage and Pedagogy: The British Institution in the Early Nineteenth Century." *Art History*, vol. 5, no. 1 (March 1982), 59–72.

Gaspar, David Barry. " 'Rigid and Inclement:' Origins of the Jamaica Slave Laws of the Seventeenth Century." In *The Many Legalities of Early America*, ed. Christopher L. Tomlins and Bruce H. Mann, 93–96. Chapel Hill and London: University of North Carolina Press, 2001.

George, M. Dorothy. *London Life in the Eighteenth Century*. London: Penguin, 1965.

Gerzina, Gretchen. *Black London: Life Before Emancipation*. New Brunswick: Rutgers University Press, 1995.

Glasson, Travis. *Mastering Christianity: Missionary Anglicanism and Slavery in the Modern World*. New York: Oxford University Press, 2012.

Glynn, Ian, and Jennifer Glynn. *The Life and Death of Smallpox*. Cambridge: Cambridge University Press, 2004.

Goldsmith, Oliver. *A History of The Earth and Animated Nature* (1774). In *The Works of Oliver Goldsmith*. London, 1806.

Gradish, S. F. *The Manning of the British Navy During the Seven Years' War*. London: Royal Historical Society, 1980.

Graves, Algernon, and William Vine Cronin. *A History of the Works of Sir Joshua Reynolds P. R. A.* London: Henry Graves, 1899–1901.

Greene, Donald. *Samuel Johnson's Library: An Annotated Guide*. University of Victoria, BC: English Literary Studies Monograph Series No. 1, 1975.

Greene, Jack P. *Evaluating Empire and Confronting Colonialism in Eighteenth-Century Britain*. Cambridge: Cambridge University Press, 2013.

Gregory, Jeremy, and John Stevenson. *Britain in the Eighteenth Century, 1688–1820*. London: Longman, 2000.

Grosvenor, Ian, and Rob Chapman. *West Africa, West Indies, West Midlands*. Sandwell Department of Education, 1982.

Hailes, Lord. *Decisions of the Lords of Council and Session from 1766 to 1791*, selected by M. P. Brown. Edinburgh: William Tait, 1826.

Hargrave, Francis. *A Complete Collection of State-Trials and Proceedings for High-Treason and other Crimes and Misdemeanours*. 4th ed. Vol. XI. London, 1781.

Harwood, Thomas. *The History and Antiquities of the Church and City of Lichfield*. London: Cadell and Davies, 1806.

Hawkins, John. *The Life of Dr. Samuel Johnson (The Works of Samuel Johnson, Vol. I)*. London, 1787.

———. *The Life of Samuel Johnson, LL.D.*, ed. O M Brack, Jr. Athens and London: University of Georgia Press, 2009.

Hawkins, Laetitia-Matilda. *Memoirs, Anecdotes, Facts and Opinions*. London: Longman, 1824.

Hecht, J. Jean. *Continental and Colonial Servants in Eighteenth Century England* (Smith College Studies in History, Vol. XL). Northampton, MA: Department of History, Smith College, 1954.

———. *The Domestic Servant Class in Eighteenth-Century England*. London: Routledge & Kegan Paul, 1956.

Higman, B. W. *Jamaica Surveyed: Plantation Maps and Plans of the Eighteenth and Nineteenth Centuries*. Jamaica: University of the West Indies Press, 2001.

A History of Hertfordshire (Victoria County History), ed. William Page. London: Institute of Historical Research, Vol. II, 1908, and Vol. III, 1912.

A History of the County of Stafford, Vol. 14: Lichfield (Victoria County History), ed. M. W. Greenslade. Oxford: Oxford University Press for the Institute of Historical Research, 1990.

Hoare, Prince. *Memoirs of Granville Sharp*. London: Henry Colburn, 1820, repr., Orchard Clyst, n.d.

Hochschild, Adam. *Bury the Chains: The British Struggle to Abolish Slavery*. London: Macmillan, 2005.

Holdsworth, William. *A History of English Law, Vol X*. London: Methuen, 1938.

Hoole, John. *Five Letters and a Dream of Johnson*, ed. Gordon Turnbull. Privately printed for The Johnsonians, 2010.

———. *Journal Narrative Relative to Doctor Johnson's Last Illness Three Weeks Before His Death Kept by John Hoole*, ed. O M Brack, Jr. Iowa City: Windhover, 1972.

Hopkins, Mary Alden. *Dr. Johnson's Lichfield*. London: Peter Owen, 1956.

Hudson, Nicholas. "From 'Nation' to 'Race': The Origin of Racial Classification in Eighteenth-Century Thought." *Eighteenth-Century Studies,* vol. 29, no. 3 (1996), 247–64.

———. *Samuel Johnson and the Making of Modern England.* Cambridge: Cambridge University Press, 2003.

Hyde, Mary. "Not in Chapman." In *Johnson, Boswell and Their Circle,* ed. Mary Lascelles et al., 286–319. Oxford: Clarendon Press, 1965.

Ingledew, John. "Samuel Johnson's Jamaican Connections." *Caribbean Quarterly,* vol. 30, no. 2 (June 1984), 1–17.

———. "Some New Light on Francis Barber, Samuel Johnson's Servant." *Notes and Queries,* vol. 31 (1984), 8–9.

Johnson, Douglas. "The Last Days of Frank Barber." *Transactions of the Johnson Society* (1986), 17–21.

Johnson, Samuel. *An Account of the Life of Dr. Samuel Johnson, from his birth to his eleventh year, written by himself.* London: Richard Phillips, 1805.

———. *A Commentary on Mr. Pope's Principles of Morality, Or Essay on Man,* ed. O M Brack, Jr. New Haven and London: Yale University Press, 2004.

———. *Diaries, Prayers and Annals,* ed. E. L. McAdam, Jr., with Donald and Mary Hyde. New Haven: Yale University Press; Oxford: Oxford University Press, 1958.

———. *Early Biographical Writings of Dr Johnson,* ed. J. D. Fleeman. Westmead, Farnborough: Gregg International, 1973.

———. *The Idler and Adventurer,* ed. W. J. Bate, John M. Bullitt, and L. F. Powell. New Haven and London: Yale University Press, 1963.

———. *A Journey to the Western Islands of Scotland,* ed. Mary Lascelles. New Haven and London: Yale University Press, 1971.

———. *The Letters of Samuel Johnson,* ed. Bruce Redford. Oxford: Clarendon Press, 1992–94.

———. *Poems,* ed. E. L. McAdam, Jr., with George Milne. New Haven and London: Yale University Press, 1964.

———. *Political Writings,* ed. Donald J. Greene. New Haven and London: Yale University Press, 1977.

———. *The Rambler,* ed. W. J. Bate and Albrecht B. Strauss. New Haven: Yale University Press, 1963.

———. *Samuel Johnson's Prefaces and Dedications,* ed. Allen T. Hazen. Port Washington, NY: Kennikat 1937.

———. *A Voyage to Abyssinia,* ed. Joel J. Gold. New Haven and London: Yale University Press, 1985.

Johnsoniana: A Collection of Miscellaneous Anecdotes and Sayings of Dr. Samuel Johnson, ed. J. W. Croker. London: Henry G. Bohn, 1845.

Johnsonian Miscellanies, ed. George Birkbeck Hill. Oxford: Clarendon Press, 1897.

Jones, William R. "Barber, Francis (c. 1745–1801)." *Oxford Dictionary of National Biography*.

Jordan, Winthrop D. "American Chiaroscuro: The Status and Definition of Mulattoes in the British Colonies." *The William and Mary Quarterly*, Third Series, vol. 19, no. 2 (April 1962), 183–200.

Joye, Gillian. "Peter Joye's Charity School, St. Ann, Blackfriars in the Eighteenth Century." Unpublished thesis, 1990, Guildhall Library, London.

Judge, Roy. "The Morris in Lichfield." *Folklore*, vol. 103, no. 2 (1992), 131–59.

Kendall, H. B. *The Origin and History of the Primitive Methodist Church*. London: Edwin Dalton, 1905.

Kitson, Peter. " 'Candid Reflections': The Idea of Race in the Debate over the Slave Trade and Slavery in the Late Eighteenth and Early Nineteenth Centuries." In *Discourses of Slavery and Abolition*, ed. Brycchan Carey, Markman Ellis, and Sara Salih, 11–25. Basingstoke: Palgrave Macmillan, 2004.

Lambert, Elizabeth R. *Edmund Burke of Beaconsfield*. Newark: University of Delaware Press, 2003.

Larsen, Lyle. *Dr. Johnson's Household*. Hamden, CT: Archon Books, 1985.

Lawrence, Maureen. *Resurrection*. Unpublished play, first performed 1996.

Leslie, Charles, and Tom Taylor. *Life and Times of Sir Joshua Reynolds: with notices of some of his Contemporaries*. London: John Murray, 1865.

Lewis, Michael. *A Social History of the Navy 1793–1815*. London: George Allen & Unwin, 1960.

Liebert, Herman W. *The Bear and the Phoenix: John Wilkes's Letter on Johnsons Dictionary Newly Reprinted in Full With a Note on Johnson and Wilkes*. Privately printed for The Johnsonians, 1978.

Lloyd, Christopher. *The British Seaman 1200–1860: A Social Survey*. London: Paladin, 1970.

Lofft, Capel. *Reports of Cases Adjudged in the Court of King's Bench*. London, 1776.

Long, Edward. *Candid Reflections upon the Judgment . . . on what is Commonly Called the Negroe-Cause*. London, 1772.

———. *History of Jamaica*. 3d ed., London, 1774.

Lyon, David. *The Sailing Navy List: All the Ships of the Royal Navy—Built, Purchased and Captured—1688–1860*. London: Conway Maritime Press, 1993.

Mannings, David. *Sir Joshua Reynolds: A Complete Catalogue of His Paintings, The Subject Pictures Catalogued by Martin Postle*. New Haven and London: Yale University Press, 2000.

Martin, Peter. *Edmond Malone Shakespearean Scholar: A Literary Biography*. Cambridge: Cambridge University Press, 1995.

———. *Samuel Johnson: A Biography*. London: Weidenfeld & Nicolson, 2008.

Martin, S. I. *Britain's Slave Trade*. London: Channel 4 Books, 1999.

———. *Incomparable World*. London: Quartet Books, 1996.

McEnroe, Natasha. "The Dictionary Garret: Anatomy of a Room." Unpublished conference paper delivered at "Celebrating Johnson's Dictionary," Pembroke College, Oxford, 26–28 August 2005.

———. "17, Gough Square." *New Rambler* (1998–99), 32–37.

McGuffie, Helen Louise. *Samuel Johnson in the British Press, 1749–1784: A Chronological Checklist*. New York and London: Garland, 1976.

Meldrum, Tim. *Domestic Service and Gender 1660–1750: Life and Work in the London Household*. Harlow: Pearson Education, 2000.

"Meteorological Journalist" [John Holt]. "An Excursion from Walton to London." *Gentleman's Magazine* (1793), 619–20.

Meyers, Jeffrey. *Samuel Johnson: The Struggle*. New York, Basic Books, 2008.

Middleton, Richard. *The Bells of Victory: The Pitt-Newcastle Ministry and the Conduct of the Seven Years' War 1757–1762*. Cambridge: Cambridge University Press, 1985.

Minney, Sarah. "The Search for Dido." *History Today*, vol. 55, no. 10 (2005), 2–3.

Mitchell, Rosemary. *Picturing the Past: English History in Text and Image, 1830–1870*. Oxford: Clarendon Press, 2000.

Morgan, Philip D. "Black Experiences in Britain's Maritime World." In *Empire, the Sea and Global History: Britain's Maritime World, c. 1760–c. 1840*, ed. David Cannadine, 105–33. London: Palgrave Macmillan, 2007.

Morison's Dictionary of Decisions 1540–1808. 1801–7.

Mortimer, Thomas. *The Universal Director; Or, The Nobleman And Gentleman's True Guide To The Masters And Professors Of The Liberal And Polite Arts And Sciences*. London, 1763.

Murphy, Arthur. *An Essay on the Life and Genius of Samuel Johnson, LL.D.* In *Johnsonian Miscellanies*, ed. George Birkbeck Hill, I, 353–488. Oxford: Clarendon Press, 1897.

Murray, T. J. "Dr Samuel Johnson's Movement Disorder." *British Medical Journal,* vol. 1 (1979), 1610–14.

Myers, Norma. *Reconstructing the Black Past: Blacks in Britain 1780–1850.* 1996; repr. Abingdon: Routledge, 2004.

Nokes, David. *Samuel Johnson: A Life.* London: Faber and Faber, 2009.

Northcote, James. *The Life of Sir Joshua Reynolds.* 2d ed. London: Henry Colburn, 1819.

Norton, Mary Beth. "The Fate of Some Black Loyalists of the American Revolution." *Journal of Negro History,* vol. 58, no. 4 (October 1973), 402–26.

O'Connell, Sheila. *London 1753.* London: British Museum Press, 2003.

Overholt, John, and Thomas A. Horrocks, eds. *A Monument More Durable Than Brass: The Donald and Mary Hyde Collection of Dr Samuel Johnson.* Cambridge, MA: Houghton Library, Harvard University, 2009.

Owens, Felicity, and David Blayney Brown. *Collector of Genius: A Life of Sir George Beaumont.* London and New Haven: Yale University Press, 1988.

Paley, Ruth, Cristina Malcolmson, and Michael Hunter. "Parliament and Slavery, 1660–c.1710." *Slavery and Abolition,* vol. 31, no. 2 (June 2010), 257–81.

Patterson, Orlando. *The Sociology of Slavery.* London: MacGibbon and Kee, 1967.

Pennington, Edgar Legare. "Thomas Bray's Associates and Their Work Amongst the Negroes." *Proceedings of the American Antiquarian Society,* n.s., vol. 48 (1938), 311–403.

Penny, Nicholas, ed. *Reynolds.* London: Royal Academy of Arts, 1986.

Phillips, Caryll. *Foreigners: Three English Lives.* London: Harvill Secker, 2007.

Picard, Liza. *Dr. Johnson's London: Life in London 1740–1770.* London: Weidenfeld and Nicolson, 2000.

Piozzi, Hester Lynch. *Anecdotes of the Late Samuel Johnson LL.D. During the Last Twenty Years of His Life,* ed. Arthur Sherbo. London: Oxford University Press, 1974.

———. *The Piozzi Letters, Vol. 5, 1811–1816,* ed. Edward A. Bloom and Lillian D. Bloom. Newark and London: University of Delaware Press and Associated University Presses, 1999.

Pittock, Murray. *James Boswell.* Aberdeen: AHRC Centre for Irish and Scottish Studies, 2007.

Pottle, F. A. "The Dark Hints of Hawkins and Boswell." In *New Light on Dr Johnson: Essays on the Occasion of His 250th Birthday,* ed. Frederick W. Hilles, 153–62. New Haven: Yale University Press, 1959.

——. *The Literary Career of James Boswell Esq.* Oxford: Clarendon Press, 1929.

Prior, James. *Life of Edmond Malone, Editor of Shakespeare.* London: Smith, Elder, 1860.

Pye, Ursula. "John Phillips—An Eighteenth-Century Hatter." *New Rambler* (1981), 43.

Quinlan, Maurice J. "Dr. Franklin Meets Dr. Johnson." In *New Light on Dr. Johnson: Essays on the Occasion of His 250th Birthday,* ed. Frederick W. Hilles, 107–20. New Haven: Yale University Press, 1959.

Reade, Aleyn Lyell. *Johnsonian Gleanings.* 11 parts, 1909–52, repr. New York: Octagon Books, 1968.

——. *The Reades of Blackwood Hall and Dr Johnson's Ancestry.* London: privately printed by Spottiswoode and Co. Ltd, 1906.

Reddick, Allen. *The Making of Johnson's Dictionary 1746–1773.* Rev. ed. Cambridge: Cambridge University Press, 1996.

Reynolds, Frances. *An Enquiry Concerning the Principles of Taste, and of the Origin of Our Ideas of Beauty, etc,* Augustan Reprint No 27. Los Angeles: William Andrews Clark Memorial Library, 1951.

——. "Recollections of Dr. Johnson." In *Johnsonian Miscellanies,* ed. George Birkbeck Hill, II, 250–300. Oxford: Clarendon Press, 1897.

Rizzo, Betty. "The Elopement of Francis Barber." *English Language Notes* (September 1985), 35–38.

Roby, John. *Members of the Assembly of Jamaica.* Montego Bay: Alex Holmes, 1831.

Rodger, N. A. M. *The Command of the Ocean: A Naval History of Britain, 1649–1815.* London: Allen Lane, 2004.

——. *The Wooden World: An Anatomy of the Georgian Navy.* London: Fontana, 1988.

Rogers, Nicholas. *The Press Gang: Naval Impressment and Its Opponents in Georgian Britain.* London: Continuum, 2007.

Rogers, Pat. *Johnson and Boswell: The Transit of Caledonia.* Oxford: Clarendon Press, 1995.

Roughley, Thomas. *The Jamaica Planter's Guide.* London: Longman, Hurst, 1823.

Sancho, Ignatius. *Letters of the Late Ignatius Sancho, an African,* ed. Vincent Carretta. Harmondsworth: Penguin, 1998.

Schama, Simon. *Rough Crossings: Britain, the Slaves and the American Revolution.* London: BBC Books, 2005.

Schwartz, Richard B. *Daily Life in Johnson's London*. Madison: University of Wisconsin Press, 1983.

Sharp, Granville. *A Representation of the Injustice and Dangerous Tendency of Tolerating Slavery, or of Admitting the Least Claim to Private Property in the Persons of Men, in England*. London, 1769.

Shaw, William. *Memoirs of the Life and Writings of the Late Dr. Samuel Johnson*, ed. Arthur Sherbo. London: Oxford University Press, 1974.

Sherwood, Marika. "Black School Teachers in Britain in the Eighteenth and Nineteenth Centuries." *History of Education Researcher*, no. 81 (May 2008), 41–51.

———. "Blacks in the Gordon Riots." *History Today*, vol. 47, no. 12 (1997), 24–28.

Shyllon, F. O. *Black People in Britain 1555–1833*. London: Oxford University Press, 1977.

———. *Black Slaves in Britain*. London: Oxford University Press for the Institute of Race Relations, 1974.

Slater, Michael. *Charles Dickens*. New Haven and London: Yale University Press, 2009.

Smith, John. "Memoir of Samuel Barber, a Local Preacher." *The Primitive Methodist Magazine*, X (1829), 81–90, 118–28.

Smith, Robert Worthington. "The Legal Status of Jamaican Slaves Before the Anti-Slavery Movement." *Journal of Negro History*, vol. 30, no. 3 (July 1945), 293–303.

Smollett, Tobias. *The Letters of Tobias Smollett*, ed. Lewis M. Knapp. Oxford: Clarendon Press, 1970.

Steevens, George. "Anecdotes by George Steevens." In *Johnsonian Miscellanies*, ed. George Birkbeck Hill, II, 312–29. Oxford: Clarendon Press, 1897.

Stephens, W. B. "Literacy in England, Scotland and Wales, 1500–1900." *History of Education Quarterly*, vol. 30, no. 4 (Winter 1990), 545–71.

Suarez, Michael F. "Johnson's Christian Thought." In *The Cambridge Companion to Samuel Johnson*, ed. Greg Clingham, 192–208. Cambridge: Cambridge University Press, 1997.

Syal, Rajeev. "Dr. Johnson's Black Servant Proved to Be My Ancestor." *Sunday Telegraph* (London), 18 April 1999, 21.

Tableaux anciens et du xix siècle argenterie meubles et objets d'art du xviii siècle tapis appertenant à la comtesse A. de Casteja. Paris, 1983.

Tadmor, Naomi. *Family and Friends in Eighteenth-Century England*. Cambridge: Cambridge University Press, 2001.

Teelucksingh, Jerome. "The 'Invisible Child' in British West Indian Slavery." *Slavery and Abolition*, vol. 27, no. 2 (August 2006), 237–50.

Thistlewood, Thomas. *In Miserable Slavery: Thomas Thistlewood in Jamaica 1750–1786*, ed. Douglas Hall. Kingston, Jamaica: University of the West Indies Press, 1999.

Thraliana: The Diary of Mrs Hester Lynch Thrale (Later Mrs Piozzi) 1776–1809, ed. Katharine C. Balderston. 2d ed. Oxford: Clarendon Press, 1951.

Tompson, Richard S. *Classics or Charity? The Dilemma of the Eighteenth-Century Grammar School*. Manchester: Manchester University Press, 1971.

Turnbull, Gordon. "Not a Woman in Sight." *Times Literary Supplement*, 18–25 December 2009, 19–21.

———. "Samuel Johnson, Francis Barber, and 'Mr Desmoulins['] Writing School." *Notes and Queries*, forthcoming.

Twigger, Robert. *Inflation: The Value of the Pound 1750–1998*. House of Commons Library Research Paper 99/20, 23 February 1999.

"Vicinus," "Bishop-Stortford School destroyed; its Library preserved." *Gentleman's Magazine* 1795, Vol. LXV, Pt II, 892–93.

Wain, John. *Frank*. Oxford: Amber Lane Press, 1984.

———. *Samuel Johnson*. 2d ed. London: Macmillan, 1980.

———. "This Is Your Scholar! Your Philosopher!" *Transactions of the Johnson Society* (1976), 5–20.

Waldstreicher, David. *Runaway America: Benjamin Franklin, Slavery and the American Revolution*. New York: Hill and Wang, 2004.

Wall, Cecil, H. Charles Cameron, and E. Ashworth Underwood. *A History of the Worshipful Society of Apothecaries of London, Vol. I, 1617–1815*. London: Oxford University Press for the Wellcome Historical Medical Museum, 1963.

Walvin, James. *Black and White: The Negro and English Society 1555–1945*. London: Allen Lane, 1973.

———. *Black Ivory: Slavery in the British Empire*. 2d ed. Oxford: Blackwell, 2001.

———. *The Black Presence: A Documentary History of the Negro in England, 1555–1860*. London: Orbach and Chambers, 1971.

———. *The Zong: A Massacre, the Law and the End of Slavery*. New Haven and London: Yale University Press, 2011.

Waterhouse, Ellis K. "Study of a Black Man by Joshua Reynolds." In *The Menil Collection: A Selection from the Paleolithic to the Modern Era*, 111–15. New York: Harry N. Abrams, 1987.

West, Benjamin. *Recollections of the British Institution for Promoting the Fine Arts in the United Kingdom*. London: Simpkins and Marshall, 1860.

Wheeler, Roxann. *The Complexion of Race: Categories of Difference in Eighteenth-Century British Culture*. Philadelphia: University of Pennsylvania Press, 2000.

White, Jerry. *London in the Eighteenth Century: A Great and Monstrous Thing*. London: The Bodley Head, 2012.

Whyte, Iain. *Scotland and the Abolition of Black Slavery, 1756–1838*. Edinburgh: Edinburgh University Press, 2006.

Wiecek, William. "*Somerset:* Lord Mansfield and the Legitimacy of Slavery in the Anglo-American World." *University of Chicago Law Review,* vol. 42 (1974), 86–146.

Williamson, Edward. "Dr. Johnson and the Prayer Book." *Theology* (October 1950), 363–72.

Wilson, Erasmus. *The History of the Middlesex Hospital During the First Century of Its Existence*. London: John Churchill, 1845.

Wiltshire, John. *Samuel Johnson in the Medical World: The Doctor and the Patient*. Cambridge: Cambridge University Press, 1991.

Winder, Robert. *Bloody Foreigners: The Story of Immigration to Britain*. London: Little, Brown, 2004.

Windham, William. *The Diary of the Right Hon William Windham 1784 to 1810*, ed. Mrs. Henry Baring. London: Longmans, Green, 1866.

Wise, Steven M. *Though the Heavens May Fall: The Landmark Trial That Led to the End of Human Slavery*. Cambridge, MA: Da Capo, 2005.

Index

References to FB and SJ are to Francis Barber and Samuel Johnson, respectively. References in **bold** are to illustrations.